The Essential Spirit

Book Sponsored by
California Lutheran Homes and Community Services
Glendale, California

The Essential Spirit

Providing Wholistic Services to and with Older Adults

Edited by
DONALD R. KOEPKE

Foreword by
CHARLES FAHEY

PICKWICK *Publications* · Eugene, Oregon

THE ESSENTIAL SPIRIT
Providing Wholistic Services to and with Older Adults

Pickwick Publications
An Imprint of Wipf and Stock Publishers
199 W. 8th Ave., Suite 3
Eugene, OR 97401

www.wipfandstock.com

PAPERBACK ISBN 13: 978-1-62564-916-4
HARDCOVER ISBN 13: 978-1-4982-8688-6

Cataloguing-in-Publication Data

The essential spirit : providing wholistic services to and with other adults / edited by Donald R. Koepke ; foreword by Charles Fahey.

xvi + 224 p. ; 23 cm. Includes bibliographical references.

ISBN 13: 978-1-62564-916-4

1. Older Christians—Religious life. 2. Aging—Religious aspects—Christianity. 3. Church work with older people. I. Fahey, Charles. II. Koepke, Donald R. III. Title.

BV4580 .E87 2016

Manufactured in the U.S.A.   01/18/2016

It has been said that aging is not for sissies. Some persons spiritually decline as they grow older ending in despair as their core beliefs crumble under the weight of age. Others thrive, not because they don't have challenges, but because their spiritual focus reveals other perspectives that are more important and vital for life than the challenges. These people are not defined by the physical, emotional, and social that often are a part on the experience of aging but by the hope, courage, and an inner strength that comes from their core beliefs, their "Essential Spirit."

It is to people such as these:
those who crumble
and those who thrive
that this book is dedicated.
You are
my teachers and mentors,
who by living your faith,
taught me about mine

"The spiritual is elusive not because it lurks behind ordinary phenomena (life) but because it is inter-woven within the phenomena."

—D. E. Capps

Contents

Foreword by Msgr. Charles Fahey, SJ | *xi*
Preface | *xiii*
Acknowledgments | *xv*

Introduction: The Essential Spirit | 1
—Donald Koepke MDiv, BCC

This introduction will provide a definition of spirituality that will be used and further explored by each of the chapters below. Spirituality is defined as a person's core beliefs that are influenced by all of the domains of life, only one of which is religion. Everyone might not have a religion, as culture defines a religion, but everyone has a spirituality.

PART I: PRINCIPLES BEHIND OLDER ADULT SPIRITUALITY

1 Spirituality, the Sacred Domain: Core Concepts and Implications for Practice for Older Adults | 11
—Jocelyn McGee, PhD, Kenneth Pargament, PhD,
   and Aaron Silverbook, BS

This chapter shares a paradigm of how the spiritual works within individual persons, giving caregivers and other professionals an insight into the inner workings of clients and residents of long-term care. In addition the chapter explores therapeutic goals for spiritual care from the perspective of religious leaders, social workers, nurses, and hands-on long-term care staff such as Certified Nursing Assistants (CNAs). Spiritual assessment strategies will be shared that includes questions revealing personal spirituality that are acceptable to theists and non-theists alike.

2 Finding Meaning in Perceived Meaninglessness | 26
—James Ellor, PhD, DMin, LCSW, ACSW, BCD, DCSW, CSW-G

One of the most pressing spiritual needs and challenges experienced by both family and professional caregivers of the elderly is that of finding meaning in old age. Existential Psychotherapy suggests that there is no inherent meaning in a world that is impersonal and devoid of meaning except for those meanings that are attributed by the individual. A discussion about how Viktor Frankl understands this essential need for meaning, as well as ways this concept can help service providers effectively engage the spiritual challenges found in the latter years.

3 Spirituality and the Brain: We Know in Part | 42
—Paul Dobies, OD

This chapter will discuss recent brain research and understanding provides physiological evidence for the use of spirituality to enhance the provision of service with older adults by any discipline. The author suggest that the need for and core of the spiritual because "we do not know that we do not know."

4 Religion: Friend or Foe? | 59
—Peggy Price, DMin

Often religious issues are ignored for fear of accusation of proselyting or exploring irrelevant material. This chapter will advocate for the inclusion of the client's religious thought and practice as a means of enhancing the service provision by persons of all disciplines. The author will advance the notion that if a client is theistic and the service provider does not include the client's use of personal religious perspectives an essential part of the person is lost. Clinically helpful insights from all of the great world religions will be discussed.

PART II: PRACTICAL STRATEGIES FOR ENGAGING THE SPIRITUALITY IN OLDER ADULTS

5 Fostering Spirituality in Dementia: Looking Beyond Cognition | 75
—Cordula Dick-Muehlke, PhD

In this hyper-cognitive culture, the experience of dementia asks a deeply spiritual question: "What does it mean to be human?" Does a person have to be able to cognate in order to be accepted as being human? If a person's spirituality is their core values and beliefs, how does a family member or caregiver engage the spiritual of persons with mild cognitive impairment, moderate dementia, advanced dementia when their ability to engage in meaningful conversations becomes more and more limited.

6 The Essential Spirit in Caresharing | 92
—Marty Richards, LICSW

Caregiving has often been envisioned as a one-way experience with the caregiver doing the giving (active, dominant) and the care receiver doing the receiving (passive role). This chapter will explore a new paradigm of "Caresharing" where both the "giver" and the "receiver" are partners in the task of providing care.

7 Caregiving: Body, Mind, and Spirit | 111
—Giovanna Piazza, MDiv, BCC

This second chapter on caregiving is included because it creatively explores the task of caregiving by examining archetypical patterns of belief among caregivers and corresponding patterns of behavior which could be problematic in healthy self-care. A few of the archetypes examined are: the Ghost, the Martyr, and the Perfectionist. Specific spiritual practices are suggested for each archetype.

8 Touching Spirits: Programming for Meaning and Connection | 122
—Nancy Gordon, MSLS, MDiv

The activity professional is a key person in the lives of residents in a long-term care community. In fact they can be an essential spiritual leader in the way that activities are developed, scheduled, and implemented. The author asks the essential activity question: "What is being accomplished through our activity program? Entertainment that fills the hours until one dies or events that touch the heart, is filled with meaning, and encourages growth of core beliefs?"

9 Using Rituals to Engage the Spirit | 142
—Rabbi Richard Address, DMin, PhD (honorary from HUC–JIR 1999)

Many rituals, both religious and secular, have been practiced throughout the life of the client and thus may assist the client to find insight to their lives as well as cope with the many challenges of old age. To give a client, even one with very limited cognition, a cross to hold, a yarmulke to wear, or a rug on which to pray, allows that client to again connect with their core of being, an experience is not cognitive but experiential.

10 Transforming Suffering into Spiritual Energy: The Practice of "Dedicated Suffering" | 155
—Jane Thibault, PhD

The many physical, psychological, and social challenges often evoke in older adults a perception of suffering. The driving force of this chapter is to address suffering, cope with suffering, even gain meaning in suffering through a process called dedicated suffering.

11 How Diminished Income Can Result in Whole Persons | 173
—Donald Koepke, MDiv, BCC

Finances, or the lack thereof, whether real or imagined, weigh heavily on the hearts of older adults. "Will I have enough to see me through these 'golden years' that is filled with opportunity but also struggle and tragedy?" "What is going to happen if I run out of money?" This chapter explores the spirituality of money and its place in aging by encouraging clients to search their core beliefs regarding money and its role in their lives. The chapter will provide insights and even the words for service providers of all disciplines to effectively address issues surrounding money with their clients.

12 Death and Dying: The Final Act of Living | 193
—G. Jay Westbrook, MSG

Providing service to the dying has long been a recognized province of spiritual care. Dying exposes the effect of core beliefs and values throughout the client's life. Most hospice providers are highly skilled with engaging a client's spirituality. This chapter will expand those skills so that persons of all disciplines, both within and outside hospice, can hear and appropriately respond to this most personal of all experiences of life: dying.

**Epilogue—Looking in a Mirror: What Do I Want to Be
When I Grow Up** | 211
—Nancy Gordon, MSLS, MDiv and Donald Koepke, MDiv, BCC

Spirituality is such a personal component to the life of a client that it is essential that the service provider becomes aware of his or her own spiritual journey and beliefs. The goal is that this awareness might assist providers to avoid coloring the clients experience and beliefs with their own. Strategies for exploring the provider's personal theistic or non-theistic view of spirituality will be shared thus providing the clinician with a personal foundation for effectively engaging the spirituality of the client.

Contributors | 223

Foreword

This timely compendium is a useful contribution to the field of aging, to long-term care, and also to those individuals and institutions that care for the dying.

In recent days some persons express the conviction that they are "spiritual" but not "religious." On the other hand, neither religious bodies nor persons who consider themselves religious have abandoned "spiritual" or "spiritually" as both institutionally and personally antithetical to their conception of religion.

While there seems to be little appetite to clarify this conundrum in the public market place, the concept, broadly utilized, is generally perceived an integral facet of the human journey. It is important to all. At least a working understanding of the various nuances embodied in the concept and explored in this book is useful to all, especially to those attempting to assuage the anxieties and other hurts of others.

This volume includes the insights of a number of thoughtful, experienced people who have dealt extensively and intensively with various nuances of spirituality in a variety of real life situations both as clinicians and academics. Their individual and collective insights offer a rich menu of ideas valuable for those for whom this reality is important both personally and professionally.

The timeliness of this work is underlined by the recent report of the Institute of Medicine: "Dying in America: Improving Quality and Honoring Individual Preferences at the End of Life." The distinguished panel who contributed to this work noted that the spiritual needs of the individual and their loved ones should be a concern of all who are attendant upon the patient approaching death. Individuals and institutions in this arena should assure that there is not only sensitivity to addressing this need but persons well prepared be available to those in need. The Essential Spirit can be of valuable assistance in meeting these objectives.

Msgr Charles Fahey, SJ
Past Chair, Board of Directors, American Society of Aging
Professor of Aging Studies Emeritus, Fordham University

Preface

This book was years in birthing. It began in 1994 when I was a chaplain at UCLA Medical Center. There was a highly skilled and practical social worker on my unit who understood boundaries and, at times, became the self appointed definer and enforcer of those boundaries. There were the events and decisions that were the province of the physician, others the psychiatrist, still others the social worker. But she didn't have a clue as to what the role of the chaplain was or could be. The sad thing was neither did I even though I came to chaplaincy after twenty-seven years serving in congregations. Because of this social worker I discovered that my seminary training equipped me to be a theologian in the pulpit, a pseudo-social worker in home visiting, and a junior-shrink in the counseling office. My skill set and even my language was the same as social workers, psychologists, and even physicians. So what did I bring that was unique to the interdisciplinary table during rounds at the hospital?

One item was spiritual assessment. Strangely I had never heard of spiritual assessments either in seminary or in the parish. Assessing a patient's spirituality was indeed unique. But what was spirituality and how did it affect behavior, even healing? It wasn't until I became a chaplain in retirement communities that I begin to discern a glimmer of a definition that worked not only for theists like myself, but the many non-theists that I had come to know and respect at UCLA. That glimmer, that spark, was fanned into a flame when I joined the American Society on Aging and its constituent group, the Forum on Religion, Spirituality, and Aging (FORSA). It was in FORSA that I found a group of interdisciplinary professionals who were seeking the same answers as I. While many had a many years head start I was a dedicated and fast learner. I found a professional and personal home in FORSA.

At the same time, my relationships with persons of other disciplines outside of FORSA continued to be frustrating. Even as I gained confidence and the words to express what I was experiencing as I explored the spiritual lives of older adults, persons of other disciplines continued to debate spirituality efficacy or worse, just ignored any attempt on my part to convince them otherwise. I consciously tried to avoid the tendency for a professional to believe that everyone else should get behind their view of the human, their understanding on health, their view of the world, as if psychiatry, social work, nursing, or physiology was "God's greatest gift to the world." I was trained as a pastor who often have big heads or big egos, but as I explored the interplay between old age and the spiritual I became convinced that while other disciplines addressed an essential component in the lives of older people, only spirituality truly looked at the person as a whole. As spiritual caregivers, I and others in FORSA became increasingly aware that the social, psychological, physical aspects of life separated the patient—separating them into parts, rather than addressing them as a whole. So much of healing, be it sociological, psychological, or physiological, is based upon how each client receives and integrates the bio-medical model so rampant within health care in American today.

So this book became a desire, a wish, a hope, a glimmer in my eye. I didn't expect the network of persons both in and outside of FORSA would embrace the idea as strongly as they have. But as I began to recruit, I only had one "No, not right now" response. Many of these persons are my mentors in gerontology. Many I had come to appreciate the passion for older adults and spirituality that surpassed my own. While I believe that anyone interested in older adults will be helped by the insights that my friends have shared in these pages, the target audience are professionals who are providing services to and with older adults.

In the last two years my perspectives have been revisited and even challenged because of the views of the authors in this book. Other personal beliefs have been sharpened as they are given voice and words. I trust that this book will encourage you to go deeper into this realm of the spirit so that the fine work that you are presently providing older adults via your discipline will be enhanced and become more effective and fulfilling as you become aware of and use *The Essential Spirit*.

Donald Koepke

Acknowledgments

Even with the expertise of a fine publisher like Wipf and Stock, there are many costs involved to edit and market a book such as *The Essential Spirit*. My thanks go to the vision and generosity of California Lutheran Homes and Community Services of Glendale, CA for the grant that has made the publication of this book a reality. I also want to acknowledge their passion and financial expertise that will enable all proceeds from this book to offer financial grants to other worthy nonprofit organizations that promote the use of spirituality in aging.

Introduction

The Essential Spirit

—Donald Koepke, MDiv, BCC

Spirituality is the aspect of humanity that refers to the way individuals
seek and express meaning and purpose and the way they experience
their connectedness to the moment, to self, to others, to nature, and to
the significant or sacred.[1]

I HAD BEEN A twenty-seven-year veteran as a parish pastor when I began
work as chaplain at the Alhambra Retirement Community in Alhambra,
California, a California Lutheran Home. I was very new to chaplaincy, having just completed a residency year of CPE (Clinical Pastoral Education)
at UCLA Medical Center. I was sad to have left the hustle and bustle of the
medical center behind me. The intellectual vibrancy plus the excellence of
proving care was intoxicating. It was the place where I had begun my training in chaplaincy. Little did I know that my training was just beginning and
that my teachers would be residents in long-term care.

Besides independent and assisted living, the Alhambra had a fifty-five-
bed skilled care unit filled with people in wheelchairs. My initial observations were that many residents seemed to be resigned to life there in the
SNF, perhaps simply waiting for death to rescue them, while others had eyes
that still burned with life. Both sets of residents ate at the same dining room,
ate the same food, lived in identical rooms, received care by the same staff,
and yet some were so alive that I hardly believed my eyes. Upon further
observation I noticed that both groups, save those with acute dementia, had
similar chronic conditions. In fact, some who were the most engaged with

---

1. Definition from Puchalski et al., "Improving the Quality."

life had greater physical and emotional conditions than the others. I wondered why, so I began to listen, and learn from my teachers.

I discovered (or more honestly I was taught) that their embracing of life beyond their condition did not come from better physical and emotional care. There was something more, something intangible, something powerful and yet beyond what could be touched, tasted, heard, seen, felt, and proved. What I discovered was a deep personal intrinsic spirituality that enabled them to have hope in the midst of struggle and joy in the midst of pain. That experience began a journey of learning. I wanted to understand how a person's spirituality affected their aging and how their aging affected their spirituality. What I found was a perspective that changed my life and my perspective on life that has finally given birth to this book, *The Essential Spirit*.

This book is intended to advocate for a greater role and awareness of spirituality not only in long-term care but throughout the health care industry. I have asked friends from around the county to contribute in areas of care that they have studied for much of their life. Their offerings provide the nuts and bolts of providing quality and effective spiritual care. My job is to present the heart of spiritual care, sharing the essence of what my teachers have taught me.

WHO IS THE HUMAN PERSON?

The human being is more than the sum of his/her parts. The essential part of a human being can not be seen in CAT scans, blood tests, or psychological profiles alone. Persons are essentially spiritual in that their core beliefs, a spiritual self, developed over a lifetime. This spiritual self are the glasses through which a person interprets the world about them, including what is happening to them physically, socially, and psychologically. At the same time, the physical, social, and psychological experiences of life effect and expand one's spirituality. D. E Capps is quoted by Pargament and Krumrei as saying, "The spiritual is elusive not because it lurks behind ordinary phenomena [life] but because it is inter-woven within the phenomena [life]"[2] It is this core belief, a person's spirituality, which guides and even drives how that person perceives, integrates, and reacts to the physical/social/psychological experiences in their lives. Just as spirituality affects each domain of life, each domain also affects one's spirituality, one's view of the world.

Figure 1 below seeks to visualize this process. Instead of spirituality being but one domain of life, spirituality is essentially the core

2. D. E. Capps as quoted in Aten and Leach, *Clinical Assessment*, 93.

of the domains influencing and being influenced by each domain as it is experienced. Thus, a person's spirituality is both dynamic and inclusive of all experiences in life, making spirituality difficult to define or even grasp by both the person themselves and any inquisitor. ps]

Domains of Life

THE ESSENTIAL SPIRIT IS MORE THAN RELIGIOUS BELIEFS

While every religion seeks to guide and nurture the spirituality (core beliefs) of the person, spirituality is greater, deeper than religion. Save for exceptionally aware individuals, people who are called "saints" by Christians, "wali" by Muslims, Arhats or Bodhisattvas among Hindus, and *Tzadik* (righteous) in Judaism, a person's spirituality is always greater than a person's religion because spirituality is formed by so many experiences in life other than religious thought and perspectives. Many people have asked: "What is spirituality? How is it defined?" What I believe that they are asking is for a cognitive, empirical, logical definition. But spirituality is not cognitive. It is subjective, not objective, and even experiential. Spirituality is of the heart not the head. At its best, religion, or the cognitive world, provides the words that allows a person to interpret their inner core, through awareness and reflection. A person's spirituality, one's core values and beliefs, are continually in a process of becoming as they encounter new perspectives within their lives that are more varied than simply religious beliefs and values. Many of these perspectives are conscious. I wonder, however, if most are experienced in the unconscious self that is formed by experience not thinking. Like the famous paradigm of the philosopher Hegel, thesis, antithesis, synthesis, suggests that a person's life is continually changing as new events are encountered that either support or challenge those core values and beliefs.[3] Figure 2 seeks to visually chart this phenomena though the number of categories that influence one's core belief(s), a person's spirituality, is infinite in number limited only by what each person deems as being important and thus affective of these core beliefs. That is why a person does not have to be religious in order to have spirituality. Jesus of Nazareth once quipped "Where your treasure is, there your heart will be also."[4] What is it that is treasured by a person, sought by a person, desired by a person? In chapter 1 Pargament and McGee picture spirituality as that which is "sacred" in a person's life—their so-called "sacred cows." That which is treasured defines who we are, how we think, what we pay attention to, what we value. The domains noted in figure 1 above might end up believing that power is the most important thing in life. Some persons might "choose" wealth, or philanthropy, or selfless giving of time. I don't know from where it developed, but a recent therapeutic encounter revealed that I didn't feel like an evil person; I actually believed that I was evil incarnate, an insight to my core beliefs that I had never recognized before, but a belief that shaped my life enormously. Such is the power of belief.[5]

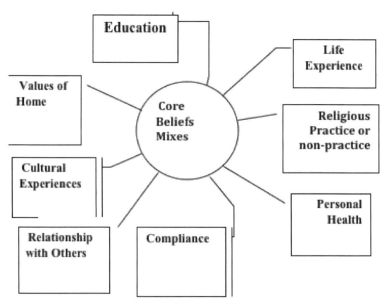

3. While Hegel suggested in *The Science of Logic* (1812–16) that logic progresses by encounter with differing views (a dialectic), the so-called Hegelian Dialectic used here is more attributed to an earlier philosopher, Johann Gottlieb Fichte.

4. Matt 6:21, RSV.

5. For a deeper study of the power of belief read Lipton, *The Biology of Belief*.

THE ESSENTIAL SPIRIT AS EXPERIENCED IN AGING

One of the chapter authors in this book, Jane Thibault (chapter 10), correctly describes the experience of aging as a "natural monastery."[6] To enter a monastery a person must surrender old habits and beliefs in favor of living within a new paradigm designed to break through personal defenses. At the same time, to enter a monastery one has to surrender individualism for the inter-commitment of the community. One lives alone in a solitary room providing time for contemplation, while at the same time, lives communally. In monastic life, inconvenience, afflictions, even suffering is expected and embraced as being the doorway to deeper knowledge of one's real values and beliefs.

Such is also the way of aging. All the disciplines of aging-care view the experience of aging as a decline. Physicians seek to plug the holes and stem the tide of an inevitable physical tsunami. Social workers encourage the elderly to focus on their strengths rather than their weaknesses, calling attention to what they can do rather than on what they cannot do. Psychologists help a person cope (survive) with all of the finitudes of the latter years. Only a view of the spirit, encompasses aging as a time of potential growing and becoming. Only spiritual care views the challenges of aging as a potential advantage, a window to the soul, the core, of who we are, a potential "golden age" *not in spite of* physical, psychological, and sociological challenges, *but because of* these challenges as the person is "forced" to explore the depths of what it means to be human. Am I human if I can't think cognitively? I wonder how Descartes would answer because of his dictum "I think therefore I am." Yet is a major league pitcher less of a person if an arm is broken? Is a person less when they become the "cared-for" rather than the caregiver?

Thus *The Essential Spirit*. Spirituality is the window into what it means to be human. To deny or ignore a person's spirituality due to fears of offense, or the so-called separation of church and state, or the policies of an institution, or the learned ethics of professional practice is to miss the "something more" that is essential to understanding, and thus treating effectively the whole person. To engage and learn from *The Essential Spirit*, clinical providers of care are able to use the principles of their profession in the most effective way possible. Dr. David Felton MD, a research immunologist, concluded "If you [physicians in the audience] are not prescribing spiritual practices to your patients . . . you are doing them a dis-service."[7]

6. Thibault, "Aging as Natural Monastery," 3.

7. David Felton, Grand Rounds Presentation, February, 2004, King Drew Medical Center, Los Angeles. Dr. Felton shared results of his research on immunology which demonstrated that when a patient practices spiritual actions the "good stuff" of their immune system goes up while the "bad stuff" goes down.

It is important to state that spirituality is dead unless it is expressed, lived, and integrated within the self. For an older adult, or anyone else for that matter, to become aware of and then be able to intentionally use their spirituality, their core beliefs take discipline, perseverance, and more than a little courage. The reason is that engaging one's spirituality requires becoming deeply aware of not only one's strengths, but limitations as well. Paul Dobies in chapter 3 uses the metaphor of an automobile. He suggests that owning a car gives its owner identity, a sense of independence, and even control. So if owning a car gives identity like religion, then driving that car is spirituality. Spirituality is how one uses the car, good and not so good. As noted above, core beliefs are sculptured by many life experiences, many of which might not be pleasant to uncover. In fact, the more that older adults become aware of the existence of their spirituality, they become intensely aware of the personal barriers and deceptions that threaten and obscure their attempt to follow that internal compass. The resulting inner tension and turmoil is the core of spiritual distress. But exploring that distress, what core beliefs work and those that inhibit, can be a window into the core of the persons and an engagement with their essential self.

THE PURPOSE OF THIS BOOK

This book, like a good appetizer, is designed to increase your desire for more. *The Essential Spirit* only scratches the surface of the power that lies behind including spirituality in providing quality service to older adults. Each chapter focuses on a specific challenge of aging and also how engaging the spiritual, the belief system and core of the person, can result in insight bringing wholeness and healing to the whole of the person. Figure 3 below illustrates *The Essential Spirit* in terms of the chapters of this book. The goal: to advocate that persons of all disciplines engage the spirituality of their clients so that their interventions might be as lasting and as effective as possible.

I also call your attention to the epilogue that is written especially for you, the reader personally. It is authored by me and Nancy Gordon, my successor as Director of the CLH Center for Spirituality in Aging. It is written in the first person, sharing personal insights and experiences that hopefully will engage your perspective on your own aging and how it affects and is affected by your personal core beliefs, your spirituality.

Finally without denying or even minimizing the challenges of aging, each chapter will demonstrate methods of caring for the spirit that can revitalize a person's perspective on life and thus bring quality to life, even if those challenges don't go away. The concepts in this book are not designed to make all readers a spiritual-care specialist. That is the role of the client's spiritual advisor/local clergy and/or the chaplain of your facility. At the same time, this book is not intended to negate the value of other disciplines. Instead it is hoped that family caregivers and service providers of all disciplines will find that the effectiveness of their efforts are quantifiably enhanced and improved by paying attention to *The Essential Spirit*.

REFERENCES

Aten, Jamie D., and Leach, Mark M., eds. *Clinical Assessment of Clients' Spirituality*. Washington, DC: American Psychological Association, 2009.

Lipton, Bruce H. *The Biology of Belief*. Carlsbad, CA: Hay, 2008.

Thibault, Jane Marie, "Aging as a Natural Monastery." *Aging and Spirituality: Newsletter of the ASA's Forum on Religion, Spirituality and Aging* 8 (Fall 1996) 3, 8.

RECOMMENDED READINGS

Aten, Jamie D., and Mark M. Leach. *Spirituality and the Therapeutic Process*. Washington, DC: American Psychological Association, 2009.

Cohen, Gene D. *The Mature Mind: The Positive Power of the Aging Brain*. Cambridge, MA: Basic, 2009.

Fischer, Kathleen. *Winter Grace*. Nashville: Upper Room, 1998.

Highfield, Martha Farrer, and Carolyn Cason. "Spiritual Needs of Patients: Are They Recognized?" *Cancer Nursing* 6/3 (1983) 187–92.

Koenig, Harold G. *Aging and God: Spiritual Pathways to Mental Health in Midlife and Later Years*. New York: Haworth, 1994.

Moody, Harry. *Religion, Spirituality and Aging*. Binghamton, NY: Haworth Social Work, 2005.

Moody, Harry, and David Carroll. *The Five Stages of the Soul*. New York: Anchor, 1997.

Pargament, Kenneth L. *Spiritually Integrated Psychotherapy: Understanding and Addressing the Sacred*. New York: Guilford, 2007.

Thibault, Jane Marie. *A Deepening Love Affair: The Gift of God in Later Life*. Nashville: Upper Room, 1993.

Van Hook, Mary, Beryl Hugen, and Marian Aguilar. *Spirituality within Religious Traditions in Social Work Practice*. New York: Wadsworth, 2001.

PART I

Principles Behind Older
Adult Spirituality

1

Spirituality, the Sacred Domain

Core Concepts and Implications for Practice for Older Adults

—Jocelyn McGee, PhD, Kenneth Pargament, PhD, Aaron Silverbook, BS

DRAWING ON THEORY, RESEARCH, and clinical practice, Pargament's seminal work, *Spiritually Integrated Psychotherapy*, offers a highly accessible and well thought out system for understanding and evaluating the role of spirituality in life.[1] This chapter of the *Essential Spirit* will highlight some of the core concepts and practice implications derived from Pargament's work, which the reader may use to develop a more spiritually sensitive clinical practice. The primary aim of this chapter is to offer practical information for clinical providers from multiple disciplines that work with older adults and recognize the essentiality of addressing spirituality in their care. The chapter will start out with a description of spirituality as the sacred domain. We will then consider how people engage in the search for the sacred, focusing more specifically on: (a) how people discover the sacred, (b) the various pathways they take in an effort to conserve or hold on to the sacred, and (c) how they may respond to struggles in the search for the sacred through coping and transformation. We will conclude with some suggestions and guidelines around spiritually sensitive care.

---

1. Pargament, *Spiritually Integrated Psychotherapy.*

DIVERSE PEOPLE, DIVERSE DEFINITIONS

It seems that there are as many ways to understand spirituality as there are human beings. Just last semester, a highly diverse class of graduate students in my (JSM) course Spirituality in Clinical Practice at the University of Alaska Anchorage (UAA) were asked about their conceptualizations of spirituality and how they perceived spirituality to play out in their clinical practice. Not surprisingly, there was no consensus on how to define spirituality. Some equated spirituality with religion while others believed that spirituality transcends religion. Some viewed spirituality from an individual perspective while others believed that spirituality could only be experienced within the context of a community. The class was unable to come to consensus around these terms, and the students were surprised when I shared with them that many older adults equate spirituality with religion in contrast to the evolving trend in our culture toward a view of these constructs as polar opposites.

The students expressed a range of ideas about how spirituality should be addressed, if at all, in clinical practice. The majority of students recognized that spirituality was somehow important for good patient care but did not have a full grasp of: (a) how their patients would express their spirituality within a clinical context; (b) how spirituality could be a source of strength or struggle in the life of an individual, family, or community; or (c) how their own spiritual beliefs and practices might impact the care of their patients.

As you read the *Essential Spirit*, you too are likely attempting to understand how these issues impact your work with older adults. We hope that the concepts presented here will expand your understanding of people and their problems from a spiritual perspective and influence your ability to provide more spiritually integrated care to older adults and their families.

DEFINITIONS AND CORE CONCEPTS

Pargament's definition of spirituality as "a search for the sacred"[2] was particularly helpful to my students as they began their journey of discovering how to integrate spirituality into their clinical practices. In this section, we will unpack this definition and provide you with several key concepts for understanding the sacred as it pertains to providing care to older adults. The sacred, at its core, has to do with God, higher powers, or transcendent reality. The representations of divinity that go into the *sacred core* are

2. Pargament, *Psychology of Religion*.

specific to each person and are influenced by religious traditions, culture, communities, family, and individual life experiences and development.

Radiating out from this core are the relationships, places, experiences, and objects of daily life that take on sacred status through their association with that person's *sacred core*.[3] These objects, which form the *sacred ring*[4] are imbued with sacred significance through the process of *sanctification*.[5] That is, they become sacred through their association with the transcendent. For example, an older adult may perceive the divine when glimpsing a snowy mountain peak, hearing the waves of the ocean crash against the shore of a sunny beach, or sitting quietly in a garden and watching a sparrow as it drinks from a fountain. Another may view the baking of bread and consuming it with loved ones as a sacred gift from God. Values, beliefs, character traits, and strivings may also be deemed sacred if they are associated with what is perceived as holy for that person. Virtually anything can be held as sacred by a person; this point has important implications for the provision of spiritually sensitive care to older adults, especially those residing in long term care facilities whose activities, interactions, and relationships may represent nothing less than the face of God.

It is important to recognize that there is considerable diversity in what particular older adults perceive as sacred in their lives; that is, individuals can vary in the elements that make up their sacred core and ring articulates three varieties of the sacred: a) the self; b) the relational; and c) place and time. Consistent with this conceptualization of the varieties of the sacred, a recent mixed-methods study on spirituality among people who were diagnosed with mild Alzheimer's disease (AD) revealed that *sacred relationships*, for them, were particularly important and fell into several categories: a) relationship with the transcendent (i.e., God, higher power, spirit); b) relationship with the spiritual community (i.e., church, synagogue, mosque, spirituality group); c) relationship with significant others (i.e., family and friends); and d) the relationship with the self.[6,7] For example one man coping with AD described his relationship with the transcendent in this way: "What is most sacred to me is that I would rely on God for any help that I need." Several were fearful of losing this connection with God as the disease progressed, as expressed by one man: "I guess I have thought more about if you lose your cognitive awareness and ability, do you lose

3. Pargament and Mahoney, "Spirituality."

4. Pargament, *Spiritually Integrated Psychotherapy*.

5. Pargament and Mahoney, "Sacred Matters."

6. McGee et al., "Spirituality."

7. McGee and Myers, "Sacred Relationships."

your ability to conceive [of] God?" Pertaining to the sacred relationship with the spiritual community, participants expressed how important their spiritual community was to them. For example, one person said: "It is very supportive, we have several [individuals who] have AD." One woman described how she perceived sacredness in her relationship with a significant other: "My salvation is my daughter . . . She is my strength . . . I know the Lord is involved, and I think He sent her to me. She moved here to be with me . . . that is sacred." Another man stated: "[My] relationship with friends is sacred. Friendships and loyalty and being loyal to friends . . . those are the things that are most sacred." In describing his sacred relationship with himself, one man put it this way: "Well, the most sacred thing to me is the love . . . I have for myself."

Additionally, the spiritual or sacred relationship between professional caregivers and their patients has begun to receive more attention in the research and clinical literature. Several authors have identified and described the elements of this spiritual connection. These include: the capacity of the provider to be mindfully attuned to and present for the patient,[8] the ability of the provider to offer therapeutic inspiration,[9] the ability of the provider to relate wholeheartedly to the patient in the fullness of their humanity with an I-Thou orientation,[10] and a focus on transformational present moments.[11] Each of these elements of the spiritual relationship between caregiver and patient may serve as an ingredient of positive change.

In our recent work, we have been exploring one particular aspect of the spiritual relationship between professional caregivers, or providers, and their patients —sacred moments—as a potentially key contributor to positive change in providers, patients, and the helping relationship.[12] Sacred moments, we believe, are brief periods of time where patient and/or provider experience certain spiritual qualities in the context of the professional relationship or the therapeutic encounter; these qualities include transcendence, ultimacy, boundlessness, interconnectedness, and spiritual emotions.[13,14]

The first sacred quality, transcendence, refers to perceptions that an experience or object has surpassed ordinary understanding and moved

8. E.g., Bruce et al., "Psychotherapist Mindfulness."

9. O'Grady and Richards, "Role of Inspiration."

10. Buber, *I and Thou.*

11. Stern, *Present Moment.*

12. Pargament et al., "Sacred Moments."

13. Lomax et al., "Perspectives."

14. Pargament and Mahoney, "Sacred Matters."

into the realm of the extraordinary or supernatural. An example is when seven eagles circled above my home as I walked my friends to their cars the day after my husband died (JSM). For years, my husband had told me that if he died before me, every time I encountered a hawk or an eagle, it would be a reminder that he was with God. This profound experience could not be explained in any ordinary sense and transcended rational explanation. It was extraordinary, supernatural, and in essence sacred for all who experienced it, which was remarkable given our differing religious and spiritual orientations (i.e., Christian, Buddhist, spiritual only, and atheist). The second sacred quality, boundlessness, involves experiences in which time and space appear to be limitless, endless, extending beyond all normal boundaries. Quoting Elkins on this sacred quality: "Eternity breaks in, an eternal present."[15] Ultimacy or "the essential and absolute ground of truth, the foundation for all experience"[16] has to do with what is perceived as "really, real."[17] Perceptions of deep and mutual understanding and caring are markers of the sacred quality of interconnectedness.[18] Finally, spiritual emotions involve a sense of uplift, awe, humility, mystery, gratitude, joy, peace, and serenity. These emotions can be facilitated in variety of ways to provide spiritually sensitive care to older adults.

Findings from our studies suggest that sacred moments, within the context of a therapeutic relationship, represent an important ingredient for provider and patient well-being as well as highlight the value of attending to the spiritual dimension of this relationship.[19] Indeed, for the fifty-eight mental health providers we surveyed in our first study, the degree to which a patient encounter was considered sacred was strongly correlated with their perceptions of greater patient gains, therapeutic relationship gains, provider gains, and overall work motivation. These findings were largely replicated in our second study of 519 patients who had received mental health care in the year before our study. One patient described a sacred moment within the context of the therapeutic relationship this way: "It was sacred to me because I knew, all the way to my spirit that I was not alone in this anymore and that I had not only my therapist on my side but it brought home that God was pained by what I went through."

---

15. Elkins, *Beyond Religion*, 126.

16. Ibid., 39.

17. Geertz, *Islam Observed*.

18. Pargament et al., "Sacred Moments."

19. Ibid.

In concluding this section on definitions and core concepts about spirituality as it pertains to working with older adults, we would like to leave you with few take-home points:

- the sacred may be experienced in a variety of ways. Think broadly then about what a particular older adult may have sanctified and what holds meaning and purpose to them in the context of clinical care;

- integrating and attending to the sacred domain in older adult care should be important to clinical providers from multiple disciplines as it may emerge in a variety of clinical settings;

- the sacred is present in many aspects of life, even the so-called mundane, and may be a powerful resource for connection and healing both among and between providers and patients;

- providers should attempt to work towards helping older adults strengthen sacred relationships with the transcendent, the spiritual community, the important people in their lives, and the relationship with the self.

Now that we have defined spirituality and the sacred domain, we turn our attention to how people live out their spirituality in their search for the sacred.

SEARCHING FOR THE SACRED

In our discussion of what it means to search for the sacred, we make a critical assumption: people are not merely reactive beings but also active agents in their lives, striving towards the goals and destinations they hold significant.[20] Individuals and communities can find significance in many goals: material, physical, psychological, social, and spiritual. The pursuit or attainment of significance typically results in a sense of value, worth, and importance in individuals, families and communities.[21] For many, the spiritual or sacred is at the center of their strivings providing an overarching frame under which all other goals are subsumed.

A poignant example of the sacred guiding other aspects of life comes from my research on resilience in elderly guardians of orphaned and vulnerable children in Malawi, Africa last summer (JSM). When I asked an extremely impoverished elderly widow who is the guardian of several orphans about her experience, this remarkable woman stated, "I know it is the

20. Pargament, *Spiritually Integrated Psychotherapy*.
21. Pargament, *Psychology of Religion and Coping*.

will of God that I care for these orphans. When I care for these orphans, I care for all of Malawi, I care for the world." Despite the fact that she was in very poor health herself and lacked adequate food or water, she engaged in strenuous manual labor (e.g., digging pit latrines) to provide for the basic needs of the orphans in her care. She viewed this work as a sacred pursuit and found deep meaning in her goals and strivings which were rooted in her connection God.

The search for the sacred is for many people the force that motivates, organizes, and directs their lives. It is a distinctive, dynamic process that evolves over the course of the lifespan (see figure below). In brief, the search begins with the revelation, recognition, or discovery that something is sacred. A path is then forged to conserve and foster the relationship with the sacred. Challenging life experiences, however, can disrupt a person's spiritual journey resulting in spiritual struggle. As a result, the person may temporarily or permanently disengage from the spiritual search, or radically transform his/her understanding of the sacred. Three important processes then are involved in the search for the sacred: a) discovery; b) conservation; and c) transformation; each which will be discussed briefly below.

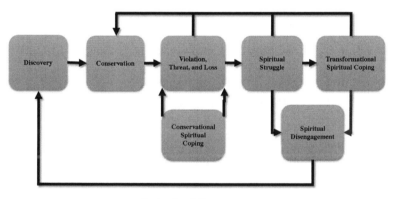

Sociocultural Context

Adapted from Pargament (2009) with permission

Discovery

The experience of discovering the sacred often begins in childhood; however, discovery or rediscovery may occur at any point in the lifespan. The students in my Spirituality in Clinical Practice course (JSM), as one of their assignments, were asked to reflect upon when they first encountered or became aware of the sacred in their lives. One student experienced an intuitive connection to the divine through nature at the age of two. Another student discovered the sacred through the liturgy in the church of her youth where her parents worshipped. Another first experienced the sacred while traveling on a train to university as a young adult, feeling a sense of awe when she encountered the lights of the large metropolitan city of Shanghai.

Researchers and professionals in the area of spirituality and health have often tried to reduce the search for the sacred to purportedly more basic motivations. Thus, religious and spiritual involvement has been conceptualized as ways to reduce anxiety, achieve connection and community, exert self-control, or find meaning in life. Certainly, spiritual involvement may serve many of these and other psychological and social purposes. But it is important not to reduce spirituality to purely psychological, social, or physical drives. The search for the sacred appears to be a distinctive motivation in and of itself. In fact, a case could be made that spiritual motivation may underlie other motivations.[22]

The discovery of the sacred has important implications for working with older adults. A growing body of research suggests that:

- the sacred becomes an organizing force in peoples' lives;

- people draw on the sacred as a resource of support and meaning in their lives;

- the sacred can be a source of powerful spiritual emotions such as awe, uplift, gratitude, and humility;

- the loss or violation of sacred aspects of life can be especially disorienting and painful.[23]

One of the most powerful implications of the discovery of the sacred is that once found, people are motivated to conserve or hold on to the sacred. The sacred becomes a habitat, a place to be, a place people long to return.

Conservation

There are numerous pathways for conserving or holding on to the sacred, once discovered. Most religious and spiritual traditions view the idea of the path as essential to the spiritual life.[24] For example, the word *Tao* within Taoism literally means "the Way," the "Eightfold Path" leads to enlightenment in Buddhism, and the "Five Pillars of Islam" is important to followers of Allah. Within different religious and spiritual systems, individuals may

22. Pargament, "Searching for the Sacred."
23. Pargament and Mahoney, "Sacred Matters."
24. Schmidt et al., *Patterns of Religion.*

take a path of learning about life's greatest truths through reason, intuition, or revelation (the pathway of knowing); enacting their religious or spiritual understandings of the world through ritual and practice (the pathway of acting); and through daily relationships with family, friends, and others in the community or world (the pathway of relating). Each individual may have a preferred mode for connecting with the sacred, or what Pargament has referred to as a spiritual orienting system,[25] or may simultaneously engage in each of these paths. At different points in development or with disease or disability, a specific path may become more predominant. For instance, people with AD have been observed to connect with the sacred through participating in sacred rituals (the pathway of acting), such as the Eucharist or singing well-known songs from their religious history, rather than engaging in study of scripture or other religious or spiritual writings (the pathway of knowing) with disease progression.

Although these spiritual orienting systems tend to help people maintain stability in their lives, trauma or transition including illness and disability, the challenges of aging may severely test a person's sacred search or predominant path, resulting in movement onto a different path: the path of spiritual coping. This path has similar components to other paths; it is made up of thoughts, practices, relationships, and experiences. However, the pathway lends itself specifically to dealing with challenges, threats, and/ or desecration or harm to the sacred. There are a number of spiritual coping methods, which we will describe, but let us first turn to a brief discussion about spiritual desecration.

At times, people experience a profound level of violation and disrespect towards the sacred aspects of their lives. The most apparent examples are circumstances that result in extreme horror and traumatic loss, such as the September 11, 2001 attacks and other instances of violent unexpected death or disability. In a study to measure a linkage between PTSD, anguish, and spiritual impact, when queried, approximately half of the respondents said that the event was both an offense against them and against God.[26] Indeed greater perceptions of the event as a desecration were linked to stronger feelings of anger, depression, and post-traumatic stress. This level of threat may also be observed when an individual has experienced a profound individual loss, such as a death of a loved one regardless of cause, especially if the relationship was viewed as a sacred representation of the transcendent. Likewise, an individual with AD may view cognitive decline as a sacred threat or loss to the core of their personhood.[27]

25. Pargament, *Spiritually Integrated Psychotherapy.*
26. Mahoney et al., "The Devil."
27. McGee et al., "Spirituality."

There are a variety of ways people utilize spiritual coping to persevere or reaffirm a connection to the divine in the face of loss, violation, and threat. When Gallup and Lindsay surveyed the population of the United States, they found that 80% of people pray when faced with a spiritual crisis and 64% report that they read the Bible or other spiritual literature. What's more, the benefits of spirituality accumulate over time. In a longitudinal study in 2004, Brown, Nesse, House, and Utz measured how well a widowed group fared in contrast to a control in dealing with their major stressors.[28] The widowed group reported that their spirituality had become more important to them; what's more, this increase in spiritual belief was tied to a decline in grief.

Pargament, Koenig, and Perez describe several specific forms of conservational religious coping.[29] For example, benevolent spiritual reappraisals involve redefining a stressor through religion or spirituality as potentially beneficial. An example comes from an elder who was diagnosed with multiple sclerosis and viewed the physical changes he was experiencing as an opportunity to focus more on his spiritual life. Spiritual support, another conservational method, involves searching for love, care, and connection with the sacred that may involve the spiritual community as well as the transcendent. It may grow out of prayer, mediation, ritual practices, nature, art, and even perception of a direct spiritual encounter with the sacred. An example is a woman who was diagnosed with mild AD participating in a movement meditation practice daily to connect to "Spirit" to help her feel loved and connected. Spiritual purification, another type of religious coping, is often used when a person perceives his or her own actions as offenses against God. Among the many examples of spiritual purification are the acts of repentance, liturgies of atonement, and confession (public or private).

Struggle and Transformation

At times, however, in spite of his/her conservational efforts, the individual may not be able to sustain the search for the sacred through religious coping, and spiritual struggles may emerge. Struggles refer to tensions and conflicts about sacred matters within oneself, with others, or with the supernatural.[30, 31] Spiritual struggles may be transient, such as a brief period of time of feeling angry or punished by God, or may be longer lasting. These

28. Brown et al., "Religion and Emotional Compensation."
29. Pargament et al., "Many Methods."
30. Pargament et al., "Spiritual Struggle."
31. Exline, "Religious and Spiritual Struggles."

struggles may lead people to experience profound pain, and deep questions about their own value, purpose, efficacy, or purpose in the wake of tragedy.[32]

Spiritual struggles take many forms. Exline, Pargament, Grubbs, and Yali identify several domains which we will briefly summarize here.[33]

- The first domain involves negative thoughts and feelings about God or the relationship with God (*divine domain*).

- The second domain pertains to concern that the devil or evil spirits are attacking the person or is the source of negative events (*demonic domain*).

- The third domain involves negative feelings about the spiritual community or institutions (*interpersonal domain*).

- The fourth domain for spiritual struggle involves wrestling with the ability to follow moral principles which can lead to excessive fear or guilt in people about their perceived offenses (*moral domain*).

- The fifth domain involves being concerned that one has doubts or questions about his or her beliefs (*doubt domain*).

- The sixth domain has to do with *ultimate meaning* or a concern about a lack of deep meaning and purpose in one's life.

For some, struggles lead to temporary or permanent disengagement from the sacred quest. Zuckerman interviewed a variety of apostates, formally religious people who chose to leave their religious communities. Many described a period of significant struggle with the dogma of their traditions, religious hypocrisy, and conflict with religious leaders. Those unable to find ways to reconcile their conflicts within their religious communities were more likely to disengage from their faith traditions.[34]

Other people stay involved in the search for the sacred, and experience more profound spiritual transformation, revising their understanding of the sacred or the pathways they take to reach their sacred destinations. Pargament describes the most significant forms of spiritual transformation including: a) sacred transitions; b) revisioning the sacred; and c) centering the sacred.[35] The rites of passage communities participate in after the death of a community member is an example of a sacred transition. Although the form of these rites vary significantly from culture to culture, they are ultimately aimed at marking a momentous occasion both for the deceased and

---

32. Hill et al., "Conceptualizing Religion."

33. Exline et al., "Religious and Spritual Struggles Scale."

34. Zuckerman, *Faith No More.*

35. Pargament, *Spiritually Integrated Psychotherapy.*

the mourners, and facilitating a transition in sacred statu—for the deceased, from living to dead; for the loved ones, from regular member of the community to mourner.

Another form of spiritual transformation, revisioning the sacred, can be found in Harold Kushner's book, *When Bad Things Happen to Good People*, which describes his own painful process after the loss of his fourteen-year-old son. Kushner transformed his understanding of the divine from a loving, all-powerful Being to a loving, but limited God.[36]

One final form of spiritual transformation, centering the sacred, involves creating new visions of the sacred which are realigned within the person's values and strivings. This process is most clearly illustrated by spiritual conversion. But it can take other forms as well, such as the shift in an individual's significant goals from the destructive pursuit of bitterness and anger to the sacred values of forgiveness and peace of mind after a loss. Three processes are involved in the process of centering the sacred: a) recognizing the limitations of current strivings; b) letting go of these strivings; and c) placing the sacred at the center.[37]

It is important to note that once a transformation occurs and the sacred is, in essence, rediscovered, the task for the individual shifts to conserving the sacred as it is newly understood. In this sense, the search for the sacred continues to evolve over the lifespan.

GUIDELINES FOR ADDRESSING SPIRITUALITY IN CLINICAL PRACTICE

It is essential to receive training in order to develop the skills necessary to effectively and sensitively address spirituality in clinical practice with older adults. Importantly, Pargament notes that our patients do not leave their spirituality outside of the treatment setting. Their spirituality is a core component of who they are and may serve as a source of solution or even a difficulty in clinical practice.[38] It is also important for clinical providers to recognize that they too do not leave their spirituality outside of the treatment setting. Clinical providers may be intolerant or insensitive to the spiritual aspects of their client's issues resulting in less effective or failed treatment outcomes. Spiritual literacy on the part of the provider is integral to addressing spirituality in clinical practice; competencies in this area

36. Kushner, *When Bad Things Happen*.

37. See Pargament, *Spiritually Integrated Psychotherapy* for further discussion.

38. Pargament, *Spiritually Integrated Psychotherapy*.

include spiritual knowledge, openness, tolerance, self-awareness, and the ability to remain authentic.

There are several unhelpful tendencies that clinical providers may demonstrate when attempting to integrate spirituality into clinical practice.[39] First and foremost, providers must guard against their own spiritual biases or tendency to hold stereotypical views regarding the beliefs and practices of older adults from certain religious or spiritual traditions. Older adults from the same religious tradition can hold diverse and sometimes divergent religious perspectives. Additionally, because many providers in the health care arena lack training in spirituality integrated care and may be secular themselves, they may suffer from spiritual myopia or difficulty seeing the spiritual dimension of problems. Or they may take a global, undifferentiated perspective toward spirituality and as a result miss some important aspects of care. Some providers understandably have spiritual timidity or a concern about addressing spirituality in clinical practice. I have often heard providers say that they routinely avoid addressing spirituality in their clinical practice because they feel ill equipped in this domain (JSM). In contrast, some providers demonstrate spiritual over-enthusiasm. That is, they see spirituality as the source of most clinical problems as well as the solution and then overlook other important factors. Some providers may show a spiritual cockiness, overestimating their competence in addressing spiritual issues. Finally, the inability to tolerate ambiguity or the desire to reduce complex problems to simple or definitive solutions may serve as a pitfall to providers attempting to integrate spirituality into their clinical practice. In essence, helping providers to develop an awareness of their own spiritual beliefs and biases goes a long way towards enhancing care with older adults.[40]

In concluding our discussion of core concepts for integrating spirituality into clinical practice with older adults, we would like to leave you with a few specific recommendations.

- First, it is important to ask elders about what they hold as sacred. In doing so, you may uncover a host of resources and strengths that may be tapped into which could lead to enhanced health and well-being.

- Second, learn about elders' spiritual pathways. Be alert to both traditional and nontraditional spiritual pathways and sources of sacredness. If an elder is having difficulty following a preferred spiritual pathway, due to disease or disability, you could suggest that they begin

39. Ibid.

40. For discussion on this topic see the epilogue, Gordon and Koepke, "Looking in the Mirror."

to engage in another spiritual pathway. In essence, you can assist elders in developing *spiritual compensatory strategies*, which may lead to health and wholeness if they are no longer able to engage in a previously employed pathway.

- Third, consider how elders' major losses and stressors are impacting them spiritually. Ask yourself, is this elder experiencing spiritual struggle in the wake of this loss. Affirm their willingness to engage in a deep discussion about the nature of the loss and their spiritual thoughts and feelings around the loss. Normalize any feelings of anger with God, as these feelings may be a source of great distress for an elder.

- Fourth, encourage elders to draw on their spiritual resources to sustain/conserve their faith and spirituality. Remember the importance of *sacred relationships* as an important resource for older adults, including their relationship with you as a clinical provider. When needed explore transformational resources to facilitate profound change.

- Finally, remember that you and the older adults you serve may experience *sacred moments* in the context of clinical practice which may facilitate life-changing opportunities for meaning and growth for all.

REFERENCES

Brown S. L., et al. "Religion and Emotional Compensation: Results from a Prospective Study of Widowhood." *Personality and Social Psychology Bulletin* 30 (2004) 1165–74.

Bruce, Noah G., et al. "Psychotherapist Mindfulness and the Psychotherapy Process." *Psychotherapy: Theory, Research, Practice, Training* 47/1, (March 2010) 83–97. http://dx.doi.org/10.1037/a0018842.

Buber, M. *I and Thou.* New York: Scribner's, 1970.

Elkins, D. N. *Beyond Religion: Eight Alternative Paths to the Sacred.* Wheaton, IL: Quest, 1998.

Emmons, R. A. T*he Psychology of Ultimate Concerns: Motivation and Spirituality in Personality.* New York: Guilford, 1999.

Exline, J. J. "Religious and Spiritual Struggles." In *APA Handbook of Psychology, Religion, and Spirituality*, edited by K. I. Pargament, 1:459–76. Washington, DC: American Psychological Association, 2013.

Exline, J. J., et al. "The Religious and Spiritual Struggles Scale: Development and Initial Validation." *Psychology of Religion and Spirituality* 6 (2013) 208–22.

Gaer, J. *Wisdom of the Living Religions.* New York: Dodd, Mead, 1958.

Geertz, C. *Islam Observed: Religious Developments in Morocco and Indonesia.* New Haven, CT: Yale University Press, 1966.

Hill, P. C., et al. "Conceptualizing Religion and Spirituality: Points of Commonality, Points of Departure." *Journal for the Theory of Social Behaviour* 30 (2000) 51–77.

Kushner, H. *When Bad Things Happen to Good People*. New York: Schocken, 1981.

Lomax, J. W., J. J. Kripal, and K. I. Pargament. "Perspectives on 'Sacred Moments' in Psychotherapy." *Perspectives* 168/1 (2011) 12–18.

Mahoney, A., et al. "The Devil Made Them Do It: Demoralization and Desecration of the 911 Terrorist Attacks." Paper presented at the annual meeting of the American Psychological Association, Chicago, IL, August, 2002.

McGee, J. S., and D. R. Myers. "Sacred Relationships in the Context of Living with Mild Alzheimer's Disease." *Generations* 38/1 (2014) 61–67.

McGee, J. S., et al. "Spirituality, Faith, and Mild Alzheimer's Disease." *Research in the Social Scientific Study of Religion* 24 (2013) 221–57.

O'Grady, K. A., and P. S. Richards. "The Role of Inspiration in the Helping Professions." *Psychology of Religion and Spirituality* 2/1 (2010) 57.

Pargament, K. I. *The Psychology of Religion and Coping: Theory, Practice and Research.* New York: Guilford, 1997.

————. "The Psychology of Religion and Coping? Yes *and* No." *International Journal for the Psychology of Religion* 9 (1999) 3–16.

————. "Searching for the Sacred: Toward a Non-reductionistic Theory of Spirituality." In *APA Handbook of Psychology, Religion, and Spirituality*, edited by K. I. Pargament, 1:257–74. Washington, DC: American Psychological Association, 2013.

————. *Spiritually Integrated Psychotherapy: Understanding and Addressing the Sacred.* New York: Guilford, 2009.

Pargament, K. I., H. G. Koenig, and L. M. Perez. "The Many Methods of Religious Coping: Development and Initial Validation of the RCOPE." *Journal of Clinical Psychology* 56/4 (2000) 519–43.

Pargament, K. I., J. W Lomax, J. M. McGee, and Q. Fang. "Sacred Moments in Psychotherapy from the Perspective of Mental Health Providers and Clients: Prevalence, Predictors, and Consequence." *Spirituality in Clinical Practice* 1/4 (2014) 248–62.

————. "With One Foot in the Water and One on the Shore: The Challenge of Research on Spirituality and Psychotherapy." *Spirituality in Clinical* Practice 1/4 (2014) 266–68.

Pargament, K. I., and A. Mahoney. "Sacred Matters: Sanctification as a Vital Topic for the Psychology of Religion." *International Journal of the Psychology of Religion* 15 (2005) 179–98. doi:10:1207/s15327582ijpr1503_1.

————. "Spirituality: The Discovery and Conservation of the Sacred." In *Handbook of Positive Psychology*, edited by C. R. Snyder and S. J. Lopez, 646–59. New York: Oxford University Press, 2002.

Pargament, K. I., N. Murray-Swank, G. Magyar, and G. Ano. "Spiritual Struggle: A Phenomenon of Interest to Psychology and Religion." In *Judeo-Christian Perspectives on Psychology: Human Nature, Motivation, and Change*, edited by W. R. Miller and H. Delaney, 245–68. Washington, DC: APA, 2005.

Schmidt, R., et al. *Patterns of Religion*. Belmont, CA: Wadsworth, 1999.

Stern, D. N. *The Present Moment in Psychotherapy and Everyday Life.* Interpersonal Neurobiology. New York: Norton, 2004.

Zuckerman, P. *Faith No More: Why People Reject Religion*. Oxford: Oxford University Press, 2012.

2

Finding Meaning in Perceived Meaninglessness

—James Ellor, PhD, DMin, LCSW, ACSW, BCD, DCSW, CSW-G

As Maria Cruse talks about her life one cannot help feeling her emptiness. At 82, she is surrounded by pictures of family, some of whom have died; some live far away, some live closer. Mrs. Cruse lives with her eldest daughter's family. Maria's husband of fifty-five years died five years ago. Two of her sons have also died, one while serving in the U.S. Army in Iraq and one from a motorcycle accident. She has two other daughters who live in other parts of the state or across the country. In her life Maria has experienced grief, yet also significant joy and many important relationships. These days, however, she seems to be searching for what it all means. Why did the events of her life happen the way they did and what difference did it all make?

Mrs. Cruse is not alone in her later years as she asks these questions. Pastors, social workers, and family members often experience these same feelings as well as encountering persons like Mrs. Cruse, who have lived long lives and outlived many of the people that they care about. Such persons begin to ask questions of the meaning of their lives. Counselors listening to seniors are often able to find appropriate reason to suggest a diagnosis of depression and treat accordingly. As any counselor prepares to work with such a person, she or he is called on to reach into her or his experience and selects the techniques needed to provide support for the client. The technician who repairs a car would reach into a tool box and might select a screwdriver or wrench, very concrete devices to repair the car. In counseling the thought process between experiencing the client, perceiving their needs, and determining how to help are somewhat less mechanistic.

One of the key issues that Mrs. Cruse is expressing reflects her search for meaning. Frequently, without knowing anything about existential or Logotherapeutic methods, seniors spontaneously ask meaning oriented questions. While not every paradigm for helping clients to explore issues of life, few offer the tools to address the search for meaning. Existential approaches such as Logotherapy allow for a dialogue with both meaning as well as the spiritual needs that might lay behind the client's search. In this chapter the basis for the search for meaning will be explored in an effort to support the practical use of the search for meaning when working with older adults.

THE EXPERIENCE OF MEANINGLESSNESS

Clients like Mrs. Cruse are expressing the classic symptoms of meaninglessness. The challenge for the person listening to her is to walk with her to discover meaning. Meaning by itself is just a word that if twenty people were asked to define, would render fifteen, or twenty would provide different definitions. However used in this context, the concept of meaning according to Viktor Frankl as well as other existential psychologists reflects a rich combination of philosophy and psychology that can offer comfort at times of suffering and hope for persons struggling with self-understanding.

Viktor E. Frankl, MD, PhD is well known as the founder of the third Viennese School of Psychiatry that he named Logotherapy. Dr. Frankl wrote his first published article at the request of Sigmund Freud. Functionally, Frankl found a great deal of good in the work of Sigmund Freud. He notes that the purpose of his work is to expand beyond the current options in psychotherapy. Frankl often talked about himself as a "dwarf standing upon the shoulders of a giant yet the dwarf can see farther than the giant himself."[1] He goes on to suggest that there is something beyond in life that identifies the limits of Freudian Psychotherapy.[2]

As Frankl's ideas grew in relation to philosophy, he began to embrace the philosophy of Phenomenology. Frankl subsequently referred to the work of Sigmund Freud as "reductionistic."[3] Freud as a physician was focused on isolating specific diagnostic intrapsychic explanation for feelings and behaviors experienced by the client. Frankl understood that reduc-

---

1. Frankl, *Doctor*, 3.

2. Ibid., 4.

3. Fuller, *Psychology and Religion*, 243.

tionism is the exact opposite for a search for those phenomena of human existence that cannot be reduced to lower dimensions. As Frankl's ideas grew he moved to the Adlerian School. Some scholars to this day would simply call Frankl's work an expansion of the work of Alfred Adler, which Frankl would, in part, agree with. Yet, Frankl developed a much stronger philosophical basis for his ideas largely from the work of Max Scheler. Max Scheler's was an existential philosopher[4] whose work focused broadly on human character. Unlike Ludwig Binswanger's work, which is credited by Rollo May as bringing existential philosophy into psychology,[5] emphasized the basic existential dynamics of being versus non-being and thus the fragile nature of the human experience. Scheler and thus Frankl assumed the conditions of existence and while not ignoring them, move to what might be called the next level, the more positive elements of the quest to discover meaning. It is generally well known that Viktor Frankl survived the German Holocaust of World War II, however, Frankl is very clear to note that he had written the manuscript that outlined and defined Logotherapy prior to the war. He was able to hold onto the manuscript through his time in the Warsaw ghetto, but upon arrival at Auschwitz, he had to surrender his coat in which the manuscript had been sewed. One of the ways he found meaning in his suffering in this dreadful place was to find scraps of paper to attempt to reconstruct his text, "Doctor and the Soul."[6] Frankl was clear that the world should know that Logotherapy was created from his clinical practice and only field tested at the death camp.

Frankl identifies "Logos is a Greek word which denotes 'meaning.' Logotherapy focuses on the meaning of human existence as well as on man's search for such a meaning."[7] In Logotherapy, the search for meaning, rather than the Freudian pleasure principle, offers the primary motivational force for humanity.[8] When we compare this perspective with other approaches to existential psychology where existence is the basis for anxiety and life's quest to manage this anxiety, Frankl's concept of meaning assumes existential anxiety, but suggests that it is not the primary motivation for a life well lived. Rather, human beings search for the meaning of their life's realities. This points the person to a more purposive, even positive, approach to understanding human existence, which includes finding meaning even in suffering.

4. Frings, *Mind of Max Scheler*.

5. May et al., *Existence*.

6. Frankl, *Doctor*.

7. Frankl, *Man's Search*, 121.

8. Ibid.

Sometimes the best way to understand a phenomena is to explore its opposite. The experience of meaninglessness is understood by Frankl as the absence of meaning. Dr. Frankl suggests that patients see therapists today due to "feelings of futility. The problem that brings them crowding into our clinics and offices now is their 'existential vacuum' a term I coined as long ago as 1955."[9] Frankl suggests that this feeling of meaninglessness is reflective of existential frustration. For example, clinicians have observed that the experience of reactive depression from an identifiable grief situation does not generally come on all at once, but progresses through identifiable stages, from the event that the patient is reacting to into grief, and then sometimes into depression or complicated grief. With regard to meaning, Frankl observes that the patient first experiences what he refers to as the existential vacuum, a "state of inertia, boredom, and apathy."[10] When this state continues, it can progress into existential frustration. Existential frustration reflects the hindrance in finding meaning by any number of factors in one's life, including a lack of direction in the search for meaning. Zaiser notes that "global phenomena like aggression (criminality), addition (taking legal and illegal drugs, also the problem of obesity), and depression (committing suicide) are not fully understandable unless recognizing such an existential vacuum, existential frustration, or feeling of meaninglessness underlying them."[11]

The experience of meaninglessness then is more than lethargy or a lack of motivation to live life to the fullest. Meaninglessness is grounded in the existential reflection of human existence. Life for the average human being is filled with beginnings and endings that bracket each experience. The experience itself, however, is then interpreted by the client. The task of the provider using Logotherapy is to initiate a combination of listening and educating to help the client to better understand that at times she or he may be helpless to change events, but they are always in control of how they view these events and at times can even change them by virtue of reshaping their attitude toward them. For Frankl he knew from his life experience that the world can take anything away from an individual, except for her or his right to choose how to interpret the world.[12]

Critical to Logotherapy is the concept of phenomenology. Frankl understands that at the heart of phenomenology is human perception. One can always view the same glass as half empty or half full. To explain this

---

9. Frankl, *Unheard Cry*, 24.

10. Zaiser, *Working on the Noetic Dimension*, 84.

11. Ibid.

12. Frankl, *Doctor*.

notion Frankl employs the concept of Dimensional Ontology. Frankl employs the visual image of a soup can. If a light is shined on the soup can from the top, the shadow image will be that of a circle, but if shined from the side, the shadow will be that of a rectangle. It is the same can, but when viewed from these two perspectives, it casts a different shadow. An essential tenet of Logotherapy is to suggest that humanity is capable of choosing which image to perceive, the glass half full or half empty.[13],[14]

Meaninglessness is the clinical condition that service providers face when an older adult such as Maria have to live with the reality that life is not always filled with ideals and dreams. The reality of human existence can at times be harsh and filled with sadness. However, Frankl insists that meaning can always be found if the client is pointed to reflect upon, thus awakening their "will to meaning."[15] The patient's task is "to find his way to his own proper task, to advance toward the uniqueness and singularity of his own meaning in life."[16]

ESSENCE TO EXISTENCE

Traditional existential philosophy starts with existence and moves to essence. Stated another way, something has to exist in order for there to be aspects of the existence that might be referred to as the essence of existence. While there is significant controversy as to the moment of existence between conception and birth, to existential philosophy the focus is on existence as the starting point. Something has to exist before it can be understood by its component parts or essences. An existentialist might describe such essences as reflecting personality, or cultural experience, or race. Each of these essential elements come together for the clinician to paint a picture of the existence of the client. Frankl, like the Lutheran theologian Paul Tillich,[17] takes the unique position that there is something that is deeper that predates the moment of existence for the person. For Paul Tillich, following the biblical understanding of the spirit descending on humanity. In more common terminology, the soul or spirit comes from God at the point of existence and then returns to God at the point of death. It is this spirit, or depending on one's theological perspective, soul, that is the difference between life

13. Frankl, *Psychotherapy and Existentialism*, 23.

14. For more discussion see Koepke's introduction to this book.

15. Frankl, *Will to Meaning*.

16. Frankl, *Unconscious God*, 56.

17. Tillich, *Systematic Theology*.

and death that Dr. Frankenstein could not replicate.[18] For Frankl, there is something greater in the person than their human existence. While often clear in his lectures that he leaves theology to the rabbis, as a psychiatrist he attends to the existential elements of human existence. Yet, in his later writings, he begins to talk about the search not just for meaning, but "ultimate meaning."[19] Within this context Frankl notes, "when setting out to discuss the meaning of meaning I referred to the meaning as something 'down to earth.' However, it cannot be denied that there is also some sort of meaning that is 'up to heaven,' as it were; some sort of ultimate meaning, that is a meaning of the whole, of the 'universe,' or at least a meaning of one's life as a whole. At any rate it is a long-range meaning."[20],[21]

Frankl and Tillich both knew each other. However, before they were acquainted, they were both familiar with the work of Martin Heidegger. Heidegger's existential philosophy contributed to both of their thoughts in this matter. Yet each takes Heidegger in a different direction. While Frankl continues to base existence in the human experience, suggesting that it must have its origin in ultimate meaning, he offers very little detail. Tillich[22] in his *Systematic Theology* spends hundreds of pages with this connection and all of the various ramifications. In Tillich's work he understands both a human spirit and a divine spirit. The human spirit originates in heaven, but is the essence of the existence of being human. The human spirit *can* reach out to the divine spirit reflecting human free will, but for Tillich the divine spirit *is always* reaching out to the human spirit. This same free will is present for Frankl, but he confines his reflections to emphasize what Tillich would call the human spirit.

In a dialogue between Dr. Frankl and Dr. Melvin A. Kimble, videotaped by Terra Nova Films[23] at the annual meeting of the American Society on Aging, Frankl suggests that any European when confronted with the German word for *spirit* would need to understand which type of spirit is being discussed. In German the word spirit is Geist. Depending on which suffix is used, Geistig or Geistlich, the word Geist or spirit can refer to spirit in the religious sense or spirit in the interhuman human spirit which Frankl understands as self-transcendence. Where Tillich makes the

---

18. King-Hele, *Erasmus Darwin*.

19. Frankl, *Man's Search*.

20. Frankl, *Man's Search*, 142–43.

21. See the introduction where Koepke discusses spirituality as one's core belief in "The Essential Spirit is more than religious beliefs."

22. Tillich, *Systematic Theology*.

23. Frankl and Kimble, *Conversation*.

distinction between Geistlich and Geistig by talking about spirit, with a small "s" and Spirit with a capital "S" Frankl makes no such distinction. Bulka notes that "the translators of Frankl's works used the term spirituality loosely, thus distorting the precise meaning that is evident from the German. Frankl in his own English writings carefully avoids this misuse by using the terms 'noölo'ical' an' 'noëtic,' to differentiate the psychological and psychic, respectively, from the spiritual dimension in its religious sense."[24] For Frankl, the spiritual aspect of the person is found within the noölogical dimension. notes, "the noölogical dimension may rightly be defined as the dimension of uniquely human phenomena." It is within this dimension that Frankl understands "man's search for meaning."[25] Notice that this reflects the human relationship to one another, not the religious understanding of the transcendent relationship between the Divine and humanity. This use of the noölogical (psychological) dimension offers a clue as to how to help clients to find meaning since it suggests that transcendence must be present. Therefore meaning is often found in the capacity for reaching out and being reached by others.

One of the key tenets of existential therapies is understanding human nature holistically. The image of the traditional pie with one slice of the person being the physical, one the emotional, and one the social, which is Adlerian thought or G'anger Westberg's concept of the physical, emotional, social and spiritual as the essential aspects of the person, both conceive of the human person as a sum of parts. In existential therapies the metaphor of the pie is not to identify the slices, but rather to engage the basis for unity after the slices have been removed. In short, how do these aspects of the person interact. For Logotherapy, one might argue that the pie pan is the vessel that shapes and contains the pie. This pie pan is the noölogical dimension. The noölogical dimension reflects the essence of human existence. A. R. Fuller notes, "This distinctively human dimension is said to transcend, but also embrace, the instinctual and bodily dimensions of human life."[26] This higher dimension Frankl calls the "noölogical dimension" or "dimension of the noëtic."

To fully understand Logotherapy, then, professionals need to first consider the role of the mind in human existence. Philosophy and to some extent psychology have evolved over the centuries from observations that the heart is the center of human existence. An example is in ancient Egypt where they observed that when the heart stops the person is dead.

24. Bulka, *The Search*, 47.
25. Ibid.
26. Fuller, *Psychology and Religion*, 243.

In biblical Hebrew thought, wind or the lungs (Heb. *ruach*) were central as in their medical and spiritual existence. A person who is not breathing is dead. This made sense in terms of the soul. The entrance of the soul is when a child first breathes. At the end of life, the last thing that one can observe is a sigh when the last breath rushes out, and with it the spirit that dwells within the person. Today it is clear that both heart and lung functions are controlled in the brain. Thus, as the result of modern medicine, humanity for the most part embraces the mind as the center of the person. It is clear in Frankl's writing that it is the working of the mind that render the capacity to discover meaning. As a corrective of the work of Freud who sought in all his work to discover the biological source of feelings, Frankl sees the capacity of the mind as offering the full focus for existence through the noölogical (human) dimension. This observation is consistent with the interpretation of the human experience that is the basis for self-understanding and thus self-transcendence. Self-transcendence reflects the capacity to connect and essentially reach out to care for the other person. This self-transcendence is all too often shut down as persons turn inward with depression or even serious medical illness. Frankl observed that if the professional can help the client to think about and help others, these transcendent acts can help move the person toward insight into one's own meaning in life. Indeed, for a person to fully find meaning, she/he must first rediscover transcendence.

Transcendence is not just an action. Rather it is an attitude emanating from the thought process of the person. Self-transcendence is the basis for the human capacity to relate to other persons as the capacity to reach out implies the ability to care about the other. While maintaining a freedom of choice suggesting that the person may or may not empathize or even understand the other person, the basic capacity to transcend is uniquely human. According to Frankl, transcendance is always a part of the human condition and is critical in the search for meaning. As Fuller notes, "Self-transcendence is the directedness of human life to a realm of meanings everywhere surrounding it."[27] Frankl suggests that human life relates "to something or someone, other than oneself, be it a meaning to fulfill, or human beings to encounter."[28] Frankl's concept of self-transcendence parallels the theory of the intentionality of human behavior found in phenomenology.[29] In this way Frankl challenges traditional psychotherapy to think beyond the intrapsychic and look at understanding human nature as always reaching out beyond itself. Indeed, the person who is considered incapable of caring for

27. Ibid.

28. Frankl, *Unheard Cry*, 243.

29. Fuller, *Psychology and Religion*, 244.

others fits into one of the sociopathic pathologies found in *DSM* 5. Frankl refers to intentional self-transcendence as reflective of the human capacity to discover meaning. With this capacity, the focus in discovering meaning is always on more than internal psychic processes; it also reaches out to human life not restricted to the limitations of an internal focus.

THE WILL TO MEANING

The concept of freedom of the will and will to meaning are understood by Frankl to be found in the noölogical (human) dimension. Frankl notes that there are clearly emotional and social experiences that can limit this freedom, but the sort of freedom that Frankl is referring to in the noölogical dimension is within the human capacity. He suggests that our human existence, as long as it is not neurotically distorted, is always directed toward the search for meaning.[30] Frankl follows this with the understanding that life is always expecting something of each person. The basic human question is not "What am I expecting of life?" but "What is life expecting of me?" The human answer to this should reflect Frankl's understanding that freedom is always paired with responsibility. He proposes that in the United States our understanding is only half right. We have a statue of freedom on the East Coast, but we should have a statue of responsibility on the West Coast. Since Frankl's death, the Responsibility Foundation has worked to finance a 300-foot statue of responsibility for the West Coast.[31] Frankl believed that to live in a world of absolute personal freedom is to live in anarchy. As human beings we live within a tension between freedom and responsibility.

The definition of human existence suggests that humanity has the capacity for freedom as well as responsibility. It also reflects self-transcendence. In the context of the tension between freedom and responsibility, self-transcendence is reflected in the capacity to reach out into the world. Frankl notes that human existence is always directed toward something and that something is the will to meaning. The will to meaning then is the engaged effort to discover meaning and thus to fulfill the meaning and purpose in life.[32] Key to the discovery of meaning is that it is always directed beyond the person (self-transcendence). One example of the discovery of meaning can be found in the organization, Mothers Against Drunk Driving (MADD). This organization was started by a group of women who had

---

30. For more on this concept see chapter 5: Dick-Muehlke, "Fostering Spirituality in Dementia: Looking Beyond Cognition."

31. See www.statueofresponsibiliy.com for more information.

32. Fuller, *Psychology and Religion*, 247.

all lost children in auto accidents caused by drunk drivers. The creation of this organization does not in any way bring their daughters back, but by preventing the kind of grief that they have suffered, they can find meaning in their own suffering.

THE MEANING OF LIFE

Frequently, the meaning of life is reflective of the stories of our lives. From an existential perspective, each experience that an individual has belongs to that person. However, when the individual reaches out to talk about this experience the telling of it allows it to become a story. It can be said that the sons and daughters of Abraham (Christianity, Judaism, and Islam) are the sons and daughters of the story. Stories are the substance of our experiences shared with others. As we tell the stories of our lives, the client or the listener will begin to find the themes that are consistent from one story to the next. These themes often hold clues to the meaning of the person's life. Fuller writes, "life is said to be meaningful in three ways: 1) through what we create and give to life, principally through our life's work; 2) through the values life presents us with, through the good, the true, and the beautiful; and 3) through the stance we are able to take when faced with an unchangeable fate, in particular through our attitude toward suffering."[33],[34] There are two rules that Frankl observes for the therapist who is listening to the story and walking with the client. First, no one can ever give meaning to someone else. Meaning must be discovered by the individual. The therapist can walk with and possibly help the person to interpret their stories, but the client must discover their own meaning, even if what they discover does not seem consistent with the perspective of the therapist. Second, the therapist must believe that meaning can always be found. Frequently, in existential frustration, clients struggle to choose to see other perceptions about their stories which allow them to find their meaning. The therapist must be consistently making it clear that meaning is there to be found, even when the client is experiencing the darkness of their world and even their own mistakes.

33. Ibid., 250.

34. For more discussion on suffering, see chapter 10: Thibault, "Activating Resources of the Soul amidst Suffering."

BRIDGING PSYCHOLOGY AND SPIRITUALITY

In the past twenty years the concept of spirituality has grown in use and application in counseling. The field of gerontology related to the term religion for the first one hundred years. Working in parallel with sociology, gerontologists, when relating to religion and the church, employed the concept of religiosity in their work. Religiosity reflects the behaviors of religious practice. The most common variables in the literature reflect such activities as church attendance and how often the client prays. Regarding these terms, the relationship between older adult ministries as well as social policy is reflected in the series of White House Conferences on Aging. A White House Conference on Aging is intended to allow older adults in the United States to communicate their needs directly to Congress and the administration through a series of lectures and speeches. In 1951 and 1961 while there were sections on transportation, housing, and other social services, there was also a section on religion to bridge religion with older adult services. In 1971 as the result of the election of President Nixon and his platform on strict separation of church and state, there could no longer be a section on religion. The White House Conference staff, specifically Clark Tibbits, in their effort to find an alternative, developed the concept of spiritual well-being.[35] Through the 1970s and into the 1980s the term spiritual well-being was often added to religion in the literature.[36] Spiritual well-being was developed by Clark Tibbits out of the concept of psychological well-being to refer to spiritual happiness. In 1974 a definition for the term spiritual well-being was finally developed by the National Interfaith Coalition on Aging.[37] This definition while politically useful, was challenging to researchers and clinicians alike. By the mid-1980s, in parallel with the developing use of the term spirituality in the other professions, publication of the term spirituality began to emerge.

The term spirituality is a familiar concept to the mystical traditions within Roman Catholicism, Islam, and Judaism as well as in such Eastern traditions as Hinduism and Buddhism. Unfortunately, most mainline Protestant denominations built on theologians like John Calvin and Martin Luther have not been a source of reference to this concept as it was never discussed in the founding theologies. The term spirituality started as a political correction for religion. But it is far more challenging to define in a way that can be universally embraced. Many Christians substitute the concept of

---

35. Ellor and Kimble, "Heritage."
36. Ellor and McGregor, "Word from the Editor."
37. Thorson and Cook, *Spiritual Well-Being.*

a soul for what is understood in other faith traditions as spirituality. Frankl employs both traditional religious images as well as the use of the more transcendent term spirituality in his work.

In Logotherapy Frankl understands religion to operate at the level of the specifically human. Religion for Frankl is a strictly human experience. Again consistent with Tillich's understanding of the church, Frankl sees religions and religious practices as reflective of the human experience.[38] Religion is experienced in the noölogical (human) dimension. Like any higher dimension, the noölogical dimension also encompasses the lower dimensions of biology, psychology, and sociology, yet it also relates directly to transcendence. Frankl writes, "One may be justified in defining religion as man's search for ultimate meaning."[39] Instead of employing religious terminology for this experience, Frankl turns to what Tillich's identified as spirit (small "s").[40]

Frankl's use of the noölogical dimension's capacity to incl'de religion is much like Carl Jung's understanding that religion was subsumed as a part of what Jung refers to as the collective unconscious. The collective unconscious for Jung is an aspect of the psyche that'is not necessarily within any one human's experience, but rather a part of a larger psyche and is endowed in the person from birth. Frankl rejected Jung's understanding of the collective unconscious but does understand what he calls the spiritual unconscious.

Frankl notes that Freud only understood the unconscious as an instinctual aspect of the human experience. At a very human level, all that Freud understood to be in the unconscious was locked away beneath the Ego and reflected sensory-born experiences. A significant aspect to the unconscious for Freud is that the line between conscious and unconscious was guarded by the Ego, the mediator with reality. For Frankl there is both an instinctual unconscious containing instinct and sensorial data, but also a spiritual unconscious which as part of the noölogical dimension that is reflective of the transcendence of the person (Geist). Frankl suggests that it is relatively unimportant as to the nature of the instinctual unconscious as it is fluid with what he understands as the spiritual unconscious. Frankl credits Ludwig Binswanger with this fluid relationship.[41] This is a direct contradiction with Freudian psychoanalysis. But what Frankl goes on: "I would say that being human is being responsible, existentially responsible,

---

38. Frankl, *Unconscious God*, 13.

39. Ibid.

40. See Koepke's introduction to this book.

41. Binswanger, *Existential Analysis*, 191–213.

and responsible for one's own existence."[42] He goes on to point out that all of our existence as human "is in essence spiritual."[43]

Frankl's understanding of religiousness suggests that it offers content for the spiritual unconscious. In more modern uses of these terms, the term spiritual is somewhat more mystical. If it is associated with the soul, as many Protestant laypersons might do, this insight by Frankl will not be helpful as Frankl's spiritual relates to the unconscious, not a divinely inspired mysticism. For Frankl, religion is a human invention that provides language and content for the spiritual that originates in the spiritual unconscious. The spiritual unconscious provides the basis for Geistig or human transcendence, spirit with a small "s" according to Tillich and offers the human capacity to reach out in self–transcendence to one another. It also offers the basis for the search for ultimate meaning, which reflects Geistlich (Spirit with a large "S"). But Frankl also notes that "man is incapable of understanding the ultimate meaning of human suffering because 'mere thinking cannot reveal to us the highest purpose,'" He goes on to note that "if a person cannot understand ultimate meaning, then it must be a matter of faith."[44]

Tillich understands this concept by suggesting that God is infinite where human beings are finite in their capacity to understand reality. Since no one can put a gallon of water into a can that only holds a cup, so humanity could not hold all of what God is and what God might teach us because human beings would be overwhelmed by it. To this end Tillich's systematic theology is referred to as anthrocentric theology. While most theologies are theocentric, which means that they attempt to understand how God sees humanity, an anthrocentric theological position attempts to only understand how humanity sees God. Therefore all of the perceptions are human by nature. Approaching an understanding of the spiritual anthrocentrically, the provider does not have to account for God's intentions. Religion and spirituality reflect the human condition, or in Frankl's terms the spiritual unconscious. Ultimate meaning is then based on faith, which through this lens can also be understood as human belief. Unlike theocentric approaches, Frankl and Tillich's concepts only have to account for human perception and can thus allow God to be God and humanity to be human.

---

42. Frankl, *Unconscious God*, 26.

43. Ibid., 27.

44. Frankl, *Will to Meaning*, 145.

BACK TO MRS. CRUSE

The role of the noölogical (psychological) dimension is critical to understanding the existential vacuum that Mrs. Cruse is experiencing. In a case like this one, the fact that the deaths of loved ones plays a role, suggests that both meaning and ultimate meaning will assist in understanding her crisis. Maria can look back at a life where she and her husband raised five children. It seems that each child has been a productive member of their communities. The heartache for Mrs. Cruse is that she has now lost her husband and two of her children. It is easy for older adults to see the glass half empty and focus on the losses rather than the strengths of her story. On the other side is that she bore and raised five children. She was married for fifty-five years. Thus she experienced all the joys and sorrows that are reflected in these aspects of her life. Her story is likely to be much richer than the simple listing of her being a mother and a wife. She buried a husband and two of her children. Her response to those events in her life, both good and bad, contain the seeds for reframing her life. Hers is a story that she needs to tell, for in the telling she might discover her own meaning and purpose for her life.

The service provider who wishes to use Logotherapy understands that the delimiters of life, birth and death, can be allowed to define a life, especially for one who perceives herself as being of an age where death is likely to soon be eminent. If a person lives their life focused only on these delimiters, existentialists would refer to that as "being unto death" or living to die. The focus for the care provider working with Maria needs not to focus on the stories of birth and death, but rather on the various ways that life has expected Maria to live. This reflects in part an effort to help her to see the glass as half full, rather than half empty. The provider could incorporate what Howard Clinebell would call Growth Therapy.[45] Dennis Saleebey would refer to it as a strengths perspective,[46] or Snyder and Lopez's positive psychology.[47] Logotherapy built on similar ideas from Alfred Adler employs these same concepts to support the clients to understand the delimiters of birth and death, but also to focus on all of life, including those positive aspects for their lives that are pleasant to remember and those negative ones from which we learn so much.

As the client tells her/his stories, the role of the provider is to listen for common themes in the various stories. Themes like caring relationships and successful life events, as well as the challenges of life, all need to be

45. Clinebell, *Contemporary Growth*.
46. Saleebey, *Strengths Perspective*.
47. Snyder and Lopez, *Handbook*.

understood. From these themes Maria's attention needs to be turned to seeing how these themes have been consistent throughout life and that both the good and bad are important as together they make up the life she has lived. Maria needs to be the one who puts this together, or in Frankl's terms, discovers the meaning to be found in her life, but the provider can point her in a direction that can facilitate that discovery.

Through this journey, Maria will likely discover her own transcendence. As a mother and wife she has been in many obvious caring relationships, but it is not unreasonable to suspect that there were other such relationships as well. In order to help Maria to discover the meaning in her current suffering, Maria needs to rediscover her own transcendent capacity. Often persons who fall into the existential vacuum turn inward and have a difficult time demonstrating to themselves or others their own natural transcendent capacity. Engagement of this natural transcendent capacity can be facilitated by connecting Maria with others through church activities or other community events where she can add value to the group and feel like she can continue to contribute to the well-being of her community. By placing her in activities where she feels safe, she can engage in more robust interactions later where she can experience her own transcendence allowing insight into Maria's old skills and how they relate to her stories from the past. These spiritual skills may lead her to embracing her own understanding of the quest for ultimate meaning as well. Mrs. Cruse's spiritual nature can be coaxed out of unconsciousness though transcendence with and through others to facilitate meaningful insights into both her current suffering as well as her own connection to ultimate meaning.

REFERENCES

Batthyany, A., and J. Levinson, eds. *Existential Psychotherapy of Meaning: Handbook of Logotherapy and Existential Analysis*. Phoenix: Zeig, Tucker & Theisen, 2009.

Binswanger, L. *The Existential Analysis School of Thought*. In *Existence: A New Dimension in Psychiatry and Psychology*, edited by R. May, E. Angel, and H. Ellenberger, 191–213. New York: Basic, 1958.

Bulka, Reuven P., *The Quest for Ultimate Meaning: Principles and Applications of Logotherapy*. New York: Philosophical Library, 1979.

Clinebell, H. *Contemporary Growth Therapy*. Nashville: Abingdon, 1981.

Devoe, D. "Viktor Frankl's Logotherapy: The Search For Purpose and Meaning." *Student Pulse* 4/7 (2012) n.p. http://www.studentpulse.com/a?id=660.

Ellor, J. W., and M. A. Kimble. "The Heritage of Religion and Spirituality in the Field of Gerontology: Don Clingan, Tom Cook and the National Interfaith Coalition on Aging." *Journal of Religious Gerontology* 16/1–2 (2004) 143–54.

Ellor, J. W., and J. A. McGregor. "A Word from the Editor: Reflections on the Words 'Religion,' 'Spiritual Well-Being,' and 'Spirituality.'" *Journal of Religion and Aging* 23/4 (2011) 275–78.

Frankl, V. E. *The Doctor and the Soul: From Psychotherapy to Logotherapy.* New York: Vintage, 1986.

———. "Facing the Transitoriness of Human Existence." *Generations* 14/4 (1990) 7–10.

———. *Man's Search for Meaning.* New York:Washington Square, 1984.

———. *Man's Search for Ultimate Meaning.* New York: Plenum, 1997.

———. *Psychotherapy and Existentialism: Selected paper on Logotherapy.* New York: Washington Square, 1967.

———. *The Unconscious God.* New York: Washington Square, 1975.

———. *The Unheard Cry for Meaning.* New York: Washington Square, 1978.

———. *The Will to Meaning: Foundations and Applications of Logotherapy.* New York: Meridian, 1969.

Frankl, V., and M. A. Kimble. *A Conversation with Dr. Frankl at the American Society on Aging's Preconference, 1989.* Chicago: Terra Nova Films 1989.

Frings, M. S. *The Mind of Max Scheler: The First Comprehensive Guide Based on the Complete Works.* Milwaukee: Marquette Studies in Philosophy, 1997.

Fuller, A. R. *Psychology and Religion.* 3rd ed. Lanham, MD: Littlefield Adams, 1994.

King-Hele, D. *Erasmus Darwin: A Life of Unequalled Achievement.* London: Giles De la Mare, 1999.

May, R., E. Angel, and H. F. Ellenberger, eds. *Existence: A New Dimension in Psychiatry and Psychology.* New York: Basic, 1958.

Saleebey, D. *The Strengths Perspective in Social Work Practice.* White Plains: Longman, 1992.

Snyder, C. R., and S. J. Lopez. *Handbook of Positive Psychology.* New York: Oxford University Press, 2005.

Thorson, J. A., and T. C. Cook. *Spiritual Well-Being of the Elderly.* Springfield, IL: Charles C. Thomas Publisher, 1980.

Tillich, P. *Systematic Theology.* New York: Harper & Row, 1967.

Zaiser, R. "Working on the Noëtic Dimension of Man: Philosophical Practice, Logotherapy, and Existential Analysis." *Philosophical Practice: Journal Of The American Philosophical Practitioners Association* 1/2 (2005) 83–88. doi:10.1080/17428170500226088.

3

Spirituality and the Brain
We Know In Part

—Paul Dobies, OD

Editor's note: In accepting an invitation to write this chapter, the author was asked to outline his understanding of possible relationships between the human brain and human spirituality. With degrees in psychology, vision science, and optometry, Dr. Dobies is a primary health care provider (optometry is applied neuroscience), university assistant professor, and clinical educator. By virtue of education and professional experience, the author is uniquely qualified to provide a lay person's overview of the human brain for The Essential Spirit. *As such, he places his perspective on human spirituality within a "Big Three" context—neurobiology, neurogenesis, neuroplasticity—in the hope of initiating a deeper understanding of what a shared human brain function can mean for each of us within our own religious tradition.*

SPIRITUALITY AND THE BRAIN

From a "brain" perspective, "religion" is a "top-down" (mind, heart, body) attempt to verbally codify (left brain) the normative thoughts (dogma) and behaviors (morality) of a community of believers. From a "brain" perspective, "spirituality" is a "bottom-up" (body, heart, mind) nonverbal to verbal (right brain to left brain) experience of "God's" power, knowledge, and presence. One can have "religion" and not be particularly "spiritual" and vice versa, but the goal is to develop both "bottom-up" and "top-down" flexibility over a lifetime of increasing awareness with disciplined practice. From a brain-development perspective, spirituality precedes religion. Children "know" God in their body-heart connection before they "know about" God in the mind. Spiritual development can, if healthy and supportive of life (body), generate new life (body-heart), and develop a full life (body-heart-mind) within individuals and communities. On the one hand we have "objective" brain structure and function which objectively does limit our awareness of reality. On the other hand we have the more "subjective" personal elements of human spirituality.

As we discuss the brain and spirituality, it would be wise to "tune in" to that developing "child within" who is still there "inside us" and ask him or her, "What are you sensing, feeling, thinking?" The "answers" we get will in all likelihood surprise us as we "live" that "spiritual" question. At the same time I will assume a certain "adult" maturity and wisdom on the part of my readers. I will assume we know how to identify and safeguard against both "objective" religious excesses and "subjective" spiritual pitfalls. I will assume we have sufficient maturity to avoid the "objective" excesses of religious uniformity, conformity, and groupthink, and sufficient wisdom to avoid the "subjective" pitfalls of spiritual elitism, exemptionalism (the hypocrisy of "exempting" oneself from expectations placed on others), and cultism. I will additionally assume that we are comfortable with the following propositions: God exists, God is infinite, and God is the only one who is omnipotent, omnipresent, and omniscient. In short, that means that only God is all-powerful, everywhere-present, and knowing-everything-and-everyone. That means, of course, that we exist, we are finite, and we are less than all-powerful, everywhere-present, and knowing-everything-and-everyone. In short, we know in part.

THE BIG THREE

We know in part because of human brain structure and function. This is objectively and subjectively true because of what I will call the "Big Three"— neurobiology, neurogenesis, and neuroplasticity. *Neurobiology*, as a branch of biology, studies the development and function of "neurons" (nervous system cells) organized into "nerves" (functional circuits) that process information and mediate behavior. *Neurogenesis* refers to the formation of "new neurons" throughout life. *Neuroplasticity* refers to the brain's ability to "reorganize neurons" throughout life. Why is there a connection between the brain and spirituality? Healthy spiritual development often leads to adjusting our activities in response to new situations and environments within the context of a religious tradition. An overall understanding of the Big Three will give us an objective basis upon which to consider how we adjust our activities in response to new situations and environments. For better and worse, spiritual development is limited by the limits of brain structure and function. If near-death experiences (NDEs) are any indication, communicating with each other within the limits imposed by brain structure and function, is "practice" for "knowing" God beyond those limits after natural death. Although some are negative, most NDEs are reported very positively by those who have "known" God beyond the brain.

VISUALIZING YOUR BRAIN IN YOUR HAND

In terms of structure, the human brain can be visualized as follows: Lift up your arm and open your hand in front of your eyes. Place your thumb into the palm of your open hand. Now wrap your fingers around your thumb to enclose your thumb within your grasp. Looking at this arrangement, human brain function can be described as follows: Your arm and the bottom of your hand represent the "input" coming from the physical senses of your body into your thumb which triggers the "throughput" of the emotional reactions of your heart that finally alert the cognitive responses of your mind. It's the order and interconnectedness that is important for us to visualize. This is how we developed as children—body, heart, mind—and it is how we continue to develop as adults. This is how memories are formed. We hopefully learn over time with disciplined practice to better anticipate consequences that will not only protect us from threats to our survival but also help us to recognize opportunities for thriving. The Big Three is how these structures exist and function together. The Big Three focuses on how complex "neural circuits take shape" and "regenerate" as our brain processes sensorimotor information (body), triggers emotional reactions (heart), and generates alternatives for cognitive responses (mind) in the formation of memories and thoughts.

AN APPLICATION: COMMANDMENTS AND COMMUNICATIONS

I am personally most familiar with the Judeo-Christian religious tradition. Studying the founder or founders of other religious traditions, I have seen how all great religious traditions converge back to very similar spiritual insights about loving God and one's neighbor. I am confident that all of my readers will be able to make the connections between the brain and spirituality within their own religious tradition. As but one example, I discern the outlines of brain function—body, heart, mind—in the two "Greatest Commandments" of the Judeo-Christian tradition: 1) Love God with your whole self (strength [body, physical life force], heart, mind, soul) and 2) Love your neighbor as you love your whole self (body, heart, mind, soul). This parallels the Big Three emphasis on physical sensation (body), emotional reaction (heart), and cognitive response (mind). In general terms, the brain limits our conscious awareness by "creating" a "virtual copy" of reality from what we sense, how we react, and why we respond in chosen ways to new threats to survival and new opportunities for thriving. Through this Big Three process, this "virtual (not actual) copy" of reality (note the small "r") leaves us all with a partially valid frame of reference and that we, in fact, only know in part, all of us without exception. It's how the brain is structured to function so as to not overwhelm us with information that we are unable to process (Reality) because of our physical limits.

This presents us with the reason why miscommunication will inevitably occur. If we all have a partially valid frame of reference, which one is the "right" one? This is a moot question because, by definition, no partially valid frame of reference can be "the" frame of reference for everyone, no matter how "complete" it may "appear" to any one of us. Therefore, when it comes to matters of religion and spirituality, none of us, with a partially valid frame of reference, can use words to completely encompass a God we universally say is omnipotent, omnipresent, and omniscient. This inevitable "word limitation" was noted by St. Francis of Assisi who is famously quoted as saying, "Preach the Gospel at all times and, if necessary, use words." Because we know in part, we need to realize that sometimes we truly don't know what we don't know, and, as a result, we sometimes truly don't know what we are doing! This brain-based human condition requires compassion and forgiveness for us and for others as a result.

A "FELT-SENSE"

Our physical senses (body) trigger emotional reactions (heart). This "felt-sense" happens and it alerts our thoughts (mind) to respond. The direction of information moves from body to heart to mind from a brain-based perspective. We may not be aware of this order—body, heart, mind—but this is happening within us all the time without exception. This is true for such very human experiences as trustworthiness and romance. Children are more easily "tuned in" to this felt-sense connection because the brain structures needed for cognitive thought are not yet fully developed. However, all of us can recall felt-sense examples we have had personally as teenagers and as adults.

Sharing a personal example from my own life, the emotional reaction that got triggered within me the moment I first saw my future wife was, to paraphrase what Adam reportedly said upon meeting Eve for the first time, "OMG! Where have you been all my life, Baby?" Fortunately, of course, my cognitive brain structures were sufficiently developed at the time, and I recognized I shouldn't blurt that out and scare her off. However, to this day, my wife can be in crowd of people and I will have that same felt-sense reaction even before my mind recognizes I'm seeing my wife. Fortunately for me, my wife had that same felt-sense experience for me. So there we were, face-to-face, looking at each other, completely fired up on the inside but completely "cool" on the outside. Then the real test came. In our religious tradition we exchange a Sign of Peace.[1] That means actually exercising an option to shake hands or hug another person. You can guess which one I chose. Sharing a socially appropriate Sign of Peace hug (because we're "cool") with my future wife pushed my physical senses to overload and triggered an emotional reaction so powerful that it literally took me the better part of an hour after the meeting before I could thoughtfully drive safely. For my wife, she confides all she kept sensing and feeling was "Hold me, squeeze me, just one kiss NOW!" One can't "think up" a felt-sense reaction in one's head alone. Your mind, at best, alerts you to what is actually happening in your body and heart and, if your mind is sufficiently developed, you decide based on this felt-sense information (after what sometimes seems like an eternity of milliseconds) how to respond to it. The spiritual life begins deep down in your body (input), triggers your heart (throughput), and alerts your mind (output). From my perspective, God "designed" us for romance

---

1. Within some Christian worship forms the "Passing of the Peace" is a blessing between worshippers whereby each person shakes the hand of another worshipper with the words "The Peace of the Lord is With You." If the two persons know each other well enough they might hug rather than shake hands.

both between human beings and in our relationship with God. It's how we were "designed" to move and live and have our being. Now let's look at the Big Three process in more detail.

INDIVIDUAL NEUROBIOLOGY (LIFE)

From birth, and even before birth, our senses develop from "hands-on" to "ears-on" to "eyes-on" as infants and toddlers. At birth, the most developed sense is a kinesthetic "hands-on" awareness of the body. If you have you ever seen an infant kicking legs and waving arms, you know what I mean. We bumped into things, felt things, and pleasure and pain "taught" us how to move through our environment.

The next most developed sense from birth, and developing even before birth, is an auditory or "ears-on" awareness of the body. Have you ever seen an infant turn its head to track the sound of its mother's voice? We heard things, were pleasantly or painfully surprised, and sound "taught" us how to move through our environment.

Finally, the sense least developed at birth, developing fully after birth, is a visual "eyes-on" awareness. Have you ever seen a small child reach for the moon in the night sky with their hand? We recognized things and people on sight, felt happy or frightened, and light "taught" us how to move through our environment. These three senses allowed us to get a sense of where we are in the world around us. As adults, we still develop by touching/hearing/seeing to gather kinesthetic/auditory/visual information through our hands/ears/eyes. This level of development at birth, as well as before and after birth, is the neurobiological basis for eventually communicating face-to-face with others in relationships and communities.

MAXIMIZING NEUROGENESIS (NEW LIFE)

The brain continues to grow throughout life. New neurons are helped in this process by adequate recovery from stress, a sufficient amount of sleep, and good nutrition to name a few of the most important elements. Intermittent episodes of elevated stress followed by an appropriate period of restful recovery, sleep, and nutrition sets the stage for maximizing the growth of new neurons. A lengthened period of elevated stress prevents restful recovery, disturbs sleep, and minimizes the otherwise good effects of proper nutrition. As adults we all know that fatigue is the killer of romance whether we are "in love" with another person, a profession, an idea, a cause, etc. We do have physical-emotional limits and those limits will be exceeded by chronic stress. We need to take care of ourselves in order to love our neighbor as we love ourselves. This is not selfish. It is essential for the neuronal growth that is at the heart of human spiritual development.

Chronic stress can come in the form of anything that continues to disturb a sense of "eustress" (good stress) balance between too much stress and too much relaxation. This is a very individually determined balance such that what distresses one person may actually relax another and vice versa. For example, something "bad" like the death of a loved one or losing a job or something "good" like a positively anticipated family event or starting one's education in a chosen profession can disturb that balance. In general, when we overemphasize an "eyes-on" approach to chronic stress we tend to react by taking flight and running away. When we overemphasize an "ears-on" approach to chronic stress we tend to react by freezing in place and stopping to hide. When we overemphasize a "hands-on" approach to chronic stress we will resist and fight. These reactions—run, hide, fight—form the foundation of all emotional reactions to physically perceived "bad" threats to survival and their counterbalancing states—restful recovery, sleep, nutrition—promote maximal growth and thriving. It takes a disciplined mind to discern the felt-sense difference between a eustress balance and an imbalance in life. This requires a dynamic, individually determined, examination-of-consciousness which is at the heart of spiritual development.

Once again, the recovery states—rest, sleep, eat—can be developed using the mind to achieve a certain eustress (good stress) balance between chronic distress and chronic relaxation for maximum neurogenesis. Understanding this need for developing a certain eustress emotional balance between the perception of physical stimuli and the modulating judgment of cognitive responses is essential to understanding how to survive and thrive in the spiritual life. Discerning the heart matters! This is the first stage of spiritual direction. Discover who you *are* as a human being in your body and heart, from a brain-based perspective, and then you will be in a position to help others do the same. We cannot give what we do not have.

AN APPLICATION: THE 7 "DEADLY SINS" + 2

There are nine possible "bimodal" felt-sense combinations of the eyes/ears/hands perceiving physical stimuli and triggering emotional reactions. There are "bimodal" cells in the brain supporting this approach. In essence, the brain "chooses" a primary sense and a secondary sense, leaving the remaining sense in a "shadow" state. As a result, it is possible for us to not know what we don't know in terms of information from a particular sensorimotor channel. This is particularly evident when we are either very stressed or very relaxed. It takes a robust mental discipline to support extended stretches of "being" in the eustress "zone" (which we will discuss later) to be our best selves. We tend to "miss the mark" and oscillate between a stress recovery time that is either too long or too short. When our stress recovery time is too long we are very relaxed and perhaps very blissful but not growing new neurons at a maximal rate. When our stress recovery time is too short we are chronically stressed and perhaps very productive but not growing new neurons at a maximal rate. In both cases we tend to selectively overemphasize one sensorimotor channel, get a second support sense about right, and underemphasize the remaining third major sense with minimal to no conscious awareness.

This "missing the mark state" of selective over/under attention puts us at a disadvantage in discerning a felt-sense awareness of God and leaves us variously "blind (eyes-off), deaf (ears-off), or lame (hands-off)" to God's greater reality. From a brain-based perspective, therefore, we "naturally" tend to "miss the mark" and need forgiveness because we often truly "don't know what we don't know" when we are seeing/hearing/doing in a less than complete "bimodal" way. I will use the following convention to describe the overall pattern: Dominant sensorimotor channel → secondary sensorimotor channel ("shadow" third channel). The six of the most straightforward "bimodal" approaches are:

Eyes-on → ears-on (hands-off)

Ears-on → eyes-on (hands-off)

Eyes-on → hands-on (ears-off)

Hands-on → eyes-on (ears-off)

Ears-on → hands-on (eyes-off)

Hands-on → ears-on (eyes-off)

The three remaining "bimodal" approaches are interesting. They essentially try to balance two separate channels while paying "less" attention to a channel that is actually "more" preferred but only minimally perceived, plus or minus. Sounds strange but, with practice, these remaining three "bimodal" combinations can be discerned. For these one can discern a certain "outsourcing" of the "more" preferred/minimally perceived channel to "outside sources" in an attempt to balance the remaining two. I will use the following convention to describe these variations on the overall pattern: Dominant sense "outsourced" to balance a separate channel ↔ with a separate channel

This results in the remaining three "bimodal" approaches which are:

Hands "outsourced" attempting to balance an Eyes-on ↔ Ears-on approach

Ears "outsourced" attempting to balance an Eyes-on ↔ Hands-on approach.

Eyes "outsourced" attempting to balance an Ears-on ↔ Hands-on approach

This schema provides a basis for what I am calling the 7 "deadly sins" + 2. You can find this schema of nine possible combinations thoroughly described, researched, and applied in the "Enneagram" literature and community.[2] I mention it because there appears to be a brain-based rationale for nine "bimodal" options for awareness. Here is a diagram summarizing these nine "bimodal" options where V stands for a Visual Eyes-on sense, A for an Auditory Ears-on sense, and K for a Kinesthetic hands-on sense. Once again, there are "bimodal" cells in the brain. I've included the "Enneagram" Type numbers so you can cross-reference their use by well-known respected "Enneagram" authors and teachers such as Don Riso, Russ Hudson, Helen Palmer, Dr. David Daniels, Fr. Richard Rohr, et al.[3]

In this schema, we might be spiritually "blind" (eyes-off or "outsourced"), "deaf" (ears-off or "outsourced"), or "lame" (hands-off or "outsourced"). If true, then spiritual "blindness" might lead to "issues" of pride, wrath, or *fear*. Spiritual "deafness" might lead to "issues" of gluttony, lust, or *deceit*. Spiritual "lameness" might lead to "issues" of greed, envy, or sloth. Before getting too far into the weeds of hypotheticals, let me state that I personally use readily observable nonverbal EyeClues to identify which sensorimotor channels are "on" and which are "off" in any face-to-face conversation, a formal presentation of which is beyond the scope of this chapter.

---

2. For more on the Enneagram, see Riso and Hudson, *Discovering Your Personality Type*.

3. For a country by country and a state by state listing of Enneagram teachers go to: www.enneagraminstitute.com/TeachersNext.asp#.VDM_ofldWSo.

7 "Deadly Sins" + 2			Diagnoses for Spiritual Development	Enneagram Type
greed	V → A	K off	Run → hide, detach from body, hoard a minimal life	5
sloth	V ↔ A	+ K -	Run ↔ Hide, "outsource" body's power, stay calm	9
envy	A → V	K off	Hide → run, a special victim, entitled to exemptions	4
gluttony	V → K	A off	Run → fight, hard to hit a moving target, downplay pain	7
deceit	V ↔ K	+ A -	Run ↔ Fight, "outsource" heart's desire, spin images	3
lust	K → V	A off	Fight → run, came / saw / conquered, avoid weakness	8
pride	A → K	V off	Hide → fight, blind to own needs, be helpful to others	2
fear	A ↔ K	+ V -	Hide ↔ Fight, "outsource" mind's authority, be loyal	6
wrath	K → A	V off	Fight → hide, not see one's own faults, be perfect	1

Put in a Big Three context, catching oneself in the act of recognizing which channel is "off" in a brain-based "bimodal" schema (what we are avoiding and "don't know what we don't know") can bring us the spiritual insight we need to further develop our awareness of the greater reality of God's omnipotence, omnipresence, omniscience. In short, recognizing the "missing the mark" felt-sense relationship between the potential new life of neurogenesis and the actual "bimodal" life of neurobiology is the human foundation of human spirituality. If neurobiology gives us a "sense" of "What's So" physical awareness, and neurogenesis intimately connected to neurobiology gives us a "felt-sense" of "So What" emotional-physical awareness, then what remains to be discussed is what I will call the "Now What" cognitive awareness of neuroplasticity to complete the Big Three.

SELF-DIRECTED NEUROPLASTICITY

We can choose to change our minds to change our brains. I recently spoke with one of my interns who had a less than ideal interaction with one of her preceptors in front of a patient. She is in her third year of a four-year program. In a follow-up email reply to her, I said:

The best way to "survive" any of your Preceptors and life in general is self-directed neuroplasticity. How we think will actually "rewire" our brains, this process is happening 24/7, and we all get to choose once we're aware of the neurological fact that we have choice! The neurons that fire together wire together. Our ability to intend (felt-sense emotion, you showed plenty of that yesterday so you were in a perfect place to do this!) to attend (cognitive thoughts) means that our minds CAN change our brain's wiring, literally.[4]

I then threw her a "mental life preserver" because she was, in effect, trying to hold a "mental anvil" of self-doubt, "outsourcing" her mind's authority to a preceptor (see "deadly sin" *fear* above), starting to "drown" while "swimming" against the "temptation" to be chronically stressed in her professional program. I concluded my email reply to her by saying:

It broke my heart to see you so distraught and not noticing all the positive attributes you have as a student currently and the wonderful clinician you are educating yourself to be! I do the following, even with First Years, to be sure that you all feel the positive core belief I have in your ability to choose how to develop yourselves as clinicians. Here are the questions I walked you through yesterday. I want you to remember them and practice using them every day:

1. What did you like?

2. What do you like more?

3. What do you like less?

4. What will be better still?

So glad you are doing so much better! I could hear it in the tone of your email. :)

Dr. Dobies[5]

Neuroplasticity is 24/7. Our brains are always rewiring. The informed decision we have is whether this process happens on "autopilot" or whether we self-direct it intentionally and explicitly in a disciplined way. I choose to self-direct this process toward good news but doing so is going counter to what we have inherited neurobiologically from our genetic ancestors. Back in the day, millennia ago, our progenitors survived by "negatively" assuming there always was constant danger and threat behind every bush, rock,

4. Dobies, personal email communication.
5. Dobies, personal email communication.

or tree. They survived because they could be "wrong" ninety-nine times out of a hundred but "right" the one time out of a hundred actual mortal dangers was present. Those who "positively" assumed they were safe were "right" ninety-nine times out a hundred but "wrong" the one time out of a hundred it really mattered. Now that we no longer live in caves, we have the opportunity to thrive by anticipating threat levels to our survival. The difficulty is that our brains are still living in a cave and we imagine danger to a much higher degree than is actually present in a civil society. Danger is still present but we can now take a much more rational approach to anticipating consequences. Triggered by the "input" of our physical senses, alerted by the "throughput" of our emotional reactions, we can now learn to discipline the "output" of our cognitive responses.

It's difficult to develop spiritually when physically emotionally "dead" (not discerning our felt-sense through an examination of consciousness) or weighed down by a core belief that God is the Ultimate Adversary lying in wait to punish. That was Lucifer's lie: namely, try to deceive us by "polarizing" us from and "demonizing" God. After all, any well-trained devil won't expose intentions to deceive by tempting us with evil. Temptations to destruction will come disguised in something or someone appearing good. But the good news is that God is omnipotent, omniscient, and omnipresent. Why would God want to be everywhere if God didn't enjoy being there? It is essential we do the spiritual work needed to "seek and find" that eustress[6] God-is-everywhere awareness within us and among us in community in order to support and be supported in self-directing the "natural" process of neuroplasticity.

Therefore, the first step is to humanly grow in our awareness of the felt-sense "input" and "throughput" of all three major sensorimotor channels mediated by the eye/ear/hand. The next step is to balance stress and relaxation and experience that eustress new life. Too much relaxation, perhaps making molehills out of mountains, and our minds do not need to think. Too much stress, perhaps making mountains out of molehills, and all the alerting energy remains at the physical-emotional level for survival and our minds are not alerted to think about how best to not only survive but also thrive. The best thinking occurs when the mind is sufficiently alerted by a eustress balance. This physical-emotional balance allows the thinking of the mind to modulate a response that supports and strengthens that eustress balance. In effect, we then experience a certain "bottom-up" and "top-down" reciprocal flexibility that is both the body-heart-mind development

6. Stress that is seen as healthful. From Greek: "en" good or well, plus "stress" and thus literally "good stress." http://dictionary.reference.com/browse/eustress.

of children and the mind-heart-body development of adulthood through self-directed neuroplasticity—life to the full. The "child within" (What is s/he feeling—body, heart, mind?) interdependently integrates with the self-directed "adult in community" (Who knows/decides what—mind, heart, body?) in order to *be* a human, a human "*being*" in the fullest sense of the word as distinct from a mere human "doing" in a lesser sense.

Fortunately, we still have mystics among us who experience a change our mind and behavior in response to God's gift of creation, made possible by the Big Three. Objective neuroscience confirms this is factually accurate and correct. In a real sense, this is why some of the world's greatest "sinners" (in touch with their body and heart, "missing the mark" of their mind) become some of the world's greatest "saints" (body, heart, mind flexibly integrated with mind, heart, body). This idea of "changing your mind" is expressed in various ways in all healthy religious traditions. Just as we once "knew" that the world was flat, perhaps we can now know why mystics and "sinner/saints" were correct all along. It's self-directed neuroplasticity. We are truly wonderfully made and, I believe, it is wise to choose life! In much the same way, it might be said that Descartes had the right elements but in "top-down" order when he wrote "I *think* (mind), therefore, I am (heart-body)." The Big Three confirms that the path to his summation is "bottom-up" and so I will also rewrite his elements from a brain-based perspective as "I *am* (body-heart), therefore, I think (mind)." Thinking, in terms of neuroscience, is "built" upon the "I *am*'s" of felt-sense lived experience.

In short, the so-called "higher centers" of the human neocortex structurally "rise" from, functionally "ascend" above, and are intimately interconnected together and "one" with the neural "wiring" of the so-called "lower centers" of the brain's emotional-physical structures and functions. This neural organization provides the "objective" basis for the "subjective" aspects of human spirituality. It's like driving a car. The car is an "objective" mode of transportation. The "subjective" experience of a car in operation, however, will depend upon *who* the driver is and *how* the driver is doing the driving! In much the same way, as others have said, happiness is not merely a destination to be reached (buying the car). It is also a way of travelling (driving the car). To recap what was said at the outset, "religion" is more like "owning" a car and "spirituality" is more like "driving" it. What good is a car (our humanity) that sits in a garage (a church) with us at the wheel (the pews) saying "vroom-vroom" (going through "prayerful" motions) if the engine (the Big Three) is never started and the car is never driven out of the garage into the world? Although it is satisfying to admire the car it is more satisfying still to drive it!

It is important to say this one more time: the neocortex is powered by and globally interconnected with the underlying emotional limbic system which reacts to our physical senses. It first develops humanly from the bottom-up—body, heart, mind—and then grows spiritually in responsive wisdom from the top-down—mind, heart, body. The best top-down "thinkers" are arguably the most aware of the bottom-up "child" within. This insight and lived experience is both structurally and functionally sound based on the line of human development from childhood to adulthood from a brain-based perspective.

So, if it feels good, do it? If it feels bad, don't do it? I have spent over thirty years caring for seniors (75 percent of my patients have been seventy-five years of age or older). I can attest from receiving the wisdom of their lived experience that sometimes what feels good should not be done and sometimes what feels bad should not be left undone. Wisdom is discerning the better response to the felt-sense of consolation (Wow, that feels good!) and the felt-sense of desolation (Wow, that feels bad!). How do we develop wisdom to choose what we hope will be wiser courses of action?

AN APPLICATION: METACOGNITION AND SPIRITUAL DEVELOPMENT

So what can we think about thinking (metacognition) to guide us making wiser informed decisions for spiritual development? From a brain-based perspective, the human brain is structurally not a sphere. The human brain is two hemispheres "wired" with neural circuitry travelling side-to-side between a right brain and a left brain and interconnected front and back with our emotional structures and physical sense organs. The "back" of the brain brings us "input" from our sensorimotor channels that begin the process of developing a "virtual" copy that represents *what* is "out there" in our environment. The "front" of the brain receives the "throughput" of our emotional reaction to and along with this "virtual" copy of sensorimotor "input" and *who* we are generates the "output" of our cognitive responses. The right brain gathers information from this "virtual" space representation in the present and the left brain makes decisions in "virtual" time from the past to the future alerted by the "input/throughput" received. In short, actual reality can be different from *what* "appears" to be because *who* we are interprets a "virtual" copy of *what* reality actually is. As a personal example, I am more *and* less a parallel processor for whom everything and everyone is more *and* less interconnected in a rational manner. That is why for me there is no conflict between science and religion. Science, technology, engineering, and mathematics explore the "neuro-gap" we all have between the "virtual" reality represented to us by our human brain and God's greater reality of *what* actually *is* from God's complete frame of reference. I recognize that all of us sense and feel and think within a partial frame of reference. We know in part.

Because we all know in part then, obviously, there is room for error and interesting approaches to face-to-face communication. For example, sometimes we are "left brainers" who don't need an exercise program. We get all the exercise we need jumping to conclusions! Sometimes we are "right brainers" who can't give a simple answer to a simple question. Did you ever try to pick up a fresh watermelon seed? It just keeps eluding the grasp of our fingers every time we try! Sometimes we are "stealth" communicators. Stealth "left-brain" communication asks rhetorical "questions" that are already answered (but we're not saying so directly when others think we've asked a "real" question)! Stealth "right-brain" communication gives rhetorical "answers" that are already questioned (but we're not saying so directly when others think we've given a "real" answer)! Once again, I personally use readily observable EyeClues to identify what is actually the case during face-to-face conversation, a formal presentation of which is beyond the scope of this chapter. The visual system can be fooled but the eyes of the body do not lie. The eyes are a direct structural extension of the brain and EyeClues may be an indirect functional expression of *who* decides/knows *what* in "virtual" space and time. Here is an abbreviated summary from a brain-based perspective that shows a parallel between Jungian psychological type functions and human spirituality:

Informed Decisions for Spiritual Development				
WHO	**decides**		**knows**	**WHAT**
"Front" Brain	Left-Brain, verbal, serial processing, Time		Right-Brain, nonverbal, parallel processing, Space	"Back" Brain
Jungian	**Feeling**	**Thinking**	**iNtuiting**	**Sensing**	**Jungian**
Focus	What did you like?	What will be better still?	What do you like more?	What do you like less?	Focus
Informed Decision Timeline	Past	Future	Present to Future	Past to Present	Informed Decisions Timeline
Spirituality	**Heart**	**Mind**	**Soul**	**Strength**	**Spirituality**

Communicating face-to-face with spiritual directees requires a certain empathy, emotional intelligence, and a tolerance for ambiguity developed over "virtual" space and time from a brain-based perspective which, by definition, results in a partially valid frame of reference. Once again, we do know in part.

CONCLUSION

In summary, we are wonderfully "designed" in terms of brain structure and function. Even a cursory study of the human brain will show that we are only capable of knowing in part. Along the way it is sometimes wise to embrace, reveal, approach what feels good and at other times it is wise to resist, hide, run from what feels good. Likewise, it is sometimes wise to resist, hide, run from what doesn't feel good and at other times it is wise to embrace, reveal and approach what doesn't feel good. I will leave it to you to supply an ample supply of examples encountered in your education and counseling experience. We all grow through the following four areas (eliciting questions), at different rates, at different times, by ourselves, and with different individuals and communities, throughout life:

> I know what I know (What do did I like?)—*Left-brain positive awareness*
> I know what I don't know (What do I like more?)—*Right-brain desire for positive change*
> I don't know what I don't know (What do I like less?)—*Right-brain reduced sensory awareness*
> I don't know what I know (What will be better still?)—*Left-brain relaxed skillfulness (e.g., walking)*

Even if we are experts in asking questions and giving answers, the entire process of anticipating consequences is dependent upon senses that can be fooled and emotions that leave us reacting, even frozen, in a "less" than thoughtful way, unable to respond in the face of a "gray zone" of contradictory and mutually competing "solutions" to "problems" or needs presented to us. Perhaps a better understanding of brain structure and function will serve to persuade and convince us that we do, in fact, only know in part. Nonetheless, it is vitally important to be "in touch" with all the messy limiting factors we all experience as a direct result of our limited human nature. Paradoxically, our success in being ever more "in touch" with our limited and limiting felt-sense may be the "door" through which we may yet discover God's omnipotence, omniscience, and omnipresence within each of us. It is hoped that this cursory discussion of the brain and spirituality will help us recognize our need for wise spiritual direction, receive it from wise spiritual counselors, and give it wisely to others in our care.

A PRAYER FOR THE SPIRITUAL CAREGIVER

Every time I enter the room of one of my patients I say a quick prayer:

> God, I know in part. I give you my blindness (neuroplasticity). Help me see what you see. I give you my deafness (neurogenesis). Help me hear what you hear. I give my lameness (neurobiology). Help me do what you do. You Who Are All-Powerful, Everywhere-Present, and Knowing-Everything-And-Everyone.

May my prayer be your attitude as you attempt to address the spiritual needs of those you care for whether you are clergy, doctor, nurse, social worker, psychologist, program director, financial counselor, elder law attorney, professor, or lay person. Is brain structure and function related to human spirituality? I've tried to make the case that, yes, it is as we explore our essential spirit together.

REFERENCES

Riso, Don Richard, and Russ Hudson. *Discovering your Personality Type: The Essential Introduction to the Enneagram.* Rev. ed. New York: Houghton Mifflin, 2003.

RECOMMENDED READINGS

Hanson, Rick. *Hardwiring Happiness: The New Brain Science of Contentment.* New York: Harmony, 2013.

Howard, Pierce. *The Owner's Manuel for the Brain: The Ultimate Guide to Peak Mental Performance at All Ages.* 4th ed. New York: HarperCollins, 2014.

Newbert, Andrew, Eugene D'Aquill, and Vince Rause. *Why God Won't Go Away: Brain Science and the Biology of Belief.* New York: Ballantine, 2001.

4

Religion
Friend or Foe?

—Peggy Price, DMin

"One sees clearly only with the heart.
Anything essential is invisible to the eyes."[1]

—Antoine de Saint-Exupery, *The Little Prince*

FOR PERIOD OF A year I served as a hospice chaplain. Our team included a physician, a home health care representative, a social worker, a nurse, and me. A change was made in the nursing staff, and a new nurse was hired. She seemed competent at her job, but it wasn't long before a problem arose. She took her Bible with her to every home visit. Regardless of the religious beliefs of the families she served, she would proselytize at every opportunity. Although a religious institution ran our hospice, our team had worked diligently to treat each individual patient and family respectfully when it came to individual religious beliefs or non-beliefs. After several meetings with the managing director of the hospice, the nurse resigned. Problem solved.

I chose to begin with this story because it illustrates so clearly the very reason for this chapter. All of us who are involved in caring for the elderly, who

---

1. Saint-Exupery, *The Little Prince*, 63.

are facing end-of-life issues must be willing to put our own opinions and beliefs aside and focus on the needs of those we care for. Each of us may have a particular area of caregiving, from medical workers to home health care, or serving as spiritual counselors, chaplains, or companions.

People who are nearing the end of life have many deeply held beliefs and feelings of a spiritual nature, even if they have not been involved with an organized religion for many years. They have closely held values, some spiritual, some not, which have been anchored through the years by their experiences. For some, life has shown them the power of the faith they practice. For others, life has brought evidence that supports their rejection of early beliefs. More and more, our younger generations are leaning toward being "spiritual, but not religious."

Attempting to cover the wide reach of religious beliefs in this country or the world would be a nearly impossible task. I choose instead to focus on areas of sensitivity and to raise awareness of the need to consider these deeply held beliefs in our service to our clients.

As a New Thought minister, I ascribe to a view that the Divine, the One known by many names, the Ineffable, God, is personal to each of us. My spiritual beliefs are based upon universal principles that are found in every great tradition, including philosophy and natural law. My personal upbringing was in Protestant Christianity, and I feel deeply connected to the teachings of Jesus. My present denomination is Science of Mind, and our houses of worship are called "Centers for Spiritual Living." I share this with you, because my background and the beliefs I hold and teach to others color my perspective. In no way do I have an "agenda" to persuade you to believe differently than you do now. My reason for sharing this is so that you are made aware that no matter how objective I may try to be in writing this chapter, my overall belief system may, in some ways, color what I have to say.

Approaching this topic—"Religion as Friend or Foe"—asks the question, how do we spiritually support those we care for when they are facing the challenges of serious medical conditions and end of life issues? How do those who are facing end of life issues find solace and comfort in their spiritual beliefs, or conversely, how do they deal with these issues without them?

Our closely held beliefs are personal to each of us. This is true whether one follows a highly dogmatic form of religion or whether one simply labels themselves "spiritual." Caring for people who are from differing cultures, ethnicities, and religions may at times feel uncomfortable. If we don't know their customs or practices we may feel awkward in asking them. In my opinion not asking them about their beliefs and practices can cause far more uncomfortable situations for ourselves and for those whom we serve.

As shown in the diagram in the introduction to this book, there are many factors influencing our personal spirituality. We may learn according to a specific set of principles, according to scriptural teachings, or we may find a more experiential path such as meditation, but each of us has our own unique set of experiences that color our belief systems. To honor the spiritual path of the individual is to offer them Namaste—*the spirit in me beholds the spirit in you, or the humanity in me beholds the humanity in you.*

Here is a story that attempts to answer the question: "What is spirituality?"

> God called together three of his angels and said, "Look, I have the secret of life. Where can I put it so human beings can't find it?" The first angel said, "Put it up in the stars. They won't look for it there." God pondered for a moment and said, "Hmm, one day people will explore space, and they will surely find it there."
>
> "I know!" said the second angel, who was always very enthusiastic. "Put it down at the deepest part of the sea. They will never find it there!" God became very quiet and thought about it for a moment, and then said, "No, they will undoubtedly plumb the depths of the sea and will very likely find it there."
>
> The third angel, who was often the quietest and most thoughtful said, "I think you should put it in their hearts. They will not find it there." God agreed. And now every person carries the secret of life within his or her own hearts.[2]

If you are reading this book, you are a person who is called to be of service to your fellow human beings. Whether you believe in a higher power, or need empirical evidence to validate your worldview, you have a heart that is the feeling center of your being. You may be an empath or a realist. Whatever best describes our nature, you are doing some of the most significant and important work in life—serving fellow human beings on their pathway as they move into the sunset of their lives.

Some caregivers do not feel they are spiritual at all, and therefore may resist opening any conversation relative to religion or spirituality. If the topic seems awkward to you, think of your humanity reaching out to the humanity of the person before you. From that place, we can access the deeper expressions of the human heart. It is my hope that having more information may make that action easier. My goal is to give the reader an overview that can assist them in a taking more holistic approach to caring for their clients, residents, or patients. Dr. Andrew Weil, a teacher of integrative medicine, states:

2. Anonymous, personal notes.

Despite increasing interest in spirituality in medical settings, the physicians who discuss spiritual issues with patients are more the exception than the rule. The obstacles seem to be lack of time, lack of training (doctors aren't taught how to approach and explore these subjects) and difficulty identifying patients who would welcome questions about their spiritual lives and beliefs. This is a sensitive area for both physicians and patients despite emerging evidence that spirituality can play a powerful role in healing.[3]

At the Arizona Center for Integrative Medicine that Dr. Weil directs at the University of Arizona in Tucson, physicians are trained to take "spiritual inventories" of patients as part of their medical history, to pray with patients when appropriate, and to make recommendations for their spiritual needs.

Deeply held religious/spiritual/cultural beliefs have a profound impact on the way people are served in our medical institutions, our nursing facilities, or in-home care. It is in times of crisis when many people reach deeply inside to access the words of their scriptures, the customs and practices of their faith, and the cultural parameters of their upbringing.

As one confronts the later years of life there seems to be a gradual slipping away of dignity and control. Eyesight may dim, making the enjoyment of reading more difficult. One may have the car keys taken away because they are not safe on the road anymore. Others may deal with incontinence, relying on adult diapers so as to avoid embarrassment. Tasks that once seemed easy become difficult, and pleasurable activities like gardening or golf result in stiffness of joints and aching muscles. Some people take these gradual changes in stride, accepting where they are in life while others may rail against them doing everything possible to slow the inevitable progress of aging. Facing illness and needing care adds another layer to this slow process of the loss of independence. It is a time when drawing upon the undergirding of spiritual beliefs can serve as a comfort, or it can serve as a means of bringing up deep-seated fears.

My grandfather was ill with pneumonia at the age of eighty-six. My parents brought him into their home to take care of him, and an in-home nurse was at his bedside, bathing him. Even though struggling to breathe, and in the last hours of his life, I remember his words as he quoted the Gospel of John: "Very truly I tell you, when you were younger you dressed yourself and went where you wanted; but when you are old you will stretch

---

3. Weil, "Can Spirituality," n.p.

out your hands, and someone else will dress you and lead you where you do not want to go."[4]

In the midst of a fever and the confusion of his last hours, he remembered those words—his love of the Bible and the comfort it had brought to him throughout his life was a touchstone he was able to use to understand what was happening to him.

Those of us who have chosen to be in service to others as our vocation, know that our work extends beyond the specialty we have chosen. Our work lies in getting to know the inner and outer needs of our clients. Our work is about relationship.

This chapter attempts to address both the outer, or practical aspects of considering religious and spiritual beliefs, and the more subtle, and inner aspects. We are multifaceted beings, and the more we address our patients holistically, the better served they will be. There are the practical aspects of care, and those that are more subtle or spiritual.

PRACTICAL ASPECTS OF OBSERVING RELIGIOUS/ SPIRITUAL BELIEFS

Food

As a person ages, many of life's pleasures may have fallen away, and no other area of life's enjoyment can be more important than food. We all have our favorite meals—some of us enjoy comfort foods—and live to eat—others like to enjoy foods that are good for our health—we eat to live. For many, religious dietary observances are essential to their sense of well-being. To eat foods that are forbidden, or considered unclean, can cause extreme upset and distress.

Most hospitals and large facilities offer specialized diets according to Kosher (Jewish) or Halal (Muslim) guidelines. For the average caregiver, knowledge of this topic is useful. In both Judaism and Islam, there are strict taboos when it comes to the consumption of animal products. For instance, pork is considered unclean and is never eaten. Both Jews and Muslims may eat fish without any special preparation, but certain kinds of shellfish are not consumed. There is considerable information on the Internet regarding these food guidelines. When working with patients of these religious backgrounds, it is important to observe their dietary laws.[5] Even if your patients

4. John 21:18, RSV.

5. For more information on Islamic law as related to food, go to http://islamic-laws.com/fooddrinks.htm. For more information about Kosher foods and Jewish law, go to http://www.jewfaq.org/kashrut.htm.

may have strayed from these practices, they may become important when other parts of their lives feel out of control.

Although not necessarily the food of choice for everyone, it is safe to say that a vegetarian diet is a universal diet. Hindus, Sikhs, and many Buddhists adhere to a diet free of animal protein. When working with a diverse group of people and cultures, this may be the preferred way to go.

Spiritual Practices

Spiritual practices are wide ranging and also need careful study. From the Islamic practice of praying five times a day to having quiet time for meditation, our clients need to be given a means and the support for their own personal spiritual practices.

These can range from having a time of silence each day, to chanting, to using a rosary or other prayer beads, or to actively engaging in moving prayer, as in the practice of Islam, praying five times a day. In many cases, this may be difficult for a person who is infirm, but making space for the level of ability of any form of practice is important. One bed-bound person found great solace when a insightful caregiver moved the bed so it would face Mecca and placed his prayer rug over his lower body like a lap-blanket.

Ritual Purification

Ritual purification—often known as "ablutions"—are practiced widely by many religious traditions. Assisting your client or patient in cleansing before prayer recognizes the significance of their beliefs.[6]

Prayer Beads

Many traditions use prayer beads—from the Islamic practice of reciting the 99 names of Allah on beads, to the Rosaries of Catholics and some Anglicans, to the 108 beads used in Buddhist and Hindu practices—to connect the tactile and physical world to the inner spiritual world, reinforcing with words spoken out loud or silently inward. The beads can often be fingered in times of stress as a means of calming oneself or just held in an arthritic hand.

6. For more information on each religious practice, go to http://en.wikipedia.org/wiki/Ritual_purification.

Chanting

Chanting is also used in some traditions—from making the universal sound of "Om" to a Buddhist chant to persons simply singing the word "Holy" over and over again—use of sound reaches deeply into the center of being in those who utilize this method. The Internet offers many websites about chanting, but this one is a clear and simple overview.[7]

As a caregiver, asking a gentle question such as "What do you like to do when you feel anxious or when you need comfort?" opens the doorway to supporting your client in feeling comfortable to use their practices while in your care. It shows your compassion and understanding, and blesses them with a powerful tool for healing.

Modesty

Modesty is highly important in many religious beliefs. Our clients and patients who adhere to these values will feel more comfortable and secure when they are supported in them. The value of modesty runs through many religions—Islam, Church of Jesus Christ of Latter Day Saints, and many of the earlier American sects such as Mennonite and Amish.[8]

Many people are confused about the wearing of the hijab, or headscarf, in the Muslim tradition. For many Muslim women, it is a matter of choice. Many who wear it say it is a spiritual practice that gives them an outer means of feeling their inner connection with God. Others wear it because in their country of origin it is mandatory. Other Muslim women only wear it when praying or attending services at the mosque. As caregiver, when your client is wearing the headscarf, even in bed, it is important to her that it remains in place. Even if a doctor is examining her, that scarf gives her a sense of safety and comfort.

A close friend of mine named Mark was the recipient of a heart transplant a couple of years ago. His procedure took place in a highly renowned hospital in a major metropolitan area. This hospital in known all over the world for its groundbreaking work in the area of organ transplants. Mark went through the lengthy and tenuous process of waiting for a heart donor, and had a very successful outcome. He now serves as an ambassador for the hospital, and makes weekly visits to other recipients who are waiting for a transplant. Mark is a man of faith with a wide-open mind and heart when it comes to his relationships with his patients. This is what he shared with me:

7. See http://amma.org/teachings/chanting-mantras-spiritual-practice.
8. http://en.wikipedia.org/wiki/Modesty.

One of my patients was a young Iraqi woman who was waiting for a heart. Her father and brother were in the room with her. Only the brother spoke English. She was very young, in her early twenties, and though wearing a headscarf, I could see that she was very pretty. In her own concern for her modesty, she asked her brother to ask me if it would be OK for a man to put his hands inside her body (chest cavity). I asked her if she believed that God had brought her to the hospital to be healed and to have a new chance at life. With her affirmative response, I continued by asking, "If that were true, didn't it make sense that if that action is what was required for the surgery, wasn't that also part of God's plan for her healing?" Again the young woman, and her family agreed with the logic. Finally, I asked if all of this was so, then did they need to be concerned. The family was elated by the clear answer that was apparent to them when their concerns were looked at in the context of God being the one in control. They were all pleased with the new understanding that what needed to be done would be all right.

She then asked if she would be beautiful enough for a husband if she had a scar. I shared with the father, son, and the patient that I did not know their culture, and did not want to offend anyone. If it would not violate any of their religious beliefs or moral customs, with their permission I would take off my shirt and show them my surgical scar. The father began crying in gratitude when I took off my shirt and showed how my wound was actually very small. The young women wept tears of joy.[9]

Mark told this story with tears in his own eyes.

Being respectful of everyone's body is a means of honoring their spirit. Modesty is an important value for many religious women, whether Mormon, Catholic, Jewish, or Muslim. Knocking on the door before entering a room will also be a signal of respect for the individual. There are special hospital gowns available for women that cover more of their bodies, thus reducing any anxiousness about exposure to strangers. In many cultures, modesty is equally as important for men.

9. Personal interview with author.

Music

If there can be anything more personal than spiritual beliefs, it is music. It evokes deep memories, can touch our hearts, can stimulate us, relax us, make us cry, and even heal us. Music is a pathway to the soul.

Some say that listening to Gregorian chants can lower blood pressure, that slower music can slow the heart rate. Certain hymns can bring comfort, and often do.

Music therapy is often utilized with Alzheimer's patients and in hospitals because it has a calming effect on patients.

A recent film entitled *Alive Inside* demonstrates the powerful effect on patients with dementia. As they listened to music from their era, or personal favorites, they seemed to awaken and become more coherent.[10]

I have a favorite album that I play whenever I am not feeling well. It is a compilation of music produced by Dr. Andrew Weil. The album is entitled, *Sound Body, Sound Mind*. It is one hour, twenty-four minutes in length. The music flows from bright and clear, to a deep tonal extended note, and back again. As the music plays, underneath are sound waves intended to put the brain into a relaxed state. I listen to it with headphones and I find it deeply relaxing. It always helps me feel better.[11]

ABOUT DEATH

One thing I can say with all certainty is that everyone will die. With rare exceptions, we do not know when or how. Many of us who are caregivers, stand witness to death, and see that there is no "one way" to make this transition from this life to what is next.

Our own beliefs and perhaps myths about death color the way we view it—some see it as a natural part of life, some see it as punishment, some see it as something to be feared, and some welcome it, when their own suffering has become too great.

We all entered this life without any remembrance of how we got here— our conception and subsequent birth is viewed both as a miracle as well as a natural process of cell division and a bodily response to the carrying of a new life as well as a deliverance of it. No one can tell a fetus what birth will be like, and in the same way, none of us can truly say what death is like, because we have not experienced it. Yes, there are those who have had near

10. Rossato Bennett, *Alive Inside*.

11. For more information, see http://www.drweil.com/drw/u/QAA400483/Music-For-Health.html.

death experiences, and those who have "died" and come back, but even they cannot convey in words what is happening to them.

When we are present at the death of a client or patient, we may have the uncomfortable task of informing family members or loved ones. Awareness of the many different cultural, religious, spiritual and non spiritual responses gives us an opportunity to support the survivors with care and sensitivity.

Rev. Don Koepke related his personal experience when he was in chaplaincy training at UCLA Medical Center:

> I remember telling an ER Lobby filled with a Persian family that their loved one had died. Not knowing their cultural response I was taken back with the weeping and more so the wailing that ensued. Their wailing disrupted the entire ER and it was almost impossible to move them to a more private location. From then on, when a Middle Eastern person died I first moved the family to a larger private location before telling them of the death. What a mistake caused by cultural ignorance of death ritual[12]

To list the many customs and rituals of world religions would require another chapter in this book. There are two excellent resources readily available on the Internet.[13]

Down through the ages from indigenous cultures to "New Age" spirituality, we have a universal longing for a belief in life after life. For some, it may feel uncomfortable to ask your client or patient what they believe. Hospice chaplains frequently ask these questions so that they can assist their clients in coming to terms with the finality of their lives. Sometimes family members have differing views on the afterlife, and there can be conflict over this.

I have seen situations in which a dying family member observed a different religious or spiritual belief than the one "approved" by the family. At the eleventh hour of the person's life, they attempt to "convert" them, so that they can declare "victory" in their quest to "save" them. The soft words of a caregiver, may or may not allay this situation, but it is one to watch out for. Our role as caregivers, as I have stated before, is to support our patients in their own personal choices regarding beliefs. As we are present to their thoughts and feelings, we express compassion and caring. Honoring and

---

12. Koepke, "Personal Recollection."

13. http://amemorytree.co.nz/customs.php and https://www.everplans.com/articles/funeral-traditions-of-different-religions.

respecting their families is necessary as well, but in all circumstances, the patient comes first.[14]

SPEAKING OF FAITH

In polite company, we are trained to shy away from politics and religion in conversation. When it comes to caring for our clients, politics might not be appropriate, but closely held beliefs are a different matter. We live in an increasingly diverse society, and we may encounter many different cultures and spiritual paths. This can add to the resistance to bringing up religion or spirituality at all. Chronic conditions and end-of-life concerns can cause our clients to look to their belief systems (religious or non-religious) as a source of understanding their situation.

Professional chaplains, or spiritual consultants as they are sometimes called, do an in-depth assessment of their clients. Asking for guidance from a chaplain or discussing the patient in an interdisciplinary meeting might aid everyone dealing with the client/patient in having greater insight into their needs. When these meetings are not available, then it is incumbent upon the caregiver to ask how they can be of support.

The greatest gift we can give to another is to listen to them. We may bring our own religious or non-religious beliefs with us into the room of our client. In order to fully hear them, we must learn to leave our own opinions outside the door. We are not there to persuade them to believe differently, but to hear what is on their hearts. We can listen with an open mind and heart to what needs to be said.

Listening is an art. In cases of end of life care, it is a sacred art. As each person copes with the realization that their future is limited, and that the memories they hold are precious, having someone to talk with is a precious gift. In this situation, listening is a spiritual practice.

My dear friend, Kay Lindahl, founder of The Listening Center, has written a book entitled *The Sacred Art of Listening*. In it she says, "Listening is a creative force. Something quite wonderful occurs when we are listened to fully. We expand, ideas come to life and grow, we remember who we are. Some speak of this force as a creative fountain within us that springs forth, others call it the inner spirit, intelligence, true self. Whatever this force is called, it shrivels up when we are not listened to and thrives when we are."[15]

14. For a more detailed discussion about death see Westbrook, chapter 12 "Death and Dying: The Final Act of Living."

15. Lindahl, *Sacred Art*.

While there are many ways to open a conversation about faith you might try simply asking them, "Is there some favorite book or poem you like to read or is there a prayer you like to say?" or "What has helped you to cope with this time in your life?" Again my friend Mark, the ambassador for heart transplant recipients, tells me that his experience shows that many patients do want to talk about their beliefs, and want reassurance about what is happening for them. They often ask him "How did you get through this?" and his answer is that he is a man of faith, and believed that "no matter what happened everything would turn out perfectly because he believed in a higher power."

One of his clients, a Catholic man, had many conversations with him about his own faith and belief. When it was nearing time for him to have his procedure, the man called in his priest to offer communion. Mark quietly began to leave the room as he was not Catholic, and the patient called him back. The patient had valued his conversations so much that he asked him to join with his family. Because they had been through so much together, he wanted him to have communion too. At the same time Mark shared that some patients do not have any belief at all, and he respects that as well.

ONE MORE THOUGHT

Throughout this chapter, I have been addressing a deep human need—compassion. My own experience as a pastor for nearly twenty years is that at times, we can become so exhausted that we become numb to the feelings of others. Our work calls us to give out a huge amount of psychic and spiritual energy. At times we work with people who can deplete us of energy, physical as well as psychic. It is in times like these that we can lose sight of the patient or client as a human being and see them as just "one more thing to do." This doesn't seem very compassionate or "spiritual," and in truth, it isn't. In order to maintain a sense of compassion and empathy for those we care for, we must make space to care for ourselves. The demands placed upon us can feel more like a marathon than a day at work.

Caring for others requires that we also take care of ourselves. This, too, is a spiritual practice. In the beginning I spoke of Namaste—the "Spirit" in me beholds the "Spirit" in you—or the humanity in me beholds the humanity in you. We must recognize that the regard we hold for others is also the regard we must hold for ourselves. It is impossible to give from an empty cup. It is impossible to do our best when we have depleted ourselves of rest, of nutritious foods, of recreation, of being with loved ones, and of finding some way to feed our own spirit when we are away from our charges.[16] This must be your priority, because if you do not make self-care a priority, someone else will make something different your priority.

Every human life matters. We, as caregivers, know this to be true. As we serve and do our work, we are among the most privileged of all—we are the soft voice, the comforting hand, the gentle hug, the good listener, and sometimes the midwives as our clients move into the next dimension of life. Holding what is sacred to those we serve, provides them with the grace and goodness of the human heart—and always blesses us more than those we serve.

REFERENCES

Koepke, Donald. "Personal Recollections in the ER." As told to Rev. Peggy Price. N.p, n.d.

Lindahl, Kay. *The Sacred Art of Listening*. Woodstock, VT: Skylight Paths, 2003.

Rossato Bennett, Michael, dir. *Alive Inside*.Projector Media, 2014. http://www.aliveinside.us.

Saint-Exupery, Antoine de. *The Little Prince*. Translated by Richard Howard. New York: Harcourt, 1943.

Weil, Andrew. "Can Spirituality Affect Healing?" Dr. Weil.com. 2004. http://www.drweil.com/drw/u/id/QAA342854.

16. Caring for self is a major theme of the epilogue of this book: "Looking in the Mirror."

PART II

Practical Strategies for Engaging the Spirituality in Older Adults

5

Fostering Spirituality in Dementia
Looking Beyond Cognition

—Cordula Dick-Muehlke, PhD

IN THE PREFACE TO this book, Don Koepke describes spirituality as a person's core values and beliefs that "are continually in a process of becoming" as the individual encounters new events. Heavily reliant on an individual's ability to evaluate, adopt, internalize, espouse and act upon a set of guiding principles in making life choices, Koepke's definition of spirituality clearly excludes people with Alzheimer's disease (AD) or other dementias, who gradually lose this capacity. Does spirituality dissipate when memory and other cognitive abilities needed to sustain a core set of consciously adhered to beliefs and values devolve as in the case of AD and other dementias, or does spirituality transcend the limits of Koepke's definition? Making the case for the latter, this chapter briefly reviews current knowledge about the development and progression of AD, explores the impact of cognitive impairment on values and beliefs, offers a dementia-inclusive definition of spirituality, and discusses ways to foster the spiritual pursuit for meaning, connection and self-transcendence. Ultimately, the chapter argues, fostering spirituality in people with dementia requires humility, compassion and empathy, and recognition of the ultimate value of every affected individual. When rooted in these attitudes, and characterized by positive person work,[1] interactions with people who have dementia, whether in conversations,

---

1. Kitwood, *Dementia Reconsidered*.

activities, or care, have spiritual potential to foster meaning, connection, and self-transcendence.

DEVELOPMENT AND PROGRESSION OF ALZHEIMER'S DISEASE

As Hippocrates, the father of modern medicine, first cautioned, "It is far more important to know what person the disease has than what disease the person has."[2] Our societal quest to find a cure for AD entails dissecting the disease process in a manner that can leave the affected person "in the dust" of science. While the predominant biomedical approach to AD has been rightly critiqued as a major contributor to the dehumanization of affected individuals, science lends important insights to incorporate into the larger bio-psycho-social-spiritual understanding of dementia that underpins this chapter. Identifying pathways to foster spirituality in people with Alzheimer's disease and other dementias requires knowing how these conditions affect memory and thinking abilities. As a full description of cognitive decline in the various dementias (e.g., AD, dementia with Lewy bodies, vascular dementia, and fronto-temporal dementia) is beyond the scope of this chapter, the following brief review will focus on the development and progression of AD, the primary or secondary etiology in up to 80 percent of all dementia cases.[3]

Today, AD is recognized as a decades-long process that begins fifteen to twenty years or more before symptoms first emerge[4,5] and can extend sixteen years, on average, thereafter.[6,7] In the preclinical, or "silent" asymptomatic phase, of AD, the neuropathological changes that contribute to neuronal death, senile plaques, and neurofibrillary tangles begin to accumulate in the brain, as evidenced in a variety of biological changes.[8] Earliest changes occur in cerebral spinal fluid (CSF) levels of the toxic amyloid-beta and tau proteins implicated, respectively, in the formation of senile plaques and neurofibrillary tangles. Metabolic and structural changes in the brain measured with various imaging techniques follow. Recently, amyloid PET (i.e., positron emission tomography) scans have made it possible to detect

2. http://www.brainyquote.com/quotes/quotes/h/hippocrate386231.html.
3. Magaki et al., "Comorbidity."
4. Bateman et al., "Clinical and Biomarker Changes."
5. Ringman et al., "Cerebrospinal Fluid Biomarkers."
6. Morris et al., "Mild Cognitive Impairment."
7. Zanetti et al., "Life Expectancy."
8. Jack et al., "Tracking Pathophysiological Processes."

beta-amyloid deposition in the brain during life, allowing for a "real time" glimpse into the development of AD neuropathology.[9] Use of biomarkers for early identification of AD is primarily limited to research, as results of CSF assays and amyloid PET imaging are not diagnostically conclusive in and of themselves. Hence, current diagnostic guidelines recommend use of biomarkers clinically only if needed to clarify an uncertain diagnosis made using standard procedures.[10],[11] Individuals in the preclinical phase with only biomarker evidence of AD may express concerns about their memory but continue to perform normally on traditional neuropsychological measures of memory and other cognitive abilities.

The cognitive, functional, and behavioral changes historically associated with AD begin years after the first biological changes. If and when the accumulation of senile plaques and neurofibrillary tangles in the brain reaches a threshold beyond which symptoms emerge, the affected individual progresses through a transitional stage known as mild cognitive impairment (MCI).[12],[13] In MCI, the individual develops noticeable cognitive symptoms, which the person and others cannot overlook, and, when evaluated, performs significantly worse than others of the same age and education on neuropsychological measures of memory and/or other cognitive abilities (e.g., language, executive functioning). Despite these cognitive changes, the individual with MCI continues to function well in daily life. Although some difficulties with complex living skills such as managing finances may be present, basic abilities to care for oneself are preserved. In addition to cognitive changes, the person with MCI may experience a variety of behavioral and psychological changes, with apathy, depression, anxiety, and irritability being most common.[14],[15] AD or another dementia is diagnosed when cognitive impairment becomes so severe that it compromises everyday living skills (e.g., eating, dressing). While some individuals with MCI remain stable, and others return to normal if the cognitive impairment is due to a reversible cause such as depression or a medical condition, the majority progress to AD or another dementia. Nearly half, or an average of 12 percent per year, of individuals with MCI followed for forty-eight months "converted" to AD, as compared to only 1–2 percent of cognitively normal

9. Rabinovici and Jagust, "Amyloid Imaging."

10. Albert et al., "Diagnosis of Mild Cognitive Impairment."

11. McKhann et al., "The Diagnosis of Dementia."

12. Petersen, "Mild Cognitive Impairment."

13. Petersen, Smith, et al., "Mild Cognitive Impairment."

14. Apostolova and Cummings, "Neuropsychiatric Manifestations."

15. Monastero et al., "A Systematic Review."

older adults.[16] When the suspected cause is Alzheimer's disease, MCI may take three to eight years to progress to a full-blown dementia.[17,18]

In the dementia stage of AD, the individual experiences a cascade of cognitive, functional, behavioral, and psychological changes that, across an average of eight years, eventually leads to death.[19] Cognitive changes progress in a typical pattern from early short-term memory difficulties to encompass language, reasoning, judgment, visuospatial, and executive abilities plus long-term memory. As cognition declines, so do functional abilities, with the person becoming increasingly dependent on others for assistance with eating, dressing, bathing, and other basic self-care abilities. Likewise behavioral and psychological changes continue to evolve, due to a complex interplay of neuropathological changes in the brain, medical comorbidities, psychological reactions to the disease process, and environmental factors.

Nearly all individuals with AD experience behavioral and psychological changes,[20] such as apathy, depression, anxiety, delusions, hallucinations, and wandering, however, the particular symptoms vary greatly from person to person. Most importantly, it is increasingly being recognized that behavioral and psychological "symptoms" of dementia, once primarily attributed to neuropathological brain changes, are indeed an attempt on the part of the individual to communicate unmet needs. When understood as a nonverbal language, "behavioral expressions"[21] reveal much about what the person is experiencing, from pain to social exclusion. Undoubtedly such behaviors might also reflect unmet spiritual needs. To understand these expressions, the carer must take time to do the interpretive task of translating the behavioral language to identify the unmet and find a compassionate response tailored to the individual.

Finally, in advanced AD, the individual becomes increasingly unresponsive, completely dependent on others, bedridden, and, as death nears, develops neurological problems (e.g., inability to swallow). An opportunistic infection (e.g., pneumonia) and death typically follow. While the infection may be the proximate cause of death, dementia is the underlying cause. In fact, a recent study investigating major causes of death in the United States revealed that one of three Americans age 65+ dies with dementia.[22]

16. Petersen, Smith et al., "Mild Cognitive Impairment"
17. Petersen, Doody, et al., "Current Concepts."
18. Tabert et al., "Neuropsychological Prediction."
19. Zanetti et al., "Life Expectancy."
20. Ryu et al., "Persistence."
21. Consumer Consortium on Assisted Living, "Dementia Care."
22. James et al., "Contribution of Alzheimer."

IMPACT OF COGNITIVE IMPAIRMENT ON VALUES AND BELIEFS

Turning now to the question of how cognitive impairment affects values and beliefs in AD, the biomedical perspective would most certainly conclude that they are shattered across time. Yet, the voices of people with MCI and Alzheimer's disease, and clinical experience suggest that the fate of values and beliefs in dementia is not as clear biomedicine might suggest. In actuality, both a continuity and discontinuity with previously held values and beliefs can be seen in people with MCI and AD, such that resting spirituality in a set of guiding life principles that are "continually in the process of becoming" is problematic.

In the MCI and early dementia stages of AD, the affected individual struggles with the growing dissonance between the once fully cognitively capable and now cognitively compromised self. Perceptions of oneself, for example, as competent, independent, in charge and stable, are challenged by the cognitive, behavioral, and functional changes that society views as a "living death." Embedded in a society which predominantly refers to dementia with terms having negative connotations, such as "the long goodbye," "invader," "monster," and "alien," the affected, their families, and the broader community are rendered terrified and powerless.[23] A systematic review of forty-eight studies investigating stigma in AD revealed the pervasive and detrimental nature of the negative attributions ascribed to dementia.[24] Such attributions reduce the affected individual, in the words of Erving Goffman, "from a whole and usual person to a tainted, discounted one."[25] Among individuals with AD, stigma resulted in low self-esteem, feelings of shame and humiliation, and social isolation. Negative consequences of stigma extended to (a) families who suffered from feelings of shame and moral failure, increased burden and depression, social isolation, concealment, and decreased use of services; (b) professionals through differential or delayed diagnosis and treatment, and (c) society in differential access to and use of services, and increased institutionalization.[26] Stigma has multiplicative and widespread effects as the individual with AD internalizes societal stereotypes (i.e., self-stigma), carers experience stigma by virtue of their relationship to person (i.e., stigma by association), and the entire family suffers from discrimination (i.e., public stigma). Under attack from

23. Zeilig, "Dementia as a Cultural Metaphor," 260–61.
24. Werner, "Stigma and Alzheimer's."
25. Goffman, *Stigma*, 3.
26. Werner, "Stigma and Alzheimer's."

cognitive decline and stigma, long-held values and beliefs can implode. At this point, one's core values may devolve into a distancing if not rejection of self-value, value by others, and spiritual value, or in religious terms, value by God. Similarly, cognitive decline and stigma can assault beliefs about oneself as an individual, in relationship to others, and in relationship to the divine.

Interviews of thirty-five individuals with MCI or early AD or another dementia by this author revealed that the process of cognitive decline is often experienced as "demeaning," "demoralizing," "shocking," and "frightening." Art, seventy-six at the time of his interview, noted that receiving the diagnosis AD "fractured me," splintering his sense of invincibility. "It was traumatic. I've never been to a hospital or had a broken a bone. It was shocking to find out that my body was failing me." In light of such negative subjective experiences, it is no surprise that interviewees also reported attempting to hide their cognitive difficulties (e.g., "faking it") and feeling inadequate, worried and depressed, helpless, heartbroken, and angry. While some interviewees used positive coping strategies (e.g., maintaining a positive attitude, helping others, focusing on remaining strengths, accepting the diagnosis and enjoying "a different life"), it was evident that doing so took a daily focused effort. Certainly, as highlighted by Art, "You get into a spiritual question. God, he allows evil to occur and none of us are quite sure why he does that but he does."

Answering the question of what happens to values and beliefs becomes even more difficult as AD advances into the late stage. As language wanes, first becoming illogical and later disappearing almost if not entirely, and impairment extends from forgetfulness to encompass all domains of cognitive functioning (i.e., attention, judgment, visuospatial abilities, and executive functioning plus memory and language), retaining and accessing long-held values and beliefs becomes increasingly difficult and eventually impossible. In advanced dementia, self-stigmatization persists, as expressed nonverbally through behaviors reflecting frustration (e.g., shaking fists) and depression (e.g., downward glance) over the loss of abilities. Unfortunately, such behavioral expressions are too often dismissed as part of the dementia syndrome and ignored, rather than responded to professionally and compassionately, based on a thorough analysis of potential medical, cognitive, psychological, and environmental causes.

While some individuals with advanced dementia continue to behave in ways that are consistent with known values and beliefs, others act in a totally contrary manner, surprising those closest to them. Take, for example, the staunch Catholic woman with severe dementia who is found cuddling in bed with a "strange" man in the nursing home where they live. For her husband, who views her as someone who would "never behave that way," this extra-marital closeness is a source of pain and disgust. Explanatory models for the dissonance in values and beliefs that can occur, such as a "then" vs. "now" self in dementia, do not suffice as they fail to encompass the whole self,[27] which any definition of spirituality must do. Clearly, the spirituality of "constantly becoming" values and beliefs fails here, as it excludes people with advanced dementia who do not have the cognitive capacity to engage in the spiritual process Koepke describes. Both values and beliefs require conscious choice of certain principles to guide one's life as well as adhering to, confessing, and acting upon these principles, none of which people with advanced dementia remain capable of. Here, parenthetically, it should be noted that the personal preferences (e.g., for a particular assistant, activity or food) people with advanced dementia remain able to express, behaviorally if not verbally, do not necessarily equate to underlying values or beliefs. While a historically prejudicial individual with dementia may show disfavor in being assisted by an African American aide, revealing long-held values and beliefs, that same individual may embrace assistance from this aide who is particularly kind, compassionate and knowledgeable about the individual's needs.

A Dementia-Inclusive Spirituality

To include people with dementia, spirituality must be defined in a manner that encompasses the experiential, embodied, relational, and emotional aspects of being. Rooted in what Stephen Post has described as our "hyper-cognitive" culture,[28] Koepke's definition of spirituality relies too heavily on conceptual and analytic abilities that enable a person to critically evaluate, adopt, internalize, espouse, and freely act upon a set of guiding principles. Dating back to Irenaeus in the second century, it is the human capacities of reason and free will that have been promoted as the primary if not sole ways in which the image of God (i.e., imago Dei) manifests itself in humans.[29] Such theology leads us to an exclusionary spirituality, dependent on cognition, in which people with dementia are assumed to lose their inherent godliness and deemed unable to experience meaning, connection and self-transcendence.

A deeper and broader understanding of the imago Dei can lead us, however, to an inclusionary spirituality which embraces people with dementia.

27. Koppelman, "Dementia and Dignity."

28. Post, *Moral Challenge*, 3.

29. Behr, *Irenaeus of Lyons*.

Drawing on the Eastern Orthodox tradition, Allen and Coleman affirmed personhood in dementia based on the early Christian social understanding of human nature as in the image of God. Highlighting the doctrine of Trinity, these authors pointed out that the conception of God as three in one is by implication about the identity of the human person. "Just as God is not an isolated person but is considered always in relationship, Father to Son to Spirit, so a human person is never to be considered in isolation of the rest of humanity."[30] It is this relationally focused understanding of the imago Dei which underlies the social existentialist philosophy of Martin Buber,[31] a Jewish theologian who conceived of human beings as always in relationship to the world. For Buber, the person, that is "I," exists only in dialectical relationship with the other or "Thou." Each interaction is an opportunity to treat the other as an "It," that is as a means to an end, or a "Thou," a unique individual. In comparison to I–It interactions, which objectify and diminish the person, I–Thou relating is a mutual, free, non-objectifying way of being present in the moment with each other.[32] In the constant interplay between I–It and I–Thou interactions, one's prevailing relational approach has significant consequences. I–It relating can dehumanize, while I–Thou relating can sustain personhood and, as Buber noted, create an opportunity to experience the divine.

Consequently, a dementia-inclusive definition of spirituality links the universally regarded spiritual goals of achieving meaning, connection, and self-transcendence[33] to the relational nature of God and hence humans. In other words, meaning, connection, and self-transcendence can be achieved relationally, opening the door of spirituality widely to encompass people with dementia. That is, however, if being in relationship is viewed broadly, as between bodies as well as minds.[34] As the expression and comprehension of language fails, relationship in dementia shifts from a predominantly cognitive to emotional and bodily exchange. As noted earlier, behaviors that have been stereotyped as "problems" are now better understood as a means of bodily expression.[35] In the attempt to connect to people with dementia, carers must also learn to shift their language not just from complex strings of words to simple short phrases that are easier to follow, but also to emotional and bodily communication. God, in the attempt to bring humans into

30. Allen and Coleman, "Spiritual Perspectives," 214.

31. Buber, *I and Thou*.

32. Westerhof et al., "A Buberian Approach."

33. Allen and Coleman, "Spiritual Perspectives."

34. Oppenheimer, "I Am, Thou Art."

35. Consumer Consortium on Assisted Living, "Dementia Care."

relationship with the divine, became embodied in Christ. So, the carer can join the person with dementia through the body, for example in therapeutic touch, movement, and dance.

In striving towards a deeper, broader, and fully inclusive understanding of spirituality, we must also ask ourselves whether loss of cognition in dementia, the most feared health condition among older Americans today,[36] actually represents an evolution into a purely spiritual existence. In reflecting on his wife's struggle with Alzheimer's disease, the Reverend Wayne Ewing, an Episcopal priest, "began to ask myself, could it be that, as mystics of all spiritual traditions suggest, one's loss of time and space is really a foreshadowing of an entry into the eternal?"[37] Similarly, the Reverend Robert Davis, who wrote *My Journey into Alzheimer's Disease* with the assistance of his wife, shared, "Perhaps the journey that takes me away from reality into the blackness of that place of the emotionless, unmoving Alzheimer's stare is in reality a journey into the richest depths of God's love that few have experienced on earth."[38] It is carers who have the privilege of supporting people with dementia through this "unbecoming" and experiencing what some would regard as an evolution rather than devolution of the person. In *Symphony of Spirits*, Dr. Deborah Forrest, a psychologist and nurse, described how the insights of two Cherokee nurses, Dolly and Rose, changed her view of dementia. Dolly asserted that the bodies of the patients on the geropsychiatric unit, most of whom had Alzheimer's disease or another dementia, "are crippled by disease, but their spirits are not. Their spirits aren't even touched by the disease. They are continuing to grow, no matter what happens to the physical bodies. We see and hear their spirits every day."[39] In fact Dolly and Rose maintained that they could more clearly see the spirits more of dementia than cognitively intact patients. "Since these people were closer to death, their spirit images were stronger. And since their early mental processes were suspended by their disease, their spirit natures were the only things functioning strongly within them."[40]

In light of this discussion, might we want to replace Koepke's definition of spirituality with the following? *Spirituality engages the person, at all levels of human experience, in the lifelong pursuit of meaning, connection, and self-transcendence.* Hence, it is not core beliefs and values that are continually in a process of becoming, but it is the person, at all levels, who is in the spiritual

---

36. Alzheimer's Association, *2014 Alzheimer's Disease Facts.*

37. Ewing, *Tears*, 76.

38. Davis, *My Journey*, 120.

39. Forrest, *Symphony of Spirits*, 47–48.

40. Ibid., 73.

pursuit. As we progress through life and face inevitable vicissitudes, such as Alzheimer's disease, spirituality, as a process, may engage certain aspects of the human experience more or less. Encompassing in nature, the proposed definition of spirituality allows it to be, for example, emotional as well as cognitive, inter- as well as intra-personal, and silent as well as expressive. In essence, the proposed definition of spirituality is person-centered at heart, as it not only meets but greets the individual where he or she is at.

FOSTERING SPIRITUALITY IN DEMENTIA

Our challenge—and our responsibility—is to proactively support people with dementia in the ongoing spiritual pursuit of meaning, connected- ness, and self-transcendence. Given the worsening apathy characteristic of AD, the carer must take on greater responsibility in the spiritual endeavor, intentionally drawing out and engaging affected individuals. On the one hand, carers can, for example, co-create joyous moments that lift people with dementia above confusion, frustration, and depression to experience meaning, connection, and self-transcendence. On the other hand, carers can make real widely held beliefs that quality of life is absent in dementia by co-creating the isolation that contributes to meaninglessness, discon- nection, and absorption in the losses of dementia. One person living with dementia noted, "Many think it is the disease that causes us to withdraw, and to some extent I believe this is true. But, for many of us, we withdraw because we are not provided with meaningful opportunities that allow us to continue to experience joy, purpose and engagement in life."[41] Stephen Post challenged carers, "Rather than thinking of people with dementia as out of reach because of forgetfulness or unworthy because of cognitive disability, the moral task is to bring them into discourse in creative ways."[42]

Taking on Post's challenge is so simple and yet so complex. Numerous books and websites detail invaluable strategies, including dementia-specific communication skills, approaches to challenging behaviors, and ideas for activities that draw on the individual's remaining strengths, lifelong inter- ests, creativity, and religious traditions or spirituality in the broader sense. As "how-to's" can be found so widely, this author will refrain from describ- ing these strategies but direct the reader to explore innovative approaches such as art (e.g., Memories in the Making, Meet Me at MOMA), imaginative storytelling and drama (e.g., TimeSlips, Storybox), meditative movement (e.g., Tai Chi), individualized music delivered via iPods, and small group

41. Dupuis et al., "Just Dance with Me," 240.

42. Post, *Ethical Issues*, 94.

worship during which biblical stories are enacted with wooden figures (i.e., Sensing the Sacred).[43]

Enabling people with dementia to experience meaning, purpose, and connection, however, requires more than having access to and learning dementia-specific skills to communicate, respond to challenging behaviors, and facilitate even the most innovative activities. It is just this that Kitwood recognized in drawing attention to the interpersonal environment in which an individual experiences dementia. Influenced by Buber's dialectical theology, Kitwood distinguished interpersonal attitudes, behaviors, and approaches that enhance well-being in dementia from those detrimental to the person. Relational experiences characterized by what Kitwood called "malignant social psychology,"[44] or what Kuhn and Verity later dubbed "putdowns" (e.g., infantilizing, intimidating, disempowering, and excluding),[45]diminishes and further disables the person with dementia. In contrast, relational experiences typified by positive person work, or in Kuhn's terms, uplifts (e.g., honoring, validating, empowering, and including) recognize and raise up the individual's continued personhood despite any cognitive losses. For example, rushing a person with dementia through dressing (i.e., outpacing) may meet a carer's needs but communicates disrespect. In contrast, allowing the individual to take as much time as needed to dress with the appropriate level of assistance (e.g., step-by-step instructions, modeling, physical prompts) communicates ultimate regard and maximizes independence. Increasing carer awareness of how interpersonal style can support or detract from the other's personhood is critical to transforming dementia care from a highly routinized, task-focused orientation to a truly person-centered endeavor. When cared for in milieu of healing relationships characterized by positive person work, people with dementia could, according to Kitwood, actually experience a "rementing,"[46] or improvement in functioning.

Compassion, empathy, humility, and recognition of the person's ultimate value lie at the core of healing relationships in dementia. In the absence of these, the most touted approaches to dementia care are no more than a collection of techniques designed to manipulate the confused into behaving "appropriately." When dementia-specific communication skills, person-centered approaches to challenging behaviors, and innovative activities, however, are undergirded by compassion, empathy, humility, and

43. See Gordon, chapter 8 in this book.
44. Kitwood, *Dementia Reconsidered*, 46.
45. Kuhn and Verity, "Putdowns and Uplifts," 26–28.
46. Kitwood, *Dementia Reconsidered*, 62.

recognition of the person's ultimate value, the best in dementia care is achieved. Such dementia care, as noted earlier, fosters the spiritual pursuit, facilitating meaning, connection, and self-transcendence.

And, it is just this care that people with dementia say they want. In exploring the meanings of leisure for people with dementia, Dupuis et al. found that activities offered people with dementia a "space to experience and celebrate life despite dementia,"[47] or from this author's perspective, for self-transcendence. In this study, people with dementia viewed leisure as a way to live life to the fullest and, more specifically, find opportunities to "be me, be with, make a difference, seek freedom, find balance, grown and develop, and have fun."[48] Briefly, people with dementia described leisure as providing opportunities for (1) "being me" via personally meaningful experiences; (2) "being with" or connecting with self, others, animals, and nature; (3) "having fun," that is, experiencing feelings such as pleasure, playfulness and mischievousness; (4) "making a difference" or contributing; (5) "seeking freedom" or taking breaks from everyday stress and restrictive environments; (6) "finding balance" or balancing relaxation and keeping busy; and (7) "growing and developing" by challenging the mind and body. Each of these seven qualities of leisure has an inherently spiritual dimension. When pursued in the context of healing relationships, leisure activities, as described by these authors, can fulfill the spiritual needs of meaning, connection, and self-transcendence in people with dementia.

DEVELOPING CORE ATTITUDES

How does one, then, develop the qualities of compassion, empathy, humility, and recognition of each person's ultimate value that form the basis for effectively supporting people with dementia in the spiritual pursuit? While some carers have an intuitive appreciation for people with dementia, these qualities don't always come naturally, as Reverend Thomas O'Connor shared.[49] He had to consciously choose to change his attitude. Reflecting on his visits with individuals affected by dementia in a continuing care community, O'Connor recalled finding their lives devoid of meaning. On Erikson's tipping scale of despair vs. integrity in the last stage of life, O'Connor initially perceived those he visited as weighed down in despair and melancholy. What, O'Connor asked himself, would happen if he changed his assumptions and intentionally viewed those he visited as achieving integrity

47. Dupuis et al., "Just Dance with Me," 245.
48. Ibid., 245.
49. O'Connor, "Ministry Without a Future."

and having wisdom to share even in the midst of their dementia? Once O'Connor started viewing people with dementia in this way, they taught him a different way of relating, in which a touch on the hand was more important than any amount of words, enjoying the here and now took precedence over remembering, even seemingly illogical strings of words reflected an effort to work out lingering issues, and validating the individual's reality outweighed factual truth.

Empowered with new ways of looking at and relating to people affected by dementia, O'Connor realized he would also have to change his "hypercognitive" approach to ministry. "One day," O'Connor noted, "I asked Sally what God thought of her. She responded by saying, 'God doesn't do much thinking these days.'"[50] Failing to reach Sally and others in this manner, O'Connor discovered that sensory stimulation with religious symbols that people with dementia could see, touch, hear, and smell could help him achieve his desire to "a gift . . . to know that God thinks their life has been worthwhile and God loves them and will take care of them."[51] Now wearing a Roman collar, O'Connor brought sensory items, such as a Bible, holy cards with biblical scenes, recorded hymns, and traditional prayers, to his visits. Notably, O'Connor recounted a visit in which he showed the stuffed lamb to Sally and asked her, "Do you know the story of the lost sheep?" Taking the lamb and hugging it, Sally recalled being lost in a church and found by her father. Validating Sally, O'Connor replied, "You were scared—like the lost sheep." As the exchange continued, O'Connor was able to draw the spiritual connection, stating, "Your father was a good shepherd and he took good care of you. You trusted him." And, she recalled, "He found me a number of times"[52] Using the symbol, O'Connor enabled Sally to affirm God's positive intention toward her.

By shifting his stance towards people with dementia from an arrogant, downward-looking position to a humble, compassionate, upward looking one that recognized them as "wisdom figures,"[53] O'Connor was freed to interact in new ways that deeply touched those he visited. When carers are similarly humbled, they are freed to engage in positive person work and implement innovative approaches to dementia care, such as those referenced earlier, in a manner that facilitates the spiritual pursuit toward meaning, connection, and self-transcendence. Developing humility, compassion, empathy, and a belief in the ultimate value of each individual with dementia

50. Ibid., 11.

51. Ibid., 10.

52. Ibid., 11.

53. Ibid., 7.

requires not only a conscious choice such as O'Connor made, but practice. As Buddhism teaches, one must train the mind, constantly cultivating an attitude of compassion towards all other beings.[54] Faced with a behavioral challenge such as wandering (e.g., wanting to go home), a carer hold back any impulse to react impulsively and purposely pause momentarily to reflect with compassion and empathy for the individual's suffering (e.g., feeling abandoned). With that appreciation, the carer must use knowledge of the person and dementia-specific communication and problem-solving skills in a manner that keeps the individual safe, eases the suffering, and prevents embarrassment. No short order. Yet, even if the intervention doesn't go smoothly, the person with dementia will have sensed the carer's compassion and empathy. That experience of shared humanity is ultimately the most important aspect of dementia care. And in that I-Thou moment lies the opportunity, as Buber pointed out, to experience the divine.

IN CONCLUSION

Even Koepke, with his great appreciation of people affected by dementia, has fallen into the "hypercognitive"[55] trap of American culture by defining spirituality as a person's core values and beliefs that "are continually in a process of becoming." Fitting hand and glove into the constrictive biomedical understanding of AD, with its narrow focus on cognition and the brain, Koepke's definition leaves behind people, such as those with AD or another dementia, who have lost the ability to choose, adhere to, confess, and act upon a set of guiding life principles. Based on a relational understanding of the imago Dei, this chapter has reframed spirituality as engaging the person, at all levels of human experience, in the lifelong pursuit of meaning, connection, and self-transcendence. Even more radically, this chapter has challenged the reader to consider the possibility that AD and other dementias actually free up the individual to achieve spiritual growth in new ways, through non-cognitive aspects (e.g., social and emotional) of the self that persist despite the loss of cognition. Launching from its broad and inclusive definition of spirituality, this chapter has highlighted the importance of healing relationships, characterized by positive person work, humility, compassion, empathy, and recognition of each individual's ultimate value to fostering the spiritual endeavor in dementia. It is this author's hope that readers will engage themselves in the ongoing cultivation of these qualities,

---

54. Hopkins, *Cultivating Compassion*.
55. Post, *Moral Challenge*, 3.

as well as their development in others, to ensure that people with dementia can live spiritually rich lives despite cognitive impairment.

REFERENCES

Albert, Marilyn S., et al. "The Diagnosis of Mild Cognitive Impairment Due to Alzheimer's Disease: Recommendations from the National Institute on Aging and Alzheimer's Association Workgroups on Diagnostic Guidelines for Alzheimer's Disease." *Alzheimer's and Dementia* 7 (2011) 270–79.

Allen, F. Brian, and Peter G. Coleman. "Spiritual Perspectives on the Person with Dementia: Identity and Personhood." In *Dementia: Mind Meaning and the Person*, edited by J. C. Hughes, S. J. Louw, and S. R. Sabat, 205–21. Oxford: Oxford University Press, 2006.

Alzheimer's Association. *2014 Alzheimer's Disease Facts and Figures.* New York: Alzheimer's Association, 2014. http://www.alz.org/downloads/facts_figures_2014.pdf.

Apostolova, Liana G., and Jeffrey L. Cummings. "Neuropsychiatric Manifestations in Mild Cognitive Impairment: A Systematic Review of the Literature." *Dementia and Geriatric Cognitive Disorders* 25 (2008) 115–26.

Bateman, Randall J., et al. "Clinical and Biomarker Changes in Dominantly Inherited Alzheimer's Disease." *New England Journal of Medicine* 367 (2012) 795–804.

Behr, John. *Irenaeus of Lyons: Identifying Christianity.* Oxford: Oxford University Press, 2013.

Buber, Martin. *I and Thou.* New York: Scribner, 2000.

Consumer Consortium on Assisted Living. "Dementia Care: The Quality Chasm." January, 2013. http://www.ccal.org/wp-content/uploads/DementiaCareTheQualityChasm_020413.pdf.

Davis, Robert. *My Journey into Alzheimer's Disease.* Wheaton, IL: Tyndale, 1989.

Dupuis, Sherry L., et al. "Just Dance with Me: An Authentic Partnership Approach to Understanding Leisure in the Dementia Context." *World Leisure Journal* 54 (2012) 240–54.

Erikson, Erik. *Vital Involvement in Old Age.* New York: Norton, 1986.

Ewing, Wayne. *Tears in God's Bottle: Reflections on Alzheimer's Caregiving.* Tucson: WhiteStone Circle, 1999.

Forrest, Deborah A. *Symphony of Spirits: Encounters with the Spiritual Dimensions of Alzheimer's.* New York: St. Martin's, 2000.

Goffman, Erving. *Stigma: Notes on the Management of Spoiled Identity.* Englewood Cliffs, NJ: Prentice Hall, 1963.

Hopkins, Jeffrey. *Cultivating Compassion: A Buddhist Perspective.* New York: Broadway, 2001.

Jack, Clifford R. Jr., et al. "Tracking Pathophysiological Processes in Alzheimer's Disease: An Updated Hypothetical Model of Dynamic Biomarkers." *Lancet Neurology* 12 (2013) 207–16.

James, B. D., et al. "Contribution of Alzheimer Disease to Mortality in the United States." *Neurology* 8 (2014) 1045–50.

Kitwood, Thomas. *Dementia Reconsidered: The Person Comes First.* Buckingham, UK: Open University Press, 1997.

Koppelman, E. R. "Dementia and Dignity: Towards a New Method of Surrogate Decision Making." *Journal of Medicine and Philosophy* 27 (2002) 65–85.

Kuhn, Daniel, and June Verity. "Putdowns and Uplifts: Signs of Good or Poor Dementia Care." *Journal of Dementia Care* (2002) 27–28.

Magaki, Shino, et al. "Comorbidity in Dementia: Update of an Ongoing Autopsy Study." *Journal of the American Geriatrics Society* 62 (2014) 1722–28.

McKhann, Guy M., et al. "The Diagnosis of Dementia Due to Alzheimer's Disease: Recommendations from the National Institute on Aging and the Alzheimer's Association Workgroups on Diagnostic Guidelines for Alzheimer's Disease." *Alzheimer's and Dementia*, 7 (2011) 263–69.

Monastero, Roberto, et al. "A Systematic Review of Neuropsychiatric Symptoms in Mild Cognitive Impairment." *Journal of Alzheimer's Disease* 18 (2009) 11–30.

Morris, John C., et al. "Mild Cognitive Impairment Represents Early-Stage Alzheimer's Disease." *Archives of Neurology* 58 (2001) 397–405.

O'Connor, Thomas. "Ministry Without a Future: A Pastoral Care Approach to Patients with Senile Dementia." *Journal of Pastoral Care* 46 (1992) 5–12.

Oppenheimer, C. "I Am, Thou Art: Personal Identity in Dementia." In *Dementia: Mind Meaning and the Person*, edited by J. C. Hughes, S. J. Louw, and S. R. Sabat, 193–203. Oxford: Oxford University Press, 2006.

Petersen, Ronald. C. "Mild Cognitive Impairment as a Diagnostic Entity." *Journal of Internal Medicine* 25 (2004) 183–94.

Petersen, Ronald C., Rachelle Doody, et al. "Current Concepts in Mild Cognitive Impairment." *Archives of Neurology* 58 (2001) 1985–92.

Petersen, Ronald C., Glenn E. Smith, et al. "Mild Cognitive Impairment: Clinical Characterization and Outcome." *Archives of Neurology* 56 (1999) 303–8.

Post, Stephen G. *Ethical Issues from Diagnosis to Dying: The Moral Challenge of Alzheimer's Disease.* 2nd ed. Baltimore: Johns Hopkins University Press, 2000.

———. *The Moral Challenge of Alzheimer's Disease.* Baltimore: Johns Hopkins University Press, 1995.

Rabinovici, G. D., and W. J. Jagust. "Amyloid Imaging in Aging and Dementia: Testing the Amyloid Hypothesis in Vivo." *Behavioral Neurology* 21 (2009) 117–28.

Ringman, John M., et al. "Cerebrospinal Fluid Biomarkers and Proximity to Diagnosis in Preclinical Familial Alzheimer's Disease." *Dementia and Geriatric Cognitive Disorders* 33 (2012) 1–5.

Ryu, S. H., et al. "Persistence of and Changes in Neuropsychiatric Symptoms in Alzheimer Disease over 6 Months: The LASER-AD Study." *American Journal of Geriatric Psychiatry* 13 (2005) 976–83.

Tabert, Matthias H., et al. "Neuropsychological Prediction of Conversion to Alzheimer Disease in Patients with Mild Cognitive Impairment." *Archives of General Psychiatry* 63 (2006) 916–24.

Werner, Perla. "Stigma and Alzheimer's Disease: A Systematic Review of Evidence, Theory, and Methods." In *The Stigma of Disease and Disability: Understanding Causes and Overcoming Injustices*, edited by Patrick W. Corrigan, 223–44. Washington, DC: American Psychological Association, 2014.

Westerhof, Gerben J., et al. "A Buberian Approach to the Co-Construction of Relationships Between Professional Caregivers and Residents in Nursing Nomes." *Gerontologist* 54 (2013) 354–62.

Zanetti, O., et al. "Life Expectancy in Alzheimer's Disease (AD)." *Archives of Gerontology and Geriatrics,* 49 Suppl 1 (2009) 237–43.

Zeilig, Hannah. "Dementia as a Cultural Metaphor." *Gerontologist* 54 (2013) 258–67.

6

The Essential Spirit in Caresharing

—*Marty Richards, LICSW*

THE PARADOX OF BEING CARED FOR OR BEING A CARER

Caregiving and care receiving are part of life experience. Those giving care and those cared for can be connected through blood or marriage, or they may be unrelated persons who are like "family." Others may be volunteers or paid persons brought in to assist a person with illness or disability. All give "hands on care," and most desire to be loving and supportive in the face of difficult caregiving. Although not always clearly identified, caregivers and care receivers have spiritual concerns. There can be diversity in feelings and spiritual challenges based on cultural background, family history, religious values, community expectations, or societal pressures. And, there are gender differences in perceptions of caregiving and receiving. Professionals from a variety of disciplines who walk the path with caregivers and care receivers focus primarily on the very visible physical, emotional, and mental components of the care relationship. Spiritual aspects, as noted by Koepke in the introduction of this book, are equally significant. Anyone who seeks to help others in this care journey is challenged to take these spiritual aspects take into account. This chapter will explore some of the spiritual dimensions of caregiving and receiving and will offer ideas for how spiritual support can be offered.

As Koepke notes in the introduction, all persons possess personal "truths" or core beliefs that give guidance for living and decision making. For many, these truths are shaped by "formal" religious belief systems. At the same time, personal truths can also be formed by a society's perspective on obligations to others. Core beliefs for living a just, moral life influence persons in decision making and understanding life's events. Such tenets prescribe what a person owes to another, how one lives in community, how decisions are made for the common good, and ideals about giving and receiving care. These beliefs can form "shoulds" and "oughts," often becoming hard-fast rules in the hearts of carers. Such obligations are part of the spiritual essence of caring, and can be explored as persons seek guidance for how to provided assistance to others.

In truth, the process of giving and receiving care is experienced at all ages. Parents care for young children, partners provide for each other in crisis. Persons become carers when someone in their "family" requires assistance. However, as persons age their chances becoming a caregiver increase. The mandate to care for and about others, especially elders, is foundational in many religions. "Honor your father and your mother"[1] and respect for elders are at the heart of all religions and are the basic beliefs in most cultures. Persons in caregiving relationships hear echoes of such obligations within their hearts and minds. Family members are often thrust into the roles of being cared for or being a carer with little preparation this call to care must be fulfilled even when the carer also feels (and often is) inadequate to the task. This response also happens for volunteer, non-family caregivers.

Those involved directly in this caring for/being cared struggle to understand their circumstances, because, for most, caregiving and receiving is uncharted territory. A new "status quo" develops as persons realize that their life is going to be different. The caring relationship raise challenges for a person's values and beliefs. Sometimes the caring experience call one's core beliefs into question. The caregiver role has little status, esteem, or value in society. Consider the low wages of childcare or eldercare workers. There is limited appreciation of the demanding work of providing hands on, intimate assistance to another. A caregiver overwhelmed by obligations, may act out in frustration. Persons ask questions such as: What does "going beyond the call of duty mean?" "What can I realistically do?" When a professional is aware of a person's beliefs, these queries can be explored within that particular spiritual context. Caring professionals can offer appreciation for the caring work that is being done, and emphasize its spiritual gift. There are many traditions that emphasize the idea of gift. For example, Judaism

---

1. The Fourth Commandment, Exod 20:12 RSV.

lifts up the importance of doing "mitzvah" or good acts toward one another. Christians talk about using God-given skills in the services of others. Buddhism speaks of Karma when good acts result in good consequences.[2] Viktor Frankl speaks of finding meaning in any experience.[3] At the same time a care receiver may "not want to be a burden," and thus may not honestly express feelings. Because of physical disability or even dementia, many who are receiving help are invisible in the general population. They might be considered to be "less than" more able-bodied persons.

These frustrations and difficulties are all too real. But there is a way to reframe caring relationships that stress the strengths and continued abilities of all involved. Caregiving/care receiving are holy and sacred endeavors, with opportunities to be of service to another. Many on the caregiving journey have recounted such gifts in the experience. Henri Nouwen's comments on human caring state it well. "It is a gesture that comes forth from a courageous confession of our common human need for one another and the grace of compassion that binds us together with brothers and sisters like ourselves who share with us the wonderful journey of life."[4] There is always the potential to find the divine in the person cared for and in the person doing the caregiving. Caring professionals can lift up the roles in caregiving and receiving to give voice to these universal human needs. Mother Theresa of Calcutta for example wrote about seeing Christ in the faces of the dying.

Spiritual issues underlie daily physical and emotional challenges. And as care partners wrestle with challenges in their situation, especially those around obligations and needs, the community around them may not be sensitive to their distress. Alternative perspectives for how individuals and groups around them might minister to those on the care journey may be valuable.

CARESHARING RATHER THAN CAREGIVING: THE ROLE OF RECIPROCITY

"Caresharing" is an alternative approach to caregiving and care receiving. Within this construct both the cared for and the caregiver are equal as persons of worth and value. One is not "more than" the other. They are *care partners;* both are loved by God, Allah, Vishnu, G_d, Creator, Higher Power,

2. For more discussion on this subject consult chapter 4 in this book, Price, "Religion: Friend or Foe."

3. For more discussion on Viktor Frankl consult chapter 2 in this book, Ellor, "Finding Meaning in Aging in a Meaningless World."

4. Nouwen, *A Spirituality of Caregiving,* 16.

Supreme Being, or whatever other words they may use to describe the divine in their lives. The Hindu greeting Namaste express it this way: "The Spirit in me meets the Spirit in you."[5] The concept of partnering balances give and take in the relationship.

Questions about meaning and purpose undergird caresharing. There is value in ministering to another through caregiving work; and there is inherent worth for a care receiver who, in turn, teaches basic life truths. Professionals working with care partners need to become aware of these underlying motifs, and stress their spiritual importance. I will speak more about what the care receiver offers the caregiver later.

Throughout life, persons are givers and receivers in relationships. While there has been more emphasis on giving, an emphasis on receiving is also important. The priority value of giving has resulted in skewed expectations about receiving in care partnerships. These societal attitudes can lead to awkward moments where a friend gives another a gift, but the gift recipient has nothing to give in return. But caresharing is not an equal give and take relationship. Instead caresharing is a reciprocal relationship that builds on mutual regard and deep connections. Strengths in each person are affirmed; the needs for assistance are clearly delineated. One partner may do more for the other, but that does not make the cared for "less than" the caregiver. This perspective is expressed in the notion that all people, no matter what their status is in life, are created in the image of God[6] or God-Within (mystical religions).[7] Thus interdependency is elevated as an important concept. There is the possibility for each partner can grow emotionally and spiritually even in the face of challenges.[8] The potential to learn from each other is celebrated. There is a belief in the resiliency of the human spirit, and an understanding that persons can bounce back from adversity when given support and assistance. Those working with care partners can assess the inner resources (for example, faith or humor) of both care partners as well as connect persons to outside assistance.

No matter how frail mentally or physically either is, both care partners can share the "spiritual" aspects caring. There is the chance to "recognize what is most deeply human and most deeply divine in the other person so

5. Palkhivala, "The Meaning of Namaste," n.p.

6. Gen 1, RSV.

7. While the term "mystical religions" is not precise in today's religious conversations it is used here to suggest traditions such as The United Centers for Spiritual Living, Unity, Zen (Buddhism), Sufism (Islam), Kabbalah (Judaism), Christian Mystics, i.e., Thomas Merton, Theresa of Avila, and Francis of Assisi.

8. See chapter 10: Thibault, "Activating Resources of the Soul Amidst Suffering."

that both have a chance to give and receive, to honor and learn from each other."[9]

Listening to individual stories and connecting them to others' stories and God's story may be helpful. Persons' stories are important. Inside of story, persons share their history and the dynamics of their family. Stories relate connection to community, and they illustrate how persons have experienced life challenges and coped with them over time. In the telling of the story, care partners also may raise the "unfinished business" of needs for forgiveness or dealing with myriad losses. Helpers cannot judgmentally accompany persons in caresharing, and can seek to understand the difficulties experienced by each individual in the partnership. Bearing witness to care partners' stories is an important role for a caring professional.

Embedded within the idea of caresharing is the belief that persons "serve" rather than "help" each other. "Helping" unbalances a relationship when it presumes that one person is in some way better than is the other. If a carer does too much for the cared for, the relationship equilibrium becomes precarious. Rachael Naomi Remen addresses this when she states: "We do not serve the weak and the broken. What we serve is the wholeness in each other and the wholeness of life."[10] Affirming the "wholeness" of body, mind, and spirit, even with a "frail" person, is a key spiritual support. Recognizing the "wholeness" in the caregiver is vital to providing support by the care receiver. Again, "Namaste": the god in me recognizes the god in you.

A "servant" caregiver is not superior to the cared for. Maintaining the equality between persons is the final goal. Such a perspective affirms the worth of a person's humanity. Spiritually it is the act of recognizing that they are created in the image of God. A "servant" may encourage a cared for person to make decisions on their own within the bounds of reasonable risk and their own abilities. Making such decisions also might involve making the "best of the worst choices" when there are not unlimited alternatives. Realistic limitations exist in all situations. Care partners, working with a professional helper, may sensitively sort out options while honoring the personhood of all involved.

Care partners do not exist in a vacuum but are part of larger communities. Their joys and sorrows are intertwined with the faith community and other groups, and such networks can be supportive to them. However, communities may need education about how to understand and be available to assist care partners when needed. They also can benefit from an awareness of the spiritual aspects of caring. Not being part of community, especially

9. Richards, *Caresharing*, xii–xiii.

10. Remen, *My Grandfather's Blessings*, 7.

for those who have been connected, may lead to a sense of isolation for care partners. Faith communities and other networks can be proactive in reaching out to care partners. Professionals working with care partners might offer suggestions to them on how to engage such groups.

Caresharing includes care partners' story, sharing grief and loss, dealing with needs for forgiveness between care partners, and the importance of hope.[11]

INDEPENDENCE, DEPENDENCE, AND INTERDEPENDENCE IN CARESHARING

A consideration of independence, dependence, and interdependence are central to a discussion about care partners' spiritual concerns. Through the predominant "rugged individualism" that characterizes rhetoric in the United States, persons internalize the notion that they survive and prosper by being "independent"—that they survive in the world totally on their own merit and abilities. But in reality persons are interdependent all of their lives, and an honest look at any life reveals this. Yet the cry to maintain independence is loud and persistent one as one ages and/or deals with disability.

With the population's increasing longevity, the inevitability that one will need care or give care grows. Sometimes there is a jolt of awareness of a need for caregiving when a person has a stroke or receives a terminal diagnosis. Those struggling with such chronic conditions as multiple sclerosis or Parkinson's disease see more subtle, yet progressive increments of change. At some point all dealing with illness realize that they require assistance to survive and to accomplish even the most basic tasks. Long-held values (again core beliefs about self, life, that which is beyond the self or spirituality) about independence are shaken. Over time caregivers also gradually realize parents and partners, and at times children and grandchildren, may require assistance. Those requiring care and those offering it may have differing ideas about the level of aid needed. Each may come to such realizations at different times. This can cause discord. Carer and cared for may be worlds apart in their assessment as to what is needed and expected.

While individuals have a strong sense of obligation to provide help, there may be little societal encouragement to do so. Available resources may not touch on the spiritual aspects of caresharing. Even when persons give assent to the idea of interdependence, asking for help is perceived as weakness. Care partners do not wish to rely on others for assistance. Professionals can affirm to care partners that asking for help is strength. As noted in the

11. These concepts are discussed in greater detail in Richard's book, *Caresharing*.

introduction, the embrace of one's inherent vulnerability, that one cannot go it alone, is the beginning of wisdom and essential to wholistic spirituality.

Having to depend on others due to health changes are no one's "fault." Attempts to place blame come from efforts to make sense out of chronic illness. Care partners are forced to take a realistic look at their circumstances. Having to take care of another or be dependent due to a chronic illness puts stress on otherwise well ordered, organized and predictable relationships. Physical and mental pressures are compounded when there has been a history of strained relationships. Great stress can be placed on care partners when those in the broader family network do not understand dilemmas related to dependency. In frustration a carer may place responsibility for chronic illness on the care receiver's past habits or lifestyle. While there is some truth in the assertion that negative lifestyle choices may lead to some disease processes, it is counterproductive to dwell on causation. The anguished cries of "why me" or "why my loved one" are often heard in the context of the need for giving and receiving assistance. The spiritual question is not "why," but "what now" believing that there is a light at the end of the tunnel.

Kindness and perseverance by both caregivers and care receivers is a required part of caresharing. Both persons need to try to be loving and compassionate. They may spend time seeking answers to illness questions, or performing the tasks that a particular disease process requires. Conflicts around a diagnosis and subsequent care issues are common. A person may sincerely want to provide lovingly for another and at the same time intensely dislike the illness affecting their loved one. Dilemmas in dependency cause spiritual distress. Persons may think "I don't feel worthy of such intense care when I can't give anything in return?" "How can I care for this person who I have detested all of these years?" They are part of the daily realities of caresharing; learning to live with such challenges is part of the spiritual journey.

Providing hands-on care to someone can be complicated. Care receiver dependency adds to many attendant hardships: financial, physical, emotional, mental, and spiritual. There is no magic wand that ameliorates them, but a reframing dependency into the possibility of interdependency can be beneficial. The community of faith as well as the resources in the general community can assist.

Wendy Lustbader, in her thoughtful volume on dependency *Counting on Kindness*,[12] explores in great depth what it means to have to rely on others for the most basic assistance. Depending on the compassion of others for basic needs is humbling. Caregivers, in turn, may lack sensitivity as to

12. Lustbader, *Counting*.

what the cared for feels. She reminds us that the quality of mercy is a crucial aspect of spiritual support in coping with dependency. Noting that "mercy is based entirely on exchange," she emphasizes the need for give and take in dependent relationships. "Giving help eventually embitters us, unless we are compensated at least by appreciation." By the same token, "accepting help degrades us unless we are convinced that others are getting something in return."[13] Deep spiritual concerns are embedded in these statements.

When a cared for person's only definition is "dependent," other descriptions of them as partner or parent may be lost. If these life roles are not affirmed opportunities for sharing are missed. Helpers who assist care partners can stress that interdependence is a fact for all ages and can affirm the importance of give and take in the relationship.

FEELINGS AND EMOTIONAL CONSIDERATIONS IN CARESHARING

There are mixed feelings in providing for another's intimate needs, or in realizing that one needs to depend on a caregiver for basic needs. Ambivalence is experienced because caresharing situations are fluid, and feelings often change along with worsening illness or caregiver fatigue. Ambivalence not only an emotional burden but also a spiritual concern. Carers benefit from being able to talk to counselors who non-judgmentally address the spiritual and emotional aspects of such feelings, and who stress that such feelings are normal.

Anger is common in caresharing. It is often directed at the illness process and the resultant stresses it places on both care partners. Relationship alterations can result in frustrations, and changes to long term plans and overwhelming disruptions to daily life can produce simmering resentments. Anger may surface about the illness process, fatigue, or lack of support from other family members. When a care partner's core belief that it is sinful or bad to express negative feelings, or if they perceive that anger breaks some rule in their core beliefs they may not able to acknowledge their feelings. At the same time that they believe they are obligated to care, they are feeling very unloving toward their care partner. Naming anger as a normative, understandable, and not sinful emotion can dissipate some of its power. Some have found that offering up the anger in prayer and meditation aids them to cope.[14] The role of spiritual and emotional counseling may be to assist

13. Ibid., 18.
14. See chapter 10: Thibault, "Transforming Suffering into Spiritual Energy."

persons to name and acknowledge anger and to provide a safe channel for its expression.

Sadness, loss, and grief are experienced by care partners and underlie all caresharing situations at one level or another. These emotions can be related to the myriad changes in both care partners. Grief exists around eventual death and choices made around it. Both "little" and "big" losses are present when coping with chronic illness. The new "normalcy" produces changes in long term loving relationship; the loss of spontaneous companionship is most wrenching. Deep sadness occurs when a carer assists a person who does not recognize them. One woman's comment after her mother's death illustrates this: "When her dementia worsened, I grieved for the strong person she was. After she died, I grieved for the sweet frail lady she had become."[15] Strong relationships are sorely tested by such grief, and it can feel like "too much to bear." A gentle reminder to the caregiver that the person cared for is "still in there" can affirm the human quality of each for the other.[16]

The reality that "nothing is ever going to be same again" must be addressed. Anticipatory grief for the losses that are expected is also present, but often not acknowledged. And it must be remembered that each person faces future losses in their own unique way. Compassionate listening can assist persons along their grief journey. Questions about the meaning of the losses to each care partner might be asked. In the exploration of what a loss means, care partners can work on their grieving. There is no one way to process sadness and loss, but dealing with these emotions imperative to spiritual well-being.

Both the one giving care and the one receiving it are profoundly changed by illness and disability. Opportunities for sharing may be radically altered, especially when there are mental changes. Sharing with others within the community of faith or larger group may become difficult. One gerontologist caring for a partner with dementia in grappling with the changes in ability to relate others cried out: "I knew all this when I worked with people with dementia. Now I am just overwhelmed!" This is a common feeling for carers. Grief and loss are profound, leaving persons to cry out "why us?" and "why now?" And the lament of why is often directed at God who is supposed to be a loving and caring being. This struggle has no clear answers. Really listening to what a person's is expressing, and offering walk alongside them are important spiritual gifts offered by the professional

15. Personal conversation with the author.

16. For a longer discussion of the effects of dementia, see chapter 5, Dick-Muehlke, "Fostering Spirituality in Dementia: Looking Beyond Cognition."

Yet in the middle of this very profound sadness, there can also be rewards in caregiving. Laughter, love, and joy can be shared. Sharing joy can be a profoundly spiritual experience for care partners. In dealing with what effectively becomes the new "status quo," persons can reframe relationships from what *was* to what *is* in the moment. Opportunities of sharing positive experience might be developed with the help of a third party.

There is great variation in how people experience caregiving or receiving, yet all face physical, emotional, mental, and spiritual issues. Spiritual aspects of caring and receiving are discussed in this chapter, but it really is impossible to explore one aspect of the caring process without considering the others.

SUFFERING IN CAREGIVING AND RECEIVING

Suffering can be explored and be named within a caresharing construct. Persons experience suffering throughout their lifetime; in many ways it is an expected part of the human condition, and persons struggle to make some sense out of it. All characterizations of suffering include recognition of anguish, enduring of pain, grief, and a sense of evil. Viktor Frankl in an address to the American Society on Aging's conference in Washington, DC in 1988 said it this way: "Despair is suffering without meaning."[17] Yet, each person has a unique description and timetable for dealing with suffering based on their particular circumstances. No one characterization of suffering describes everyone's experience. Attempts to make sense out of the pain related to caresharing are spiritual issues.

Most care partners desire to alleviate distress of all kinds. Some effects of disability and chronic illness cannot be fixed, and the reality of this can lead to intense spiritual pain for both care partners. And, in some ways, it is more painful to watch a loved one hurt physically, emotionally, or spiritually than it is to feel the pain for oneself. It can be more difficult for a care partner to stand by a terminally ill loved one and person, knowing that there are interventions to comfort them and yet to know that little can be done to change the final outcome than to have a diagnosis themselves.

Suffering should be ameliorated to the extent possible. Relieving physical pain, while challenging, may seem clearer than facing suffering's spiritual distress. Persons in physical pain are offered medications or other treatments. There is no such treatment for spiritual distress. The anguish of the soul when persons face chronic illness, resultant limitations, and dependency is more difficult to identify and process. When care partners find

17. Frankl, "Meaning in Aging."

no meaning in such suffering, a sense of hopelessness can result. Though care partners may or may not be able to give have verbal expression to such pains, they are omnipresent.

Suffering takes on different meanings depending on a person's religious beliefs or cultural teachings. Exploring care partners' backgrounds and related beliefs can be useful. Those accompanying care partners can explore what suffering means for the care partners individually and as part of their relationship. For those with Jewish or Christian roots, the biblical picture of Job and the lamentations of the Psalms offer glimpses of these struggles. A consideration of the Psalms might give voice to care partners' distress as well as providing catharsis and renewal. Miriam Dunson's *A Very Present Help: Psalm Studies for Older Adults*,[18] a comprehensive study of Psalms and their relevance to older adults, is an excellent resource.

As care partners talk with professionals, it often becomes apparent that the person who has a diagnosis or is visibly ill is not the only person who is "sick." All face issues related to suffering, and may have a sense that "life was not supposed be this way!" When care partners can share their feelings about suffering with each other, there is the potential for mutual understanding and comfort. Both may benefit from having a third party facilitate that discussion.

When care partners feel isolated, the anguish can be more frightening. Not all caresharers have supportive relationships with others that acknowledge such caregiving/receiving suffering. And indeed it is difficult to identify and share the spiritual distress that the losses associated with physical and emotional diminishments evoke. However, ignoring such implications of chronic illness or ill health only adds to suffering. To discount distressful realities or to attempt to suppress them often causes them to reappear later. Suffering takes a toll in caresharing.

Those around those who suffer can offer compassionate listening and affirmation that indeed the suffering is real. When communities of faith intentionally listen, they may be able to support those who are suffering. Sometimes such issues are identified through hearing a person's history and their caresharing story. Bearing witness to this story of suffering and ways that persons have overcome obstacles in the past is essential. Personal stories might be linked to biblical stories of anguish. Counselors might ask persons to visualize suffering or they might explore the care partners' personal descriptions of suffering as they have experienced it in the past or live it in the present. Hearing the metaphors which persons use to describe pain,

18. Dunson, *A Very Present Help.*

and identifying previous coping skills, may illuminate a plan for dealing with suffering.[19]

WHAT THE FRAIL TEACH THE STRONG

The affirmation that the "frail have much to teach the strong" is at the heart of caresharing. Society as a whole tends to label those with chronic illness as "problems." Even the faith community, neighborhood, or other social network may not value a former mentor in their group. They may judge them as "less than" simply because they have changed beyond the norms of the group. This is not done out of malice, but often occurs when persons do not know what to do, or have fears about their own increasing needs for help. Reframing the care receiver's role as teacher within a caresharing context can affirm their personal dignity and worth for the caregiver and the community around the care partners.

At some point all dealing with illness realize that they need assistance to survive. There may be the need to accept aid for the most basic tasks. Long-held core beliefs held about independence and dependence may be shaken to the core. "Frailty," long feared, becomes a reality.

Each person holds unique understandings of what "frailty" means, when it begins or how it is manifested. A care partner may be limited in physical and mental abilities but not frail of spirit. Others have to "fill in the blanks" for certain tasks or assist in decision making. As one becomes more dependent on another for help, there can be a shift in the balance of the relationship. At times, especially in long partnerships, commitments to "love, honor and care in sickness and health" are sorely tested. The person being cared for may have a diminished sense of self-worth. When these are not lifted up as important, opportunities for spiritual sharing are missed.

Yet much can be learned from an individual who requires assistance of one kind or another. An individual is more than their diagnosis; they are a *person* first. When a care receiver's uniqueness is not emphasized, his or her sense of personhood may be lost. When caregivers become "learners" they can see situations from the eyes of the care receiver and gain fresh perspectives. Persons who are well can also remember that they are only temporarily able-bodied, that they too may face ill health in the future.

What can be learned from those who are considered "frail"? A most basic learning is that independence is not what it appears to be. Persons state "above all I want to keep my independence." Personalizing the high

19. For a further discussion of suffering, see chapter 10: Thibault, "Activating Resources of the Soul Amidst Suffering."

value society places on this value, care partners may put a negative value on asking for help. A reconsideration of independence in the face of their physical, emotional, or mental challenges assists persons to look more clearly at interdependence. Many persons who have limits can teach interdependence to those around them. Independence knowing when to ask for needed assistance. Those considered "frail" have taught others how to be graceful receivers in a world that values givers. Those who have practiced being gracefully dependent, graciously accepting assistance from others can teach this to the more able-bodied.

It can be useful to remind those who do have a belief in and a sense of reliance on a Higher Power for strength, that God, Spirit, the Divine (or however they describe this) remains with them in their care receiving experience.

Care receivers have taught others about being grateful. Many, knowing that their time on earth is limited, are thankful for the possibilities of each new day. Those being cared for are aware of how little time is left them and they teach can the importance of living in the "now," not worrying so much about tomorrow that today's beauty is lost. This can be especially true for those who cope with dementia. Because of short long term memory limits, the "moment" becomes more precious. Learning how to be truly "present" to each other is a crucial learning for both the cared for and the carer despite mental and physical limits is a part of this.

Cared for persons can teach the lesson of appreciation. This takes many forms: gratefulness for care given, or thankfulness for companionship and love despite drastic changes. Being open to the times when appreciation is shared is a part of the spiritual journey for giver and receiver. Caregivers can affirm that love back to the person cared for.

Even in the midst of situations over which they have little control, care receivers can teach about trust. They can feel vulnerable as others minister to their needs. It takes time to develop trust, yet despite that, care receivers can forge solid relationships with those who assist them.

The frail teach the well how to cope, often in very creative ways. Humor is a particularly effective coping skill. Those who use humor well often get through particularly embarrassing predicaments with funny thoughts or jokes. The ability to laugh when confronting difficulties is something that care partners can teach others. It is a spiritual gift.

Care partners together teach a valuable lesson about love despite almost insurmountable odds. The basic needs for affection and nurture survive in spite of challenges inherent to the caresharing situation. In sharing the care, partners have taught that new ways for expression may develop out of necessity. Love remains a strong emotional between care partners.

Carers have taught others in the larger community about the value of emphasizing a person's strengths and building on them in the face of adversity. Keeping in mind that illness is only one aspect of a individual, new ways for doing things and relating to each other can be developed. Though roles and activities of daily life may need to be adapted, the "frail" are still capable of acting on their life experiences and exercising decision making within safety limitations. Understanding that they are beloved child of God, despite their circumstances, provides spiritual support to many.

With education and some coaching, the community around care partners may become a source of support and spiritual well-being. In learning how to receive care partners' wisdom, the greater community learns about reciprocity in struggles around frailty. Family, friends and others who care for persons struggling with an acute or chronic illness can learn much about living well despite limitations. Many cope with problems that seem insurmountable. Often they use the spiritual resources of faith, prayer and or meditation to aid them in this process. Helpers can take an active part in affirming these and helping persons to build on their strengths.

SPIRITUAL NEEDS OF CARERS

Within caresharing there is the belief that caregivers have spiritual needs. Jane Thibault and Richard Morgan recognize caregiving as important spiritual work, noting that caregivers must understand that "no act of love is ever a waste of time for them or the one that they care for."[20] They note that Jesus himself was a caregiver. While their book primarily explores circumstances for caregivers to persons with dementia, their reflections are provide an excellent starting point for the discussion of all carer's spiritual concerns. Caregivers lose hope and heart when they feel isolated or alone, and when they do not realize that others face similar concerns. They have a need for a community around them that understands their issues. For example, all must realize that caregiving is even more difficult when the cared for cannot actively affirm thankfulness for help given to them from their care partner.

Carers benefit from support from their faith community's or circle of friends' intentional commitment to journey with them. At times this takes the form of hands on assistance; at other times it is remembrance in thoughts and prayers and assurances that they are supported in their role. Visitors from the faith community can offer spiritual support to both care partners. Inquiring after each person's well-being helps care partners know that they are remembered by those in their religious network.

20. Thibault and Morgan, *No Act of Love*, 78.

Carers can feel burdened by wanting to provide care flawlessly. Because of their strong sense of obligation to a partner or parent, driven by a personal spirituality that not only believes that they can be perfect but demands that they are perfect, caregivers may have an idealized notion of what should be done and how they should feel. Questions around what is owed to parent or partner given their moral imperatives loom large. They may worry that they are not living up to their own standards or the expectations of those in the faith community. Care partners ponder issues about when is enough good *enough*. The care receiver's perspective can be helpful. The needs of all the persons in a caresharing relationship need to be taken into account and a caring professional can assist in sorting these out.

Professionals working with care partners often are permission givers reminding them that they are doing the best that they can within their circumstances. They may also offer resources to aid them in reducing the sense of burden. Carers can also forgive themselves by knowing that they are forgiven by a higher power when they fall short in caring. They can understand that God still loves them even or when they feel that they can no longer love someone they feel they "ought."

Thibault and Morgan stress the spiritual struggle to find meaning when a care receiver does not seem to know them. They emphasize that the soul of that care partner recognizes the kindness and compassion in any gentle act performed. Doing the task is not as important as the sharing and the connection to the cared for. And they affirm that both care partners are loved by God, and the caring that is done is important.[21] Counselors can remind caregivers of the importance of daily routine caring for another is sacred and holy work.[22]

Caregivers must be encouraged to care for themselves, and to be reminded that if they are not refreshed emotionally and spiritually, they cannot really be present to another. Often carers burn out when they have not attended to their own concerns. Helpers can pose questions about what keeps caregivers going day to day. Both carer and counselor can work together developing plans for renewal, affirming their necessity for survival. Helpers give permission for persons to do self-care.

Carers need to wrestle with the spiritual issues that accompany anticipatory grief. They know that their loved one has little time left on earth, but may find it difficult to process that. Caring professions can identify and work with this grief that can overwhelm caregivers as persons change in front of

21. Ibid., 9.

22. For further study on this subject consult chapter 5, Dick-Muehlke, "Fostering Spirituality in Dementia: Looking Beyond Cognition."

their eyes. Assisting care partners to remember the spiritual practices such as worship, prayer, contemplation of nature and ritual, and enabling them to participate in them provides benefits.

SPIRITUAL NEEDS OF THOSE CARED FOR

Care receivers also have spiritual needs that require validation. They have a yearning have their carers to them respectfully communicate, not only with words, but in actions and in kind and loving nonverbal expressions. They need to be understood as persons first and foremost. Although they may have an illness that requires them to depend on others, they still are loved by deeply God, Divine Spirit, or Higher Power. The way that a person is touched and talked to demonstrate this sense of worth that comes from the very heart and soul of the person attending to their needs.

Those receiving care need to prepare for death in a way that is congruent with how they have lived and what they believe. Their care partners and those that would minister to them have can be open to their expressions and concerns and encourage such rituals and spiritual practices that would be of help in this regard. Helpers may have to facilitate to assure that these are offered to care partners. Others around them need to really listen to and hear what they are sharing about their wishes and concerns, and to provide access to those sacraments which could support them. The sacrament of the sick is an example from the Roman Catholic tradition.[23]

Most of all, care receivers deserve to have persons around them understand that their spirit is still alive no matter what their physical or mental limitations. The essence of who they are remains in their illness process. While the outward trappings of their body or their mind may have changed their spirit remains intact.

HOPE AND THE ESSENTIAL SPIRIT IN CARESHARING

Hope is essential to caresharing. It has complex theological, psychological, and relational implications. The concept of hope can be difficult to explain, and even harder to keep in the midst of sharing care. Hope can be a noun, a verb, and a process.

While hope has many definitions, the meaning given to the concept by those caregiving/receiving help are the most important. Hope depends

---

23. For information on the sacrament of the sick and other sacraments in the Roman Catholic Church consult Trese, "Catholic Sacraments."

on one's belief and their spirituality. Hope is not unrealistic optimism about what can never be. Yet hope is integral to keeping persons alive and well spiritually, as well as physically and emotionally. It must be adaptable, realistic, reasonable and fluid. Keeping hope alive is important for spiritual wellbeing. Throughout the caresharing process, persons need to be reminded of their vision hope and those around them must be careful not to extinguish it for others, even when it seems unrealistic. Helpers can stress the importance of keeping it alive. And having a sense of hope can bring joy to all involved in caresharing.

But before care partners can be hopeful, they need to realistically look at the losses, grief and fears they face. Hope can be an antidote to the fears and concerns related to the caregiving/receiving relationship. Kathleen Fischer in *The Courage the Heart Desires* states, "Hope retains a sense of the possible, it sees a way out of the difficult."[24] Helpers can assist care partners name and talk about their fears for living with chronic illness and resultant changes. Hope helps to clarify what is occurring.

The hospice movement stresses the fact that hopes changes, and as the caresharing process advances, hope does indeed adjust. What a person hopes for in the early days of caresharing, may be transformed into something very different with the progression of the illness.

Care partners have recounted that there is a blessing in each day that is lived. Hope can be as simple as having something to get up for in the morning: seeing a grandchild, feeding a bird, or visiting with a beloved friend. The big events and the little things matter. Hope exists with joy in the opportunity to share time together. Celebrate moments in each other's presence can keep hope alive.

Faith provides strong support for many care partners. Having something or someone to believe in is important. Hope can be about believing in a power that is greater than one's self. Some persons say that they get through each day because they know that Jesus walks beside them. For some believing in afterlife keeps days more bearable as illness and mental changes increase. The belief that they or their care partner will be in a better place sustains them dark days.

Hope can also be found in relationships between the care partners and with broader networks. Relationships may take on different qualities because of illness, but they remain significant in caresharing. Knowing that someone walks alongside them has kept many care partners hopeful despite the limitations they face. Encouraging persons along the way keeps hope alive.

24. Fisher, *Courage*, 92.

Caring professionals can ask partners how they view hope. Helpers need to maintain a sense of hopefulness in their work or they convey hopelessness to those giving and receiving care. Helpers can be bridges to hope for care partners and stay strong when they the caregiver and or receiver feel that they can no longer be hopeful.

A FINAL WORD IN CARESHARING: THE IMPORTANCE OF LISTENING AND BEING "PRESENT"

Real listening is a gift that can be shared between care partners. This listening seeks to hear what is being said with all of its meanings and to understand what is not being said. It means hearing with the heart and the head.

Those who would seek to support care partners need to have a heart for listening. Really hearing a person out can reflect the care partners' essential spirit. Nouwen expresses it well: "Listening is the very active awareness of the coming together of two lives . . . where I listen, I listen not only to a story, but also with a story . . . listening is a very active form of caregiving."[25]

When a caring professional listens deeply and without judgment, he or she offers care partners space to truly share what matters to them without preconceived perceptions. Sharing one's story with another affirms life's meaningful happenings and the successful ways that persons have dealt with challenges. Care partners' stories hold the essence of each person's spirit and their history. It allows persons be heard on their own terms, and provides a lens through which helpers can to see persons wholistically. Stories also provide clues for helpful interventions.

Persons can build on past strengths to live today. Helpers may remind them of how they have coped with difficult experiences in earlier times. Out of this storytelling, ideas for coping with the present situation may emerge and thought about using adaptation and accommodation may evolve. A person who used meditation and prayer for coping may still be able to do that.

Keeping the essential spirit alive is key in caresharing. Care partners can share the spiritual through creating sacred space, using music, creating rituals, prayer and meditation, or other spiritual disciplines. The community who walks with can share sacred moments with them. Most importantly, keeping the spirit alive for care partners is honoring that which is whole in each person. It is in the small actions of caresharing that this occurs.

25. Nouwen, *Spirituality of Caregiving*, 36.

REFERENCES

Bell, Virginia, and David Troxel. *The Dignified Life: The Best Friends Approach to Alzheimer's Care: A Guide for Family Caregivers.* Deerfield, FL: Health Communications, 2002.

Dunson, Miriam. *A Very Present Help: Psalm Studies for Older Adults.* Louisville: Geneva, 1999.

Fischer, Kathleen. *The Courage the Heart Desires: Spiritual Strength in Difficult Times.* San Francisco: Jossey-Bass, 2006.

Frankl, Viktor. "Meaning in Aging." Presentation at the 1988 Annual Conference of the American Society on Aging in New York.[From Marty Richards unpublished personal notes.]

Lustbader, Wendy. *Counting on Kindness: The Dilemmas of Dependency.* New York: Free Press, 1991.

Nouwen, Henri J. M. *A Spirituality of Caregiving.* Nashville: Upper Room, 2011.

Palkhivala, Aadil. "The Meaning of Namaste." *Yoga Journal,* October 3, 2014. http://www.yogajournal.com/article/beginners/the-meaning-of-quot-namaste-quot/.

Remen, Rachael Naomi. *My Grandfather's Blessings: Stories of Strength, Refuge and Belonging.* New York: Riverhead, 2002.

Richards, Marty. *Caresharing: A Reciprocal Approach to Caregiving and Care: Receiving in the Complexities of Aging, Illness or Disability.* Woodstock, VT: SkyLight Paths, 2010.

Thibault, Jane, and Richard Morgan. *No Act of Love is Ever Wasted: The Spirituality of Caring for Persons with Dementia.* Nashville: Upper Room, 2009.

Trese, Leo. "Catholic Sacraments: Vehicles of Grace." 2006. http://www.beginningcatholic.com/sacraments.html.

7

Caregiving
Body, Mind, and Spirit

—Giovanna Piazza, MDiv, BCC

"Be kind, for everyone you meet is fighting a hard battle."

—Rev. John Watson (Ian MacLaren)[1]

MY FRIEND AMY IS a brilliant writer, director, teacher, artist. She has an eye for beauty and song and the story of people's lives. Amy can weave the personal stories of individuals into soul-revealing high art, part theater, part musical, all Truth. What makes Amy so good at her art is that she knows how to listen; she listens between the lines. Amy's own story reflects a life full of joy, pain, challenge, truth, grace, love, and loss.

In her own story, Amy tells of her ninety-year-old mother with Alzheimer's disease who, no longer able to live alone, moved in with Amy and her family. Years before Amy had cared for her brother at the end of his life as he suffered and wasted away, leaving her an "only child" in this new familial constellation. The transition was not entirely smooth, as mother moved in with daughter, son-in-law and two teenaged children, but each member

---

1. Quoted in Hendrix and Hunt, *Personal Companion*, day 198.

of the family made accommodations and soon the multi-generational household found its balance and all members were thriving.

That is, until the day that Amy came home from work to find that her mother had "instructed the gardener to cut off all of the Mexican sage blossoms that had sprung into a glorious purple sea in her back yard. The bundles lie lifeless on the ground replaced with hacked, barren stocks."[2] Amy was devastated, not because she was attached to the purple sage (though she was) but because the action caught her up short, demanding that she face what was really happening in her home and life.

The ravages of purple sage provided a metaphor for grief, loss, age, and wisdom. The unmourned losses and anticipatory grief with which Amy was living became heartbreakingly manifest in the loss of this glorious living creature in full bloom.

It was in that comparatively insignificant loss that Amy could finally allow space for the grief in her brother's death, the loss of space and privacy for her nuclear family, the erosion of her mother's memory, the exhaustion of caring for her mother (and the rest of her family), and the stress of anticipatory grief as each day brought her mother closer to death. The catharsis she experienced by letting go of the purple sage facilitated her letting go of that gargantuan bundle of grief which had begun to pass for Amy's life.

Like my friend Amy, 65.7 million people (almost a third of the adult population in the United States) are responsible for the care of another person who is ill, disabled, or aging.[3] One in every three people we meet, with whom we work, attend worship, go to school, play golf, ride the train, and shop alongside in the grocery store is caring for another person. The number is staggering. These are people we know, people carrying a heavy burden, people just like us.

Amy, and others like her, are considered informal caregivers, unpaid individuals (a spouse, partner, family member, friend, or neighbor) involved in assisting others with activities of daily living and/or medical tasks. Formal caregivers are paid care providers providing care in one's home or in a care setting (daycare, residential, care facility, etc).[4] There are 52 million informal caregivers in the U.S. providing care to adults (aged eighteen or over) with disability or illness.[5] 43.5 million of adult family caregivers care for someone fifty years of age, and 14 million care for someone who has

2. Amu Luskey-Barth, epigraph quote on Purplesagepost.blogspot.com.

3. National Alliance for Caregiving, *Caregiving in the U.S.*, 9.

4. Family Caregiver Alliance, "Selected Caregiving Statistics."

5. Coughlin, "Estimating the Impact," 1.

Alzheimer's disease or other dementia.[6] Two thirds (66 percent) of care-givers in the United States are women, and about one third of them (34 percent) care for two or more people simultaneously. The average age of a female caregiver is forty-eight years old,[7] and she spends about twenty-five hours per week in direct care of another adult. The number of hours per week in direct caregiving increases exponentially with age, so that the same woman at sixty-five is spending 30.7 hours per week and at seventy-five she spends 35.5 hours per week.[8] Caregiving is, literally, a full-time job.

The experience of taking on the role of a caregiver can, most often, be understood only in reflection. It is a more common experience to fall or slide into the role of caregiver than it is to choose the role. Similarly, caregivers find that they are well along the road of responsibility before realizing that the journey has even begun. The caregiving role can be assigned ("you're the eldest"; "you live closest to Mom"), designated by default ("now that you're not working" or "because you're a nurse") or self-appointed ("he's my father/grandmother/spouse/child; who else should care for him?"). Nevertheless, it is likely that caregiving is an aggregation of responsibilities rather than the acceptance of a defined role resulting from anything resembling informed consent.

Every day in my practice, I see people (almost always women) who began by helping out or filling in the gaps and quickly find themselves the full-time "informal" caregiver of a family member or friend. They almost always have the same question, "Now what?" which is a chronological ques-tion asked about a spiritual crisis. "Now what" usually indicates is that a loss (of center, of time, of self, of clarity, of boundaries) has occurred and it is not clear how to return to the way things were. We know, of course, that there is no going back to what has previously been a place of comfort and stability, and that inability causes all manner of uneasy feeling in the form of disappointment, frustration, anger, sadness, discouragement, resentfulness, and depression.

Somewhere down deep we know that the answer is to accept and acclimate to the "new normal" (meaning not just how things are now but how they will evolve in the short and long term), and to open ourselves to what *is* cur-rently happening rather than trying to reclaim what *was*. It is the spiritual practice of staying present to what *is*, we call mindfulness. Mindfulness is "maintaining a moment-by-moment awareness of our thoughts, feelings,

6. Alzheimer's Association, "Alzheimer's Disease Facts and Figures."

7. National Alliance for Caregiving, *Caregiving in the U.S.*, 9.

8. Partnership for Solutions, *Chronic Conditions*, 62.

bodily sensations and surrounding environment."[9] The definition can feel a bit like navel gazing, constantly taking one's emotional and spiritual temperature in the hope of discovering some new key to survival. The challenge is in observing, not judging, the feelings one observes in the moment. "Mindfulness also involves acceptance, meaning that we pay attention to our thoughts and feelings without judging them — without believing, for instance, that there is a 'right' or 'wrong' way to think or feel in a given moment. When we practice mindfulness, our thoughts tune into what we're sensing in the present moment rather than rehashing the past or imagining the future."[10]

Mindfulness practice has been shown to decrease blood pressure, increase our immune response, decrease anxiety, stress and depression, reduce violence, increase compassion, focus attention, and heighten responsiveness.[11] Mindfulness is a learned habit, cultivated through practice, which provides an awakened way of being in the world. Mindfulness, then, is not only important for caregiving but for self-care.

In dealing with those who are undergoing great suffering, if you feel "burnout" setting in, if you feel demoralized and exhausted, it is best, for the sake of everyone, to withdraw and restore yourself. The point is to have a long-term perspective.

—Dalai Lama[12]

The Maslach Burnout Inventory (MBI)[13] is meant to be used for professional caregivers but it can be simplified and extrapolated for use with informal caregivers. The MBI evaluates three factor structures to determine the degree of burnout. They are:

- Emotional Exhaustion, which measures feelings of being emotionally overextended and exhausted by one's work.

- Depersonalization (Cynicism), which measures an unfeeling and impersonal response toward recipients of one's service, care treatment or instruction.

9. Kabat-Zinn, "Mindfulness," n.p.
10. Ibid.
11. Ibid.
12. Dalai Lama quoted by http://likeateam.com/quotes-on-burnout-3/.
13. Maslach, C., & Inventory, J. S. M. B. *Manual*.1986

- Personal Accomplishment (Inefficacy), which measures feelings of competence and successful achievement in one's work.[14]

With profound apologies to Maslach et al., let us use an overly simplified version of the factor structures to determine burnout in informal caregivers. You might ask yourself:

1. Am I overwhelmed by the tasks of caregiving? How?

2. Do I feel overextended mentally, physically, or spiritually? What does that look like?

3. Who or what suffers from my caregiving decision or actions?

4. Am I behaving respectfully and patiently with the person in my care?

5. Do I cherish the mind, body and spirit of the person in my care?

6. Do I believe that my efforts are valued?

7. Do I believe that my efforts make a difference?

8. Do I believe that my caregiving is meaningful?

9. Do I believe that I am the right person at the right time to be serving in this way?

10. Am I dumping time/effort/energy into a bottomless pit of need?

11. Am I competent to care for this person in this way?

There is no pass or fail scoring on this set of questions, it is simply a guide for introspection and an indicator of the level of burnout.

Often the simple act of introspection on questions such as these will help identify the health or dis-ease within a caregiving relationship. There is no judgment on the answers; it simply is what it is. Answer the questions as they really are, rather than how you would like for them to be, and then do not judge yourself harshly if they are not the answers you expected (or other people expect of you). It is both reasonable and acceptable to dislike either the person(s) or the circumstance(s) that have brought you to this point of crisis. It is reasonable and acceptable to dislike some of the tasks required of caregiving. It is both reasonable and acceptable to feel as though you don't know what you are doing or that you are making it up as you go along. Those feelings are remarkable only in that they are shared by so many who have devoted themselves to caregiving.

14. Maslach et al., "Burnout Inventory (MBI)."

Rest and self-care are so important.
When you take time to replenish your spirit,
it allows you to serve others from the overflow.
You cannot serve from an empty vessel.[15]

—Eleanor Brownn (behavioral gerontologist and author)

WHEN YOU CRASH AND BURN

If your introspection indicates burnout, it might be worth considering whether or not your role as caregiver is benefitting or burdening the person in your care. Secure your own oxygen masks before assisting your traveling companions. This advice has been uttered by every flight attendant and self-help author in the modern era. It is an overused idiom and one that is quickly and easily dismissed as already known and thoroughly understood. And yet, it is necessary to be reminded that the only way to be helpful with respect to others is to *take care of ourselves first*. Why does this sage advice always seem anathema to caregivers? What is it about caring for self that is such a significant threat to the ability to care for others? There are some archetypal patterns of belief among caregivers and corresponding patterns of behavior which could be problematic in healthy self-care. Let us consider not only the unhealthy indications of these patterns but what self-care options might be essential for the spirit of each archetype.

The Ghost

The Ghost lacks self-worth to the extent that she becomes invisible, and therefore unconsidered. The Ghost places the value of another individual over the value of self by believing themselves to be worthless or undeserving of consideration. Using the example of the oxygen mask, the Ghost doesn't believe he is worthy of a mask. The desire of the Ghost to disappear is often attached to low self-worth and/or depression. What is essential for the spirit of the Ghost is to re-vision themselves and as valued and cherished partners, who merit consideration and attention in the caregiving equation. Ways to feed the spirit of the Ghost are:

- Look in a mirror, and write down what you see. (You didn't think you were *really* a ghost, did you?) Be objective. Notice, don't judge.

15. Brownn, "Rest and Self-Care," n.p.

- Make a list of all the things that make you unique as a caregiver and put a star next to the characteristics you appreciate in yourself.

- Consider the particular gifts you "bring to the table" in this caregiving relationship.

- Think about what you have learned as a caregiver that you did not know before.

- Think about ways you are stronger now that you have been a caregiver. How has this experience of caregiving changed your life?

The Martyr

The Martyr is willing to go to the gallows for a cause he believes to be greater than self. The Martyr is adept at meeting the needs of others but unwilling to meet (and often to know) her own needs. The Martyrs can be cavalier, routinely expecting that someone else will meet their needs. The Martyr believes that while he is securing the mask of another person, someone else should be securing his mask (think of it as mask securing in a daisy chain). The Martyr usually has unyielding rules around who should be securing her mask, and woe to you if you are the designated, but uninformed, oxygen-mask angel! What is essential for the spirit of the Martyr is to release expectation, embrace wonder and practice gratitude. Ways to feed the spirit of the Martyrs are:

- Keep a gratitude journal. Notice at least five things in a day for which you are grateful and write them down.

- Notice the many ways magic and miracles break into your day.

- Practice saying "no."

- Challenge yourself to think of your dogmatically held beliefs as flexible or, at least, negotiable.

- Conduct an inventory of expectations (what do you expect from whom and why).

- Do it yourself! At least once a day choose something to do for yourself that you would normally hope (expect) someone else to do for you. In taking responsibility for yourself (even in small things) you regain control of your life.

The Tasmanian Devil

The Tasmanian Devil whirls around, kicking up dust and producing more heat than light. It's not clear how much caregiving is actually going on when the Tasmanian Devil is around but there is a great deal of talking about how much caregiving is being accomplished. When the Tasmanian Devil leaves and the dust has settled it is often clear that no one's mask is on. What is essential for the spirit of the Tasmanian Devil is stillness. The frantic movement of the Tasmanian Devil is almost always attached to fear. Ways to feed the spirit of the Tasmanian Devil are:

- Stop, simply stop. (The world will not come crashing down, I promise.)

- Breathe (low and from the belly).

- Pay attention to the way you feel in stillness (and then don't rush to fill the void).

- Listen (the stillness will talk, what does it have to say?).

- Allow time and space for introspection.

- Identify and feel the fear. What happens when you allow the fear to surface?

  Gather and assess information, *then* act accordingly.

The Perfectionist

The Perfectionist craves a flawless external image, the unblemished ideal. The Perfectionist believes that if it looks flawless then it is flawless and with objective flawlessness as the goal; it matters little what happens behind the facade. The Perfectionist will never allow himself to be seen gasping for air, while trying to get all the right masks on all the right people at all the right times. The Perfectionist suffers greatly for her perfectionistic requirements and often has no outlet for the pain of imperfection. What is essential for the spirit of the Perfectionist is to allow for the messiness of life and the imperfection of people, including himself. Ways to feed the spirit of the Perfectionist are:

- Let a few spinning plates fall to the ground and break (maybe someone else will even clean them up!).

- Practice saying "no" (even to small things).

- Share the burden (others are willing to help, they just need to be asked).

- Allow yourself to receive (let a neighbor make your dinner or your sister do your shopping).

- Give yourself permission to deviate from the schedule (the sky will not fall down if Mom isn't up, bathed, dressed, fed and settled in every morning by 9:00).

- Squint—blur your eyes and fuzz up the edges of your well constructed life a little bit. The softer the focus, the softer the heart.

The Superhero

The Superhero swoops down at the opportune moment to set everything right. Unable or unwilling to walk the long and difficult road, the Superhero waits until the brink of disaster and then inserts him or herself into a situation where he can save the day. The Superheros are not in need of a mask because they won't be there long enough to need assistance. What is essential for the spirit of the Superhero is to become part of the whole (the family, the community, the movement, etc.). Ways to feed the spirit of the Superhero are:

- Show up and stick around (it won't be as scary or as hard as you imagined).

- Participate in the day-to-day activities of caregiving.

- Be a part of the group (identify who is the whole of which you are a part?).

- Recognize the strength of your Superhero status and use it for good not glory.

- Accept that even a Superhero has a heart that feels loss, frustration, sadness, and grief like mere mortals. Allow others to join you in those feelings and help heal you.

- Stick it out when the impulse hits to put on your superhero cape and fly away.

The whole idea of compassion is based on
a keen awareness of the interdependence of all
these living beings, which are all part of one another,
and all involved in one another.[16]

—Thomas Merton

CONCLUSION

Finally, the tools of caregiving are frequently confused with the tasks of caregiving. The tasks of caregiving are often so exhausting and overwhelming that we forget or overlook or dismiss our real purpose which is to tend to another person's body, mind, and spirit with our own. While we are lost in the life of caregiving as verb (bathing, feeding, washing, driving, watching, changing, monitoring, cooking, balancing, attending, etc.) it is easy to forget that it's not the *doing* but how it's *done*. If we could articulate a purpose in our caregiving that is less verb-oriented and more adverb-oriented (lovingly, compassionately, fully, happily, mindfully, kindly, quietly, gently, carefully, thoughtfully, joyfully, hopefully, etc.), we would increase role satisfaction and hold the key to avoiding burnout. Adverb-oriented caregiving provides purpose and meaning to the experience of caring for giver and receiver alike. And purpose may be the singularly greatest element essential for the spirit. The same gentle, loving, compassionate, kind, joyful hearts we bring to caregiving for others we must also, mindfully, bring to self-care. "Many of us follow the commandment, 'Love one another.' When it comes to caregiving, it is important to love one another with boundaries. At the same time, if we are to avoid burnout, we must acknowledge that we are included in the 'Love one another.'"[17] For the challenge to "love one another" is expanded to "love one another *as* we love ourselves."

REFERENCES

Alzheimer's Association. "Alzheimer's Disease Facts and Figures." *Alzheimer's and Dementia* 7/2 (March 2011) 208–44.

Brownn, Eleanor. "Rest and Self-Care are So Important." My Spiritual Sabbatical blog. September 4, 2013. http://eleanorbrownn.wordpress.com/2013/09/04/rest-

16. Thomas Merton quoted at http://www.brainyquote.com/quotes/authors/t/thomas_merton.html.

17. Spears and Walker, Inspired Caregiver, 68.

and-self-care-are-so-important-when-you-take-time-to-replenish-your-spirit-it-allows-you-to-serve-others-from-the-overflow-you-cannot-serve-from-an-empty-vessel/.

Coughlin, J. "Estimating the Impact of Caregiving and Employment on Well-Being." *Outcomes and Insights in Heath Management* 2/1 (May 2010) 1–7.

Family Caregiver Alliance. "Selected Caregiver Statistics." December 31, 2012. https://caregiver.org/selected-caregiver-statistics.

Hendrix, Harville, and Helen Hunt. *The Personal Companion: Meditations and Exercises for Keeping the Love You Find*. New York: Simon and Schuster, 1995.

Kabat-Zinn, Jon. "Mindfulness." http://www.greatergood.berkeley.edu/topic/mindfulness/definition.

Maslach, C., & *Inventory, J. S. M. B. Manual*. Palo Alto, University of California. Consulting Psychologists, 1986.

Maslach, C., et al. "Burnout Inventory (MBI)." http://www.mindgarden.com/117-maslach-burnout-inventory.

The National Alliance for Caregiving. *Caregiving in U.S.: 2009*. Washington, DC: National Alliance for Caregiving, 2009. http://www.caregiving.org/data/Caregiving_in_the_US_2009_full_report.pdf.

Partnership for Solutions. *Chronic Conditions: Making the Case for Ongoing Care*. Baltimore: Johns Hopkins University Press, 2012.

Spears, Peggi, and Tia Walker. *The Inspired Caregiver*. Monterey, CA: Flowspirations, 2013.

8

Touching Spirits
Programming for Meaning and Connection

—Nancy Gordon, MSLS, MDiv

THE PRIMARY TASK EVERY month for most people who are responsible
for programs in congregations, senior centers, and older adult living resi-
dences is the calendar. It must be produced by the first of the month and
it must contain a well-balanced menu of activities and programs for the
participants. The unwritten rule of creating such calendars is that they have
enough to keep the participants busy and happy, with limited resources and
little support from other staff in the organization. That is why there is an activity director after all. So in the midst of ongoing programming, the lonely
activity director is often found late in the evening at the end of the month
frantically pulling together the activity calendar for the next month.

Wendy Lustbader, social worker and noted author on aging, reflects
on how residents living in such a community feel and react when they are
greeted with this activity calendar every month. She did a series of interviews with residents of several Continuing Care Retirement Communities
(CCRCs) and found that many residents were happy with their choice to
live in such a community, rather than remain in the larger community. But
she notes,

> It was striking that each unhappy CCRC resident told me that
> they felt their lives had devolved into a series of entertainments.
> One man explained that he was insulted by the sight of the daily
> calendar posted in the lobby as though he needed to be "kept

busy" through a program of activities. He said it seemed as if he were staying at a perpetual resort, rather than living his true life. "This is too empty for me," he continued. "I need to be useful. Here, I can't even mow the lawn."[1]

Another resident she interviewed remarked, "Attending a program is not *living*." She described the weekly, facilitated current events discussion as a far cry from the spirited, engaged conversation she was used to having with friends in her neighborhood and community before she moved into the retirement community. She noted the lack of interesting conversation at the shared meals. And she reported that, "The only time I feel at home is at church on Sundays when I'm with people I've known for years and who don't live this kind of restricted life.[2] These residents were not being unkind. But they were expressing their frustration with living in an environment which was seeking to entertain them, keep them busy, but not necessarily seeking to create an environment where they were encouraged to be their authentic selves, living their lives with meaning, connection and passion.

So how do we go from the goal of keeping the older adults in our care busy and entertained to the goal of assisting them in their journey of meaning and connection and living from their passions as they age?

IT BEGINS WITH A VISION

When I entered the world of older adult services and living in January, 1998, as the Director of Growth Opportunities at Friendship Village in Schaumburg, Illinois, I was incredibly green to this whole arena. I was a mid-life, second career seminary graduate, ordained and with five years as an associate parish pastor under my belt. Friendship Village was twenty years old, and was looking for creative and meaningful programs to give them a competitive edge as they worked on bringing the physical plant up to current standards.

The Growth Opportunities program was conceived as a framework for developing those creative and meaningful programs. While faith based, Friendship Village was not denominationally based and was seeking to be a community that could serve all faiths. Nevertheless, the leadership recognized that spirituality needed to be the underlying support of all the programming — even though much of it would not be overtly religious.

1. Lustbader, *It All Depends*, 18.
2. Ibid.

As I gathered the existing staff that January I shared with them an image of a tulip blossom breaking through the snow to bloom, while a child cleared the plant's leaves and the area around the plant of snow. This, I said, was a picture of our task — to support and encourage the growth of our residents. We were beginning this endeavor during a time of change and chaos, and it would not be easy, but it was an endeavor worthy of our best work. We were seeking to create program that that touched our residents' spirits and gave them encouragement and hope.

Another image I used in communicating the vision for Growth Opportunities to both residents and staff was the image of tree, with green leaves and deep roots, along with verses from Psalm 92:"The righteous flourish like a palm tree and grow like a cedar. In old age they still produce fruit; they are always green and full of sap."[3] This was an image of flourishing, growing, fruitfulness, and vital aliveness which I wanted our program to encourage and to help produce.

And 1 ½ years into the process I wrote:

> The programs of the Growth Opportunities are based on the belief that people are capable of growth no matter what their age. Growth implies coming to maturity, to expand in any way, particularly to advance intellectually, morally, spiritually. Growth implies a process of "becoming" and developing and is possible at any age.
>
> There is the opportunity at this stage in life for reflection, for the deepening of meaning, for the exploration of the spiritual life. There is also the opportunity to appreciate the value of relationships—both old and new. There is an opportunity for new and continued learning and creativity. And there is opportunity for service.
>
> To promote growth in the residents of Friendship Village and to keep the vision of growth in front of the residents, the Growth Opportunities program is organized around three foci:
>
> 1. Social programs that bring residents together around intellectual, cultural, creative, physical, recreational and celebratory pursuits.
>
> 2. Spiritual programs that encourage and support residents in their spiritual pilgrimage.

3. Psalm 92:13a–14 RSV.

3. Service programs that enlarge the residents' capacity for service to the Friendship Village community, the wider community and world.[4]

Over the years the articulation of the program changed a bit as the organization focused on its core values and experimented with various marketing paradigms. Knowing what we were about drove the decisions we made about programming and helped to keep us focused on seeking for new ways to encourage growth in meaning and purpose and connection.

IT TAKES A TEAM

When giving a seminar for activity directors and coordinators I asked them who they worked with to plan their calendars. They all looked at me blankly and said, "No one. It's our job." It is their job to produce that calendar, but if their organization desires to create an environment where flourishing, growing, fruitfulness and vitality are hallmarks of residents' lives they need to realize that it cannot be done by one person.

Because my position was new and there were existing positions of chaplain, volunteer services coordinator, activity director and activity personnel from assisted living and the skilled nursing home, I was given the explicit responsibility to bring all these folk together and together create the program. In my subsequent years in the older adult world I have been saddened by how rarely this happens.

Not that this was always easy. People who were used to working independently from one another did not necessarily think coming together for regular meetings was a good thing. But over time the value of this sort of planning and communication became evident. We all looked forward to our annual planning meetings where we chose a theme for the year, and then looked at ways that theme could be implemented in regular on-going programming, special programs, and village wide celebratory events.

We also took advantage of our regular meetings and our big yearly planning meeting to build connections within the team. We were seeking to build a program that encouraged our residents to make new connections with themselves, others, the wider world, with nature and with the significant or sacred. Wasn't it then incumbent upon us to be planning and creating this program from a place of connectedness? We found that when we planned together the creativity and energy of the whole group created events and programs that were more-than-the-sum-of-their-individual-parts. And

4. Gordon, *Top Ten,* no Pages; online.

we found that it took the energy of all of us to carry the program; no one person could do it. When we approached it as a group project, we found ways to support one another in the individual dimensions of each person's responsibilities. And when it came to big events, we were all there, contributing to the success of the whole. And the residents just loved seeing the Director and sometimes chaplain, serving up piña coladas!

I know that many organizations are staffed in ways that create individual job responsibilities and in effect create silos that are rarely breached. Often there is resistance to doing anything that changes that. But if we are interested in creating programs that promote meaning and purpose and connectedness we need to be creative in finding ways we can bring people together to plan and create. It may mean starting informally by inviting colleagues to lunch to "brainstorm" with you. It may mean identifying folk on staff who seem to resonate with programs, even if that's not their job and inviting them to co-create with you.

Ideally the leadership for creating connected programming comes from the top of your organization, and it is leadership that recognizes the importance of this endeavor and that empowers a leader to bring everyone connected with programming and resident life together to begin the process. There may be resistance from those who are directed to come together. But remember, this is spiritual work that you are endeavoring to do, and there is almost always resistance to spiritual growth and change. But it is good work, and the residents deserve the best we can give them. And that most often happens when we create and execute as a team.

IT REQUIRES VALUING BOTH SPIRITUALITY AND RELIGION

When the CCRC residents interviewed by Wendy Lustbader complained of loss of meaning and purpose and the shallowness of the connections in their CCRC they were expressing spiritual concerns. For the sake of the long-term flourishing of residents, senior living communities need to address these spiritual issues.

Spirituality is sometimes difficult to define and for that reason two responses predominate in the retirement community world: we hire a chaplain and put spirituality in that domain or we ignore it as a concept too diffuse for us to adequately address. Hiring a chaplain can be a wonderful first step in addressing the spiritual needs of residents. But it tends to put spiritual needs into the domain of religion, and ignores those who don't practice a religion, or those who have spiritual needs not met by a religious practice. And ignoring it, or defining it too narrowly, leads to complaints like those previously quoted.

I've used two tools to think about how spirituality can infuse and shape the life of retirement communities. The first one is a re-working of the standard wellness circle of life domains used by many senior living wellness programs, where spirituality is one piece among many other pie shaped pieces. Like Don Koepke in the Introduction, I reworked the circle so that spirituality is in the center as its own circle, which touches all the other pie pieces and connects them. This diagram reminds us that spirituality is at the heart of everything we do and is the connecting factor as we serve residents.

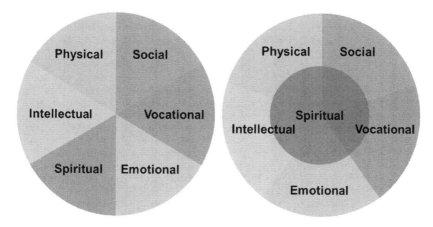

Eileen Shamy describes the centrality of spirituality when she says,

> "The word 'spiritual' embraces the essence of what it means to be human. It is concerned with personhood, identity, and the meaning of life. It is impossible to describe completely or to quantify and measure. The spiritual integrates and holds together the physical, psychological, and social dimensions of life. It integrates these dimensions into an individual person who is more than the sum of his or her parts."[5]

When we're thinking about spirituality we need to remember that it can and often does include the practice of a religion or faith tradition. The two do not need to be seen as mutually exclusive.[6] For many older adults, the primary way they experience meaning and purpose and connectedness is through the practice of their faith and following the practice and traditions that have been a part of their life up to this time. We would do well to

5. Shamy, *A Guide*, 60.
6. Ibid.

be supportive and understanding of those traditions and practices, even if they are not our own.[7]

We also need to be open to those who practice no religion, have no belief in any transcendent power or being. They too have needs for meaning and purpose and connection. And there may be those who have practiced a religion for their whole lives, but who are finding themselves unfulfilled by it, with many questions as they traverse the sometimes difficult terrain of aging. We need to have a vision of spirituality that is big enough for all that we serve. I find this definition of spirituality one that provides that breadth.

> Spirituality is the aspect of humanity that refers to the way individuals seek and express *meaning and purpose* and the way they experience their *connectedness* to the moment, to self, to others, to nature and to the significant or sacred. [8]

I like this definition because it gives room for all and it gives programmers some practical pegs on which to hang our hats. We can plan programs around meaning and purpose and connection. So let's explore this avenue.

IT REQUIRES INTENTIONALLY PROGRAMMING FOR MEANING AND PURPOSE

Viktor Frankl in his work *Man's Search for Meaning* suggests that we find meaning through three major avenues: 1) Creating a work or doing a deed; 2) Experiencing culture, beauty, nature and the uniqueness of others; and 3) Choosing our attitude.[9]

Programming for "Creating a Work or Doing a Deed"

Tapping into the innate creativity of those we serve can be a wonderful antidote to the boredom which often afflicts the days of older adults. When at Friendship Village I had a resident who was very reserved and seemed to be pretty alone in the world. She'd never married and had worked as a obstetrical nurse helping bring many children into the world. She took advantage of a memoirs writing class we offered, and enjoyed it. She told me, "Now I know how important it was that my mother died when I was two." After

---

7. For supportive religious practices, see Peggy Price, chapter 4 "Religion: Friend or Foe."

8. Puchalski, "Improving the Quality."

9. Frankl, *Man's Search*, 115.

the memoir writing class she decided that she would take advantage of the china painting class being offered by in the arts and crafts room. She took to it like a duck to water and told me, "This is why I get up in the morning. I love this!" She was someone, who I think had had very little time for creative endeavors in her earlier life. But when they were placed before her she experienced the joy of finding meaning by creating works through writing and painting.

The number of ways we can provide arenas for our residents to do a deed for someone else is limited only by our imagination. How many of our residents long to do something useful, but at the same time something, that only they in their own uniqueness can do? For many years our residents packaged awards for a Christian children's ministry. They got great satisfaction each month in seeing the big boxes of finished packets they had done and there was great mourning when the ministry decided to end that way of doing that piece of their work. It obviously filled a felt resident need to do a tangible work. One year a nursery school brought a whole class to our place each Thursday. The residents who lived in that area of the building were invited to be present each week for the pre-school session, to become teachers' helpers and special friends to the children in the class. The sparkle in the eyes of the eight to ten residents who were regular participants in the program was a joy to see. They too were experiencing meaning in doing a deed.

Programming for "Experiencing Culture, Beauty, Nature and the Uniqueness of Others"

The arena of traditional activities programs is experiences. We plan trips, we invite entertainers, we schedule interesting speakers on a variety of topics, we encourage interaction with the outdoors and with one another. Creating good experiences is at the heart of what we do. But I think a constant question for us as we do this is, "How can this experience be deepened? What would make it go beyond entertainment and/or information into meaning?"

One way that I found was to program around a theme or a subject and come at it from many angles. This practice provides several entry ways into a subject, offers differing experiences around the subject, and allows the various components on the theme to "speak" to each other during the month. One year when our winter all-Village event was a celebration of Chinese New Year we led up to it by showing films on multiple aspects of Chinese life, featured Pearl Buck's book *The Good Earth* as our "one book, one village" book group for that month, and showed the movie as well. We scheduled lessons with the proprietor of a local Chinese restaurant on how to use chopsticks, and we had a lecture from a staff member on the American missionary movement to China in the early 20th century. We featured exhibits of articles from China and aspects of Chinese life and culture. When it was time for the celebration of the Chinese New Year with the parade and Chinese musicians we were well prepared to enjoy the experience.

Another way to move toward meaning in programming is to incorporate some challenge into your planning. Often, I think, we fall into what I would call "comfort" programming. We do sing-a-longs with the old favorites from their generation. We provide arts and crafts that are easy for older hands to do. We do sitting exercise classes that follow the same routine week after week and fail to challenge the participants to extend their range of motion or the level of their exertion. We gather weekly for the same current events discussion, reminisce group, and to play the same games.

The older adults we serve do need supportive programming and routines that can be counted on. But they also need programming that challenges them to go beyond what they know and what they think they can do. And I would argue that providing programming that challenges older adults to new learnings and to doing something new and even difficult, is one way to deepen the experiences we're offering them and is a way of providing spiritual care.

It is spiritual because without challenges, problems to solve, some sense of newness and growth, life can become very boring. There isn't much joy in anything. When we meet new challenges, try new things, solve a problem — our spirits rise and expand. We have a sense of possibility, a sense of our own value, and hope that there can be another new thing tomorrow.[10]

Programming for Choosing Our Attitude

Frankl reminds us as he reflects on his experience of the Holocaust that while we cannot control the events going on around us, we can control how we respond. We can decide what our attitude to life is.

Every community or congregation or senior center has its own ethos. Some are positive and friendly and joyful. In other communities, one senses discouragement, cliquishness, and a generally negative attitude toward life. What makes the difference? The ethos of a community is a combination of history, the behaviors and attitudes of the residents over time, and the relationship of trust or distrust that exists between the residents and the administration. We don't have control over a lot of those factors, but we can

10. Gordon, "Challenge as Spiritual Care," no pages online resource.

in small and large ways contribute to an ethos that is friendly, positive and engaged.

Leading a new program in a community undergoing much change was challenging. Residents seemed to be upset about everything, from the changing programs to the food. I learned very quickly that being defensive about needed changes was not helpful. What did help was listening carefully, validating feelings of anger, loss and frustration, and when needed, admitting fault and changing the practice. I also made it clear to my staff that while we could listen to complaints carefully and respectfully, we did not have to tolerate verbal abuse. When necessary we broke off conversations until a time that they could be continued without personal attack. Sometimes older adults get in the habit of thinking they can say anything to anybody and not be held accountable just because they're old. We did our best to discourage that! By trying to consistently set limits on how we were talked to and by modeling the kind of engagement we were willing to engage in, we were able to slowly gain trust and create a better atmosphere for the community.

And we sometimes had months where we focused on a theme such as kindness or gratitude, seeking to find ways to encourage our residents to choose to practice virtuous behavior and to choose positive attitudes. Since my time at Friendship Village I have written about spiritual practices for aging. The ten possibilities that I identified as practices-to-encourage are:

1. Practice Breathing.
2. Practice Gratitude.
3. Practice Wonder.
4. Practice Creativity.
5. Practice Kindness.
6. Practice Releasing.
7. Practice Connecting.
8. Practice Resting.
9. Practice Making Music.
10. Practice Being Yourself.[11]

While this list isn't definitive by any means, it suggests practices that will help all of us who are aging navigate that journey with grace and fortitude. And can you think about how much fun it would be to focus on one of

11. Gordon, *Ten Spiritual Practices,* online resource.

these for a month, and approach the practice from as many disciplines and in as many ways as you can for both residents and staff? I think sustained and intentional programming around spiritual practices could be beneficial in helping residents to choose positive attitudes and responses to the lives they live and the challenges they face. Sustained and intentional programming around such practices can also hugely benefit the ethos and morale of a community. And this is a place where team programming by chaplains, activity people, fitness folk, the creativity leaders, dining staff and health care staff could produce amazing results.[12]

IT REQUIRES INTENTIONALLY PROGRAMMING FOR CONNECTION

The summer between my seventh and eighth grades, my family moved from a small town in central California to a small city in southern Oregon. I went from a self-contained 7th grade classroom with classmates well known to me, to a large, three-year junior high, where classes changed every hour. When school started I knew exactly two people who were in my grade. I will never forget the difficulty of that transition and the trauma of trying to figure out where to sit for lunch in what seemed like an enormous lunch room.

As I watched people move into our large retirement community, my junior high moving experience often came to mind. I was welcoming residents who were often leaving a home of many, many years. They were not only leaving a home, but in leaving their neighborhood and community, they were also leaving behind long-time connections, some of which could be sustained in their new place, but many that could not. They lost connection with people who had known them for years, and were in an environment where they had, often for the first time in many years, to make new connections with people who didn't know them and their story.

Our definition of spirituality reminds us that at its heart spirituality is about "*connectedness*" to the moment, to self, to others, to nature and to the significant or sacred."[13] Keeping these aspects of connection in mind as we create programs engages us in spiritual care in profound ways.

---

12. Frankl's third avenue of meaning-making (Attitude in Suffering) is beyond the scope of this chapter. Although never directly quoting Frankl Jane Thibault's discussion on finding meaning in suffering is very informative. See chapter 10, "Activating the Resources of the Soul amidst Suffering." Also see chapter 2, James Ellor, "Finding Meaning is a Meaningless World."

13. Consensus, *Improving the Quality of Spiritual Care*, no pages, personal notes

Connecting to the Moment

We live in a culture that emphasizes movement toward the future, and with our many ways of distracting ourselves with traditional and new media, we find that we are rarely truly present and connected to this moment. As any of us who have tried to practice mindfulness can attest, being present in this moment is not an easy discipline to learn. But we can encourage it for ourselves and for our residents. What would happen if before a meeting or an event, we took a few minutes to just breathe together, letting go of the rush to get there and the anxiety of how it will go, to just be present together? In our programming, we can incorporate movement traditions such as Tai Chi and Yoga that emphasize full attention to the breath and movement, calling our attention to this moment. We can provide creative endeavors that emphasize the flow of the process, rather than the outcome, creating a space and time for connecting to the moments of creation.

As a staff we can encourage each other in being present in this moment, letting go of our worries about what just happened and our anxiety about what needs to be done next to pay attention to what is in front of us right now. The more we are able to practice that connection, the more we will be able to be a calm, centering presence in what can be a confusing and stressful environment. That calmness, in itself, will be a gift to those we serve and perhaps also provide a bridge for their own centering connection to the moment.

Connecting to Self

Everywhere I turn I find those who are interested in spirituality saying that the purpose of the spiritual journey is so that we can become our most authentic self, so that we can be the person we were created to be. Most of us have very little time to reflect on that or even put it into practice as we raise families, tend a career and community commitments. Older adults have time and often the need to reflect on their life, what it's meant, and who they are now. But this sort of self-reflection and growth in self-knowledge is often done best in a structured, guided way. As programmers we can begin to address this need with life story groups, memoir writing, and other creative ways appropriate to our communities. Encouraging persons to become more deeply acquainted with themselves, accept their journeys and to know their true gifts and talents is a gift not only for them personally, but for our communities.[14]

14. Resources for self-reflection, see Morgan, *Remembering your Story*; Beth Sanders at lifebio.com; or *Looking Back*.

Connecting to Others

Helping residents connect to others in our communities is one of the primary ways we can serve them. We can begin by making it easy for people to be known by name by using nametags for everyone! I know that an argument against nametags is that it's "too institutional" and people don't wear nametags in their homes, and this is their home. But it's not only a home, it's a community; when we are in a community things go better if we are at least known by name. If there's initial resistance to wearing nametags, create nametag days, where affirmation (and maybe a prize or two) is given for those who wear their nametags. My office is in a community that opened five years ago; nametags were given to the initial residents and all subsequent residents. Most routinely wear them and it's a great help in the learning and remembering of names. And it's a great help to new people moving in for they don't have to try to remember all the names and faces they are meeting all at once.

It is possible to go to an event or program and walk away feeling lonelier than when you went if you perceive that everyone else is acquainted and you are still a stranger. One way to alleviate that is to take a moment at the beginning of an event to invite people to introduce themselves to someone they don't know, or don't know well. You could even give them a starter question for their conversation. For small groups always start each meeting by making sure that everyone knows who is in the group with them.

In our large community it was often difficult for people with common interests or pasts to get to know each other. So we started a program called "Coffee, Cookies and Conversation" that met once a month in each wing, and was a facilitated sharing of stories from their past around a suggested theme. Each month we put together a series of suggested topics and questions for the facilitators, who were both staff and community volunteers. Sometimes they used them; sometimes the conversation went in other directions. But through these gatherings residents who were from similar neighborhoods or who had similar growing up or vocational experiences found each other and were able to form deeper friendships on their own. Residents who participate in life story groups where stories are shared have another avenue for making connections with others on an even deeper level.

Gathering people together for support as they walk through difficult experiences is another way to facilitate connection to others. Paying attention to conversations and noticing themes that keep reappearing can be a way to notice an issue that perhaps several people would like to meet around. Support with grief in the loss of the spouse, support as a caregiver for a spouse or child, support with living with a chronic illness are all places

where creating a safe and nourishing space and time can be greatly beneficial. I think most of us of had experiences where no one else could fix the
problem, but when we felt we were being accompanied and were not walking alone we found the strength to continue.[15] Providing places of support,
facilitated by persons gifted and qualified to do so, is a significant way of
fostering connectedness, and thus providing spiritual care.

Another way to help forge connections with others is to provide a
common task. Is there a short-term volunteer endeavor that could use many
hands at the same time either within your community or in the outside
community? Doing something with others is spirit lifting and the camara-
derie that develops lasts long after the event.

And in this age of electronic devices and social media we can provide
encouragement and training for residents in using email, Facebook, Twit-
ter and other on-line modes of communication and connection. Not only
do these mediums provide opportunities for deepening connections with
family and friends, but they also provide ways for residents to connect with
others who share their passions and interests.

Connecting to Nature

Many of us experience a sense of transcendence, a sense of presence that
is much larger than ourselves when we are in an awesome natural setting.
When I moved from Illinois (cold, snowy winters and hot, humid sum-
mers!) to sunny southern California, I couldn't get over how much easier
it was to be outside and how many opportunities that communities have to
use the outdoors in their programming. Some residents have such a strong
connection to nature that they are going to be outdoors whenever possible.
But others are much more reluctant to venture out. Encouraging outdoor
trips, concerts, walks or rides to beautiful vistas are invitations for connecting to our natural world. Can we create a community garden? Is it possible
to do bird-watching walks on your campus or in your neighborhood? Is
there a nearby forest preserve or botanic garden that needs volunteers? Can
we hold exercise classes, art classes, and study groups outdoors? Anything
we can do to foster connections to nature is effort well spent.

And if there are those in our community for whom going outside is
almost impossible, how can we bring experiences of nature indoors? One of
the most joyful events that we did at Friendship Village involved bringing
nature indoors in the middle of a very cold winter. Bitter cold had kept

15. Reading some of the stories in Jay Westbrook's chapter 4, *Death and Dying: The
Final Act of Living* might evoke significant sharing.

most of our residents indoors for a week and every one was getting "cabin fever." So on a Friday afternoon my activity director and I went outside and shoveled snow into several large plastics bins, and then invited residents to come and make snowmen with us. There was much laughter that day as we created snowmen, large and small and the whole endeavor raised everyone's spirit.

Several of my Illinois residents had bird feeders on or near their windows and received much joy in watching those beautiful winged creatures visit every day. Videos of beautiful and awe inspiring natural vistas are another way to experience nature when it is no longer possible to travel to such destinations. Once again, the possibilities for creating experiences of nature both outdoors and indoors are limited only by our imagination and creativity.[16]

Connecting to the Significant or the Sacred

One of the realities of older adult life that we are loath to admit is that the time remaining is limited. One of the ways we can serve older adults well is by providing specific opportunities for connection to what is significant and sacred for them in an environment that encourages such connection. We begin to create such an environment when we are thoughtfully programming for meaning and purpose and connection, rather than creating activities for the purpose of keeping people busy.

We facilitate connection to the significant or the sacred when we support residents in their ongoing faith and religious life. Having a chaplain on staff is a tremendous help in this arena. But even without a chaplain it is possible to call on the resources of the wider community and the resources of staff and residents to find ways to assist residents in remaining connected to their faith traditions and religious communities. Koepke's article: "Providing Spiritual Care in the Absence of a Chaplain" gives some helpful hints that can be used for persons of any religious tradition.[17]

We can't program for encounters with the sacred or the significant, but we can provide spaces and places where the possibility for such encounters is more likely to happen. Is there a way we can provide a quiet corner

16. See also: The Creative Spaces Project at http:www.sensorytrust.org.uk/projects/creative_spaces/index.html.

17. Koepke, *Providing Spiritual Care* unknown date, online resource. I also recommend reading the insights of Rabbi Richard Address in chapter 9, *Using Rituals and Traditions to Engage the Spirit* where he suggests that rituals sanctify time as the attribute meaning to sometimes ordinary life events.

for meditation and prayer? Can we provide groups that together study and commit to practicing a spiritual discipline or practice?

Most of all, can we provide spaces and an ethos that encourages reflection and contemplation? I think if we look carefully at the people who radiate kindness, who live with vitality, who draw people to themselves like magnets, we will find persons who have learned how *to be* as well as *to do*. We will find people who have built contemplation and reflection into their lives.

Walter Burghardt[18] describes contemplation as "a long, loving look at the real." He suggests that our capacity for contemplation is enhanced by what he calls a "desert experience," an experience that "takes a hold of us, brings us face to face with solitude, vastness, and powers of life and death beyond our control." How many older adults do you know who have not had a desert experience?

Burghardt also posits that experiences of festivity and play expand our capacity for contemplation. Festivity resides in activity that is meaningful in itself, an activity not tied to goals. Festivity lives in the present moment, enjoys this experience, this fresh face of the real. Festivity takes usable time and withdraws it from utility. Play is more than fooling around; true play demands a sense of wonder and imagination. True play brings us more fully alive and alert to the possibilities of enjoyment in this world.[19]

These experiences prepare us for contemplation—a long, loving look at the real. And what is this "real" that we're contemplating? Burghardt gives us some suggestions. He says, "Reality is living, pulsing people, rain and rainbows, the setting sun, chocolate, music, the dying and rising Christ. Reality is not a philosophical abstraction, it is the concrete singular."[20]

When we enter into a contemplative experience of the real we are not in hurry. Rather we are "unhurried, gloriously un-harried." We can rest in this real, not "lifelessly or languidly, sluggishly or inertly, but responsively, vibrating to the throb, the pulse of the real." In our contemplation our look is not only long, it is also loving. It is not a "fixed stare, a study, or a cold, analytical examination." But it is looking from a "captivated, delighted stance that calls forth love for and oneness with the other."[21]

The result of the practice of contemplation, a long, loving look at the real, is communion, the discovery of the holy or the significant in deep

---

18. Burghardt, *A Long Loving Look at the Real*, author paraphrase, no pages

19. Ibid., 24–25

20. Author summarization of ibid., 23–27

21. Ibid., 27

thoughtful encounters with creation, with others, and with God. And it results in older adult who are truly alive. In Burghardt's words:

> What is it in summary that I would say to my contemporaries in aging? Good aging friends, our American culture needs you, needs me. But only if the younger . . . can discover in us what it means to be genuinely alive. Only if, in looking at us, they discover men and women not only grayer and more wrinkled but living more fully, more joyously than they—more fully, more joyously, than we ourselves have ever lived before. Very simply, only if they see in us what second-century Bishop Irenaeus of Lyons expressed so pithily: "God's glory—women and men alive!"[22]

IN THE END

The job of programming for older adults can be overwhelming. It's a job that's never done. It often seems to call for more resources than we think we have. So with that in mind, here are some parting thoughts.

It's Not About the Money

Yes, I had a budget, and the ability to pay for some programs. But in the end, programming for meaning, purpose and connection is not expensive. It's relational and intentional, and it's amazing how much of it actually doesn't cost very much money. What it does cost is time, for creative listening to your residents, for creative thinking and planning, and for recruiting people to help your team make great things happen. Look at every penny you are spending on programs and try to determine if the money could be stretched, used on different more creative approaches, or if there is a way to do it for free. Collaborate with organizations in your community who may have the people and resources to help, churches and synagogues, civic organizations, businesses wanting to do community service, all of them can provide helping hands and sometimes funding for programming initiatives if they can be sold on the benefits for them and for the older adults you serve

---

22. Ibid.

Don't Forget to Have Fun

Thinking about programming from a spiritual center can get pretty serious and there are many serious issues that we confront when we work with older adults. But one of the best gifts we can give is providing spaces and ways for fun and laughter. We found that programming in three to four big, all-village events with a focus on participation and taking us out of ordinary life for a few hours, reaped big benefits for the spirit of our community. And occasional fun events thrown in through the year on a more spontaneous small scale also helped. And as Burghardt points out, festivity and play increase our ability to contemplate the real.

Pay Attention to Your Own Aging Journey

Working with older adults is a wonderful opportunity for us to engage with our own aging. It is a call to be present with our own vulnerabilities and limitations. I am convinced that we can be effective in this work to the extent that we are not hiding from our own aging.[23] Henri Nouwen says this very eloquently:

> To care one must offer one's own vulnerable self to others as a source of healing. To care for the aging, therefore, means first of all to enter into close contact with your own aging self, to sense your own time, and to experience the movements of your own life cycle. From this aging self, healing can come forth and others can be invited to cast off the paralyzing fears for their future. And how can we be fully present to the elderly when we are hiding from our own aging? How can we listen to their pains when their stories open wounds in us that we are trying to cover up? How can we offer companionship when we want to keep our own aging self out of the room, and how can we gently touch the vulnerable spots in old people's lives when we have armored our own vulnerable self with fear and blindness? Only as we enter into solidarity with the aging and speak out of common experience, can we help others to discover the freedom of old age. By welcoming the elderly into our aging self we can be good hosts and healing can take place.[24]

23. See Gordon and Koepke, epilogue "Looking in a Mirror" for insights in becoming aware of one's own spirituality.

24. Nouwen et al., *Aging: The Fulfillment of Life*, 97–98.

Never forget that this is sacred work. When we seek to intentionally program for meaning and purpose and connectedness we are inviting the older adults we serve to a spiritual journey and encouraging them on that journey. And we do it best when we, too, are on that journey.

May you and your work be blessed and be a blessing.

REFERENCES

Burghardt, Walter J. "Aging: A Long Loving Look at the Real." In *Graying Gracefully: Preaching to Older Adults*, edited by William J. Carl Jr., 19–31. Louisville: John Knox, 1997.

Frankl, Viktor. *Man's Search for Meaning*. Boston: Beacon, 1959.

Gordon, Nancy. "Challenge as Spiritual Care." N.d. http://tinyurl.com/challengespcare.

———. "Top Ten Spiritual Practices for Older Adults." 2013. http://tinyurl.com/Top10SpiritualPractices.

Koepke, Donald. "Providing Spiritual Care in the Absence of a Chaplain." N.d. http://tinyurl.com/nochapspircare.

Looking Back and Giving Forward: Finding Common Ground for Positive Aging. http://www.lumunos.org/online-store/.

Lustbader, Wendy. "It All Depends on What You Mean by Home." *Generations* 37/4 (Winter 2013–14) 17–23.

Morgan, Richard. *Remembering Your Story: Creating Your Own Spiritual Autobiography*. Nashville: Upper Room, 2002.

Nouwen, Henri J. M., and Walter J. Gaffney. *Aging: The Fulfillment of Life*. New York: Doubleday, 1990.

Puchalski, Christina, et al. "Improving the Quality of Spiritual Care as a Demension of Palliative Care: The Report of the Consensus Conference." *Journal of Palliative Medicine* 12/10 (October 2009) 885–901.

Shamy, Eileen. *A Guide to the Spiritual Dimension of Care for People with Alzheime's Disease and Related Dementia: More than Body, Brain and Breath*. New York: Jessica Kingsley, 2003.

OTHER SUGGESTED RESOURCES:

Childress, Donna. "Touching the Spirit: How to Develop Programs that Enrich a Senior's Spirituality." *The Journal on Active Aging* 3 (Fall 2005) 12–16.

Cohen, Gene D. *The Creative Age: Awakening Human Potential in the Second Half of Life*. New York: Quill, 2000.

Ferrucci, Piero. *The Power of Kindness: The Unexpected Benefits of Leading a Compassionate Life*. New York: Penguin, 2006.

Friedman, Dayle A. *Jewish Visions for Aging: A Professional Guide for Fostering Wholeness*. Woodstock, VT: Jewish Lights, 2002.

Lustbader, Wendy. *Life Gets Better: The Unexpected Pleasures of Growing Older*. New York: Penguin, 2011.

Marshall, Jay. *Thanking and Blessing: The Sacred Art of Spiritual Vitality through Gratefulness.* Woodstock, VT: Skylight Paths, 2007.

Thibault, Jane Marie, and Richard L. Morgan. *Pilgrimage into the Last Third of Life: 7 Gateways to Spiritual Growth.* Nashville: Upper Room, 2012.

9

Using Rituals to Engage the Spirit

—Rabbi Richard Address, DMin, PhD (honorary)

NOT SO MANY YEARS ago, a man in his 50s, let's call him Paul, approached his clergy person with an unusual request. Paul's wife had died about a year and a half prior to this meeting. He had completed over a year of mourning. His request was simple. He asked that the following Sunday afternoon, after Sunday school had finished and the building was quiet, that he and a few close friends and family return to the sanctuary and there, at the very location where he was married and where his wife's funeral began, that a ritual be recited to allow him to remove his wedding ring. Paul needed this ritual to formalize his transition into his next stage of life. It was a very personal ritual, created by his clergy just for him and this moment, yet, done in the setting that spoke to Paul's religious tradition and community. He was asking his community, his clergy, and his God to give permission to move on with life.

Paul's choice to create a personal ritual of transition within the context of his faith tradition as well as his so called secular community is symbolic of a growing trend to re-vision and, in some cases, reinvent religious rituals in order for them to speak to new life stages and challenges that impact our lives. This trend, driven, I believe by the aging of the baby boom generation, and speaks to many issues, among them being a desire to mark special moments in religious contexts as well as a reemergence of the pursuit of a personal spirituality that often evolves outside of the parameters of traditional religious institutions. This trend of reexamining ritual's importance and a desire to explore one's spirituality becomes even more pronounced as we confront our own aging, and in doing so, our own mortality.

Spirituality is, I believe, personal. It is a way through which we live out what Koepke describes in the introduction to this book, our core beliefs. Many are core beliefs while others are not. It is practical religion. My spirituality is a way in which my religious identity is lived in the real world. It is not tied to formal affiliation with a specific denomination or group. Rather, it is how I live my beliefs, how I experience the sense of the transcendent in the world. Thus, if spirituality is theology in everyday life, then ritual serves as the formal expression of that spirituality. Ritual places my spirituality within a context of time and place. Ritual is also relational. Regardless of whether these rituals are secular or religious, they serve to celebrate a sense of relationship—with people and, with that which is beyond our own realm of understanding.

We all experience rituals. Our secular rituals are as diverse as each of us. We all have little rituals that we perform every day; our route to work, our morning routine, our bedtime routine. We have family rituals from how we celebrate birthdays to how we observe holidays. We observe sporting rituals (Super Bowl parties to wearing good luck apparel during games), eating rituals (who carves the turkey at Thanksgiving), and social rituals (annual events such as award celebrations, recognition dinners, fireworks at July 4th, etc.). These rituals connect us with elements in our life—friends, family, work groups, general society—and are often linked to regular events or moments in time.

"Rituals can be understood, in part, as methods to reduce anxiety, create meaning in life, encourage emotional expression and emotional control, foster personal identity, and promote group cohesiveness. From a spiritual perspective, though, this type of psychological and social analyses is incomplete, for rituals are first and foremost ways of connecting to the sacred, ways of bringing another world into existence that can be entered and experienced again and again."[1]

Rituals can also connect us with those elements that are outside of our own experience. These transcendent connections remind us that we are part of something greater than our own self. They help take an ordinary moment in time and elevate it to something special, even sacred. They link us to that which is beyond our own self. "Rituals reinforce the fact that a person exists within a certain context and history, and that by celebrating or recognizing an event in one's life in a formal way, that event, and thus the person, takes on an additional meaning and definition. This relational aspect of ritual is

---

1. Pargament *Spiritually Integrated Psychotherapy*, 81.

key to the power of ritual creation. It is especially important as we age, when the need for a relationship oriented life is even greater."[2] The revolution in longevity is creating new opportunities for new rituals, rituals that speak to new life stages and situations. The rituals are, at times, a reworking of a traditional, often a religious, ritual. Then, as we shall explore, there are those moments when a specific moment or event serves as a catalyst for the development of a new ritual, a personal expression of one's spiritual journey, such as the ritual for the removal of the wedding ring.

RITUALS SANCTIFY TIME

Rituals help bring meaning to life because they help sanctify time. They lift an ordinary moment into a moment of meaning, a meaning that, in a spiritual sense, helps place the participant into a sacred context. While a prayer can often be spontaneous, a ritual often will follow a prescribed script. It is the playing out of the script that we often build to a climax that gives to those participating that sense of meaning. As Lawrence Hoffman, one of the leading commentators on the role of ritual in religion, notes: "How do simple human beings find their way through the maze of things they might be. If not, primarily, through ritual?"[3] Hoffman expands this by noting that:

> Ritual is how we play out our prearranged scripts of behavior to shape specific durations of time. Since each script is repeated it prepares us to anticipate the high and low points of our lives. Without ritual there would be no meaningful use of time, except for accidental events that force us to laugh or cry on occasion. Ritual helps us minimize our dependence on chance. It arranges our life into relatively small packages of moments that matter. We want to mark special moments in our life. We do so by ritual.[4]

They often allow us to understand our past, accept an event, or begin a new transition in life. "The most meaningful rituals develop out of the shared life of a family, community, or faith group. They are often the simplest and the most lasting, handed on from one generation to the next."[5] Think about your own life and the many moments that were celebrated, observed and

2. Address, "Creating Sacred Scenarios," 224.

3. Hoffman, *Beyond the Text*, 175.

4. Hoffman, *Art of Public Prayer*, 17.

5. Robb, *Religious Rituals*, 55.

commemorated through a ritual. Rituals help tell the stories that are our lives. Imber-Black and Roberts categorized five functions that rituals serve for us.

> As you look at rituals in your life, you will find that they function in your individual development and in your interactions with others to enable *relating, changing, healing, believing and celebrating*, which are, in fact, major themes in all human existence. Any given ritual, whether it be a daily ritual, a special tradition, a holiday celebration, or a life-cycle ritual, naturally may contain one or more of these elements. A particular ritual can be shaped and re-shaped to include aspects that you deem necessary.[6]

There is, then, a certain dynamism to ritual that we often forget.

THE OLD AND THE NEW

We are witnessing a sense of freedom in that we see the revisioning of old rituals and the creation of new rituals. This is especially present in the realm of religious rituals and may have a lot to do with changing belief patterns as we age. The theology that we affirmed in our youth may be undergoing its own restructuring as we progress on life's journey. What meant something years ago may have lost that sense of meaning. When people say that a ritual has no meaning anymore, they may be saying that their own spiritual journey has taken them to a different place so that those old rituals have lost that sense of importance. Then these rituals become "empty" or, as Hoffman describe them, "ritualizations." For rituals to stay relevant, they need to be open to include the changes that an individual (or community) may encounter. As Imber-Black and Roberts wrote:

> If you have had the experience of a particular ritual becoming extremely routine, empty, meaningless, or even oppressive to you, likely this ritual no longer captures and expresses what you personally believe. Those rituals that remain alive and meaningful continue to connect with deeply help beliefs and values. Vibrant rituals have room for variations that can express changing norms and opinions while still anchoring us with a sense of shared history.[7]

---

6. Imber-Black, *Rituals for Our Times*, 28.

7. Ibid., 46.

The revolution in longevity that is now upon us is providing us with new and often creative ways of expressing ritual. For example, the website, www.ritualwell.org was created to be a site that encourages the creation and collection of religious rituals. Begun from within the Jewish world, the site states clearly that: "Ritual helps us pay attention. From the joy of recovery to the grief of a funeral, ritual helps us inhabit the breadth of human experience. When we engage in ritual, we leave the everyday and enter a space that touches and transforms us in profound and important ways."[8]

The longevity revolution has helped create a type of spiritual revolution that is often evolving outside of traditional religious denominations. Many of the traditional denominations, as a response to this spiritual wave, have themselves begun to reexamine ritual creation. Medical technology has been the foundation of this lifespan extension coupled with a greater awareness of the importance of healthy life styles. We have also witnessed a decline, or restructuring of the concept of community. We may be more "plugged-in" as a society than ever before, and that has produced a reframing of the concept of community. This need for being in community or in a relational situation becomes more important, I feel, as we age. In the new life stages that the longevity revolution is creating, we are seeing a growing desire and need for a sense of connection between human beings and, for many, with something greater than one's own self. The desire for a greater sense of intimacy and relationships is a major factor in how we, as we age, see ritual. This need for connectivity is a basic human need and can be traced back to classic religious texts—texts that can provide insight into the spiritual quest that all of us encounter as we age.

Let me suggest that the "essential spirit" that links our own aging to the use of ritual to highlight our individual journey is a spirit that is based on our fundamental need to be in relationship with others and, in a very profound and often unexpressed way, to be in relationship with some sense of meaning beyond our own existence. We find an example in the insight from Judeo-Christian classic texts: with the very first chapters of Genesis. This text describes a fundamental relationship: that our creation has within it an aspect of the sacred. No matter how you see the development of Genesis, the presence of God in the act of creation is basic. It reminds young and old alike that we share a sense of the sacred by the mere fact of our existence. Thus by the mere fact that we exist, as a representative of sacred potential, we have dignity, value, and worth. Genesis declares that our own uniqueness is something that is very powerful, very essential, and very spiritual. It reflects this wonderful insight from Martin Buber who wrote:

8. See http://www.ritualwell.org/about-ritual, paragraph 3.

"Every person born into this world represents something new, something that never existed before, something original and unique . . . that there has never been anyone like him in the world, for if there has been someone like him, there would have been no need for him to be in the world."[9] This value, that of our own uniqueness, becomes even more salient as we age. We wish to know we count for something, that our life has meaning and purpose.

Yet, that is not enough; for in Genesis 2:18[10] we are reminded that it is not good for us to be *l'vado*, alone. This little word is one of the most powerful in the Bible. We often consider this text as a basis for marriage, or being with people. Yet, it carries with it much more. I think that the idea of not being "alone" speaks as well to the desire, on a primal psycho-spiritual level, to have our lives connect with something beyond our self be it God, Allah, the Buddha, or Krishna. That connection beyond the self might be family, spouse, career, or some idealized status.

We do not wish to be alone, alone in the sense of a type of existential aloneness—a feeling of being cut off from our own soul. This idea of not being *l'vado* is basic to who we are as human beings. It speaks to a fundamental need that all human beings have: to be needed and to need, to love and be loved. It is in this search for relationships that we find meaning. "Man is declared to be that creature who is constantly in search of himself—a creature who in every moment of his existence must examine and scrutinize the conditions of his existence. He is a being in search of meaning."[11]

Why is this need for connection so powerful? Genesis chapter 3 gives us the clue. It is in this chapter that we are taught that the great fear that we all share is the ultimate aloneness of death. No matter how you may interpret the origins of this chapter, a message is clear: we are mortal. We combat this primal fear of our own death by engaging in the world, by creating and sustaining relationships, by needing and loving. Ritual is a means by which we mark moments and create scenarios that help sanctify time and, by doing so, reinforce relationships in time, and help connect us with, what may be, our higher power and sense of meaning. This relational aspect of ritual responds to the message of Genesis 3, which reminds us of our own mortality. This reality becomes ever more present as we age. This reality also wakens in us the fear, expressed by so many in our age where we are witness to declining health and dependency. We do not wish to live in pain and suffering, and we do not wish to live alone. This is why Genesis 3 is such a powerful text for it reminds us not only that we are mortal, but it asks us

9. Quoted in Levin and Prince, *Judaism and Health*, 161.

10. Tanakh: The Holy Scriptures, 5.

11. Heschel, *Insecurity*, 163.

in Genesis 3:9 what, when we are honest, is the most powerful of spiritual questions: ayekah (where are you?). We spend our entire life trying to answer this question. Ritual helps give texture, substance, and, in many ways, drama to our pursuit of how we answer this question. Ayekah points us to the questions of life: why was I born, why must I die, and why am I alive? "These are the questions that flow from God's ayekah, questions that grow in importance as we grow older and attain a deeper sense of our own mortality. To be able to truly answer God's ayekah, we must first "know" or be aware of our own unique humanity and the reality of our own mortality."[12]

There is a wonderful example from the liturgy of my community. Two prayers form part of a ritual that speaks to, what I feel, is the fragile nature of our own existence. At night, as part of the evening service, we say a prayer call the Hashkeveinu. The opening lines of this prayer are translated from the Hebrew as, "Grant, O God, that we lie down in peace and raise us up, our Guardian, to life renewed." The prayer goes on to ask that, while we sleep, a protective shield of peace be spread over us. The next morning, the ritual is that we say, as we awaken, modeh ani, which is that we give thanks that we have been given another day, another gift of life. This ritual, the nighttime prayer and the morning prayer, reminds us that sleep is, in many ways, a little death and that when we fall asleep at night, there is no guarantee that we will wake up in the morning. As we age, this simple ritual of these two prayers helps us focus on life's tenuousness and the gift that every day may bring; the gift of life.

THE SPIRITUAL EMBRACE OF LIFE

Longevity has made it possible to encounter new life stages and moments that have opened the door to creative development of new ritual. They spring, in many cases, not from the formal setting of religious life, but from the more organic, "spiritual" embrace of people. These newer rituals may be based in traditional rituals and ceremonies, but we are seeing a greater acceptance of the freedom to adapt and innovate traditional rituals to reflect new lifestyles and stages. In other words, these newly developing rituals may have one foot in tradition and one foot in some new circumstance. As one scholar noted,

> From a psychological perspective the performance of a religious ceremony has two primary functions: first, the expression and moderation of emotions, and second, the transmission of

12. Address and Rosenkranz, To Honor, 61.

information that is important to a particular religious culture. In other words, they have both an emotive component and an educational one. In order to facilitate this, ceremonies and rituals have certain key characteristics. These include repetition, the use of symbols, a recognizable and defined structure, and flexibility enabling adaptation to new circumstances.[13]

This ability to adapt to new circumstances gives us a window on the possibility of embracing new life stages and circumstances with ritual. In many cases these rituals are personal, such as Paul's request to have his clergy person create a personal ritual for him. We are seeing the creation of personal rituals allows for older adults to develop a moment of meaning that can speak to both the institutional and personal concerns.

An example from a "normal" life event is moving from one's long-time family home. In many traditions, when we move into a home there is a small ceremony that accompanies this. It is a new beginning, a major transition. Yet, when that move from a home that has been lived in for years, maybe decades, takes place, there is hardly any moment that is given to give thanks for the life that has been lived there. Usually we wait for the moving van to leave, gather the last minute boxes and head off to that next residence. A colleague, Rabbi Michael Howald, created a ritual that a family would say as they locked up that family home for the last time. It expresses gratitude for the life that was created in that home and a prayer that the next chapter in life will be blessed. In part his ritual reads:

> We honor with affection all those who crossed this threshold with us from the time we first turned the key in the lock until today. Through these doors we brought our children and welcomed our friends and family. With those who crossed this doorway we celebrated our triumphs and joys and shared our sorrows and fears. With them, we marked the holidays and the milestones of our lives. They helped make this house our home. We honor with affection all those who crossed this threshold with us.[14]

The ability to adapt and be innovative does not necessarily exclude maintaining a place in one's religious tradition. The Jewish Passover *Seder* is a perfect example. The liturgy and meal are centuries old. As the years have passed and circumstances changed, the rituals associated with the *Seder* have evolved. Modern Passover rituals contain elements that reflect modern social and political elements; from the rise in rituals celebrating feminism

13. Linke and Aronson, *Psychological Perspectives*, 82, 83.
14. Address, *Seekers of Meaning*, 35.

to ritual elements that embrace LGBT inclusion. Add to that the continuing evolution of music and prayers that often reflect current events and you have a most traditional ritual that continues to be present in today's world.

There are several examples of rituals that have been developed or should be developed that would and do bring a sense of the sacred to new life stages. As boomers age they have observed their own parents' aging and decline. There has been a growth in awareness and involvement in writing and executing medical directives and health care proxies. These are usually signed in the attorney's office with little fanfare. Yet, why not develop a ritual that takes a moment to honor what is taking place. This is a moment of great importance for it legally and literally symbolizes the fact that the person signing will eventually die. It may seem strange to have someone create a reading or small ritual that recognizes this moment as something out of the ordinary. Yet, think about it! This is a very powerful act for a person. Why not surround it with something that speaks to this from a non-legalistic perspective? This is a powerful opportunity for religious institutions to create such a small ritual that could be said as one signs these documents—a text from one's tradition that celebrates life while accepting that, as Ecclesiastes states, there is a "time to be born and a time to die."[15]

There are elements of transition and transformation in these new rituals for longevity. They recognize that aging is a transition and also support those moments of personal and spiritual transformation. The openness to create these rituals may also give older adults a fresh means of connecting with friends and religious communities, with their values, wisdom, and experience. These rituals can also be a model to younger generations, teaching them that religious rituals can speak to new experiences and help place those experiences in a sacred context. For example, I share with you a selection from a larger ritual developed by a rabbi and a congregant that was used to celebrate this congregant's turning the age of seventy. The congregant wished to do something in public to symbolize this obtaining of an age of wisdom. They developed a ceremony, made use of traditional ritual objects, such as water and candles, and non-traditional objects, such as an apple and a rose. In front of friends and family this ritual was celebrated and concluded with this prayer:

> River of light and truth, You have sustained me these many years and brought me to this place in my life's journey. Let me look out with wisdom, from the high ground of my years and experiences, over the terrain of my life. Let me gaze out toward the past and the future with a heightened sense of Your presence as

15. Tanakh, Ecclesiastes 3:2, 1444.

my guide. Let me see that growth is not reserved for any one season, and that love and fulfillment are not the exclusive provinces of the young. As today I celebrate my life's continued unfolding, I am awestruck by the wonder of my being. And so I pray that kindness and compassion may be on my lips, that strength and courage may be with me in my comings and my goings, and that I may continue to learn from and to teach those dear to me.[16]

Another challenge of modern life that cries out for a meaning-making and life-affirming ritual is when older adults choose to live together without benefit of marriage. Two people, who are alone, via death of a spouse or divorce, find each other. They choose not to be married for a host of reasons, often economic and familial. They go to their clergy person or even a caring professional to ask them to create a ceremony that celebrates that fact that they have found each other and thus will no longer be alone. This scenario, not unfamiliar to many, raises many issues. What is the role of the clergy? What safeguards may be needed to protect each individual in case of illness, incapacity, or death? This reality will challenge those clergy and caring professionals to adapt new counseling techniques to confront these new realities. Given the radical change in what makes up a family, these are not out of the ordinary questions. What then of this couple who wish a ritual that celebrates their choice? It is not a marriage. It is a celebration of cohabitation. Is there room for such a new type of ritual that speaks to what may be a growing trend? Should clergy only be seen as officiants at marriages? Here is an example of one such ritual officiated by a lay chaplain at an assisted living facility for two residents.

> Today we celebrate the loving commitment of_____and _____to each other and we share in their joy. In the Song of Songs we read, "I am my beloved's, and my beloved's is mine." This represents not only God's relationship with Israel, but also the commitment that is shared between_____and_____.
> Love lives as long as the human heart beats, as long as we draw breath. The soul reaches out to another, recognizing a kindred spirit, a receptive companion to share life's vicissitudes. Age is meaningless, for the mysteries of the heart know no temporal boundaries. Today we acknowledge their love for each other and bless their commitment:
>
> a. May they be healthy and lead productive lives.
>
> b. May they find sustenance in their relationship.

16. Address, "Creating Sacred Scenarios," 61.

    c. May they find enjoyment in each other.

    d. May their physical presence strengthen their spiritual growth

    e. May they nurture their fragility, and rely on their strengths.

    f. May their days be full and inundated with love. Amen.[17]

One of the most challenging transitional moments that families and individuals face in our society is moving someone into a long-term care facility. Many of us know the emotional, spiritual and familial stresses and strains that accompany this journey. Rabbi Cary Kozberg, a chaplain at a retirement community, developed a ritual that welcomed a new resident. The ritual included not only the resident's family and friends, but the facility's staff as well. This is a moment of significant transition. Why not create a ritual that infuses the sacred into the challenging? The opening reading in this ritual acknowledges the multiplicity of emotions that may be present in that room:

> Today we consecrate a moment of transition in the journey of life. This transition is a significant milestone. Feelings of hope and fear, of anticipation and anxiety, of sorrow and perhaps relief accompany this transition. Embarking on this new phase of the journey, we reflect on the progression of life. We contemplate the changes and the challenges yet to be faced.[18]

These examples of new rituals point the way to what may be a new and exciting period in seeking the essential spiritual spirit in our life's journey. There is this need to seek meaning in this life, to respond to those "why" questions of Genesis 3. We wish our moments to be those of meaning and connection even when the circumstances of life seem to have conspired to present us with difficult challenges. One such a moment is becoming ever more present to all of our communities. The rise on Alzheimer's and dementia cases is staggering. With an extended life span now a reality, we are seeing a frightening rise in the number of people and families who have to deal with these diseases. Many clergy colleagues have had the following scenario presented to them in one fashion or another. The situation involves a spouse who will seek out clergy for a conversation. This spouse is dealing with the care of a husband or wife, confined to an Alzheimer's facility, from which he or she will never return home. The progression of the disease has left that husband or wife unable to function, unable to care for himself or

17. Ibid., 67.
18. Ibid.

herself, unable to "know" who they are or where they are, unable to "know" the children. In the process of caring for this husband or wife, this "well" spouse has met someone with whom they share special moments. "Do religious congregation and denominations have a responsibility to speak about this issue openly and to create a document or ritual that would, in certain contexts, permit the well spouse to seek a relationship outside of the traditional understanding of marriage? Would this be a proper use of ritual, or does it demean and cheapen the concept of what a religious ritual should be?"[19]

There have been a very few attempts at discussing this possibility.

As you can imagine, a discussion as to the creation of a ritual that would reinterpret the concept of adultery in light of Alzheimer's and dementia is not high on the list of any religious institution. Yet, there may be some who are attempting to respond to the very real life situation. But does such a ritual need to be religious in nature? Perhaps a ritual can be devised by colleagues that might be helpful to persons caught in this modern challenge of life. If ritual is adaptive and serves as a way to link tradition to what is taking place in people's lives, and if, as we know, this scenario is not fiction but is being played out now, then who is to say that in some way or in some form this discussion will bear fruit.[20] This discussion is even more vital when we are expecting, according to the Alzheimer's Association, a doubling or even tripling of such cases as baby boomers age and live longer. "Such a discussion may not be for everyone or every religious tradition. Yet, to ignore the reality that an increasing number of people who are members of churches, synagogue and mosque communities are now or will be dealing with this situation is to perhaps deny them the opportunity to seek comfort, support, and guidance from their tradition."[21]

Rituals then are the pathways that allow a person's spiritual search for their own meaning to have a tangible, personal reflection in real life. They may be rooted in tradition or may spring organically from a specific need at a specific time. What is true is that they help give a human being a sense of being part of something beyond their own self. Rituals help bring meaning to specific moments of random time, elevating that time from ordinary to something that is special or holy. In this age of longevity, with new life stages emerging, the use of ritual to celebrate and commemorate these moments has never been more present.

19. Address, *Seekers of Meaning*, 52.
20. Address, "Creating Sacred Scenarios," 537.
21. Address, *Seekers of Meaning*, 56.

REFERENCES

Address, Richard. "Creating Sacred Scenarios: Opportunities for New Rituals and Sacred Aging." In *Religion, Spirituality and Aging: A Social Work Perspective*, edited by Harry R.Moody, 223–32. Binghamton, NY: Haworth, 2005.

———. *Seekers of Meaning.* New York: URJ, 2011.

———. "Till Death Do Us Part? A Look at Marriage Rituals When a Partner Has Alzheimer's Disease." *Generations* 3 (Fall 2011) 52–56.

Address, Richard, and Andrew L. Rosenkranz. *To Honor and Respect.* New York: URJ, 2014.

Aronson, Jason, and Stuart Linke. *Psychological Perspectives on Traditional Jewish Practices.* Northvale, NJ: Rowman & Littlefield, 1999.

Heschel, Abraham Joshua. *The Insecurity of Freedom.* New York: Schocken, 1972.

Hoffman, Lawrence A. *The Art of Public Prayer.* Woodstock, VT: Sky Light Paths, 1999.

———. *Beyond the Text.* Bloomington: Indiana University Press, 1987.

Imber-Black, Evan, and Janine Roberts. *Rituals for Our Times.* New York: Harper Collins, 1992.

Levin, Jeff, and Michele Prince. *Judaism and Health.* Woodstock, VT: Jewish Lights, 2013.

Moody, Harry R. *Religion, Spirituality and Aging: A Social Work Perspective.* Binghamton, NY: Haworth, 2005.

Pargament, Kenneth L. *Spiritually Integrated Psychotherapy: Understanding and Addressing the Sacred.* New York: Guilford, 2005.

Robb, Thomas B. "Religious Rituals for Life Stage Events." In *Aging and Spirituality: The First Decade*, edited by James Ellor, Susan McFadden, and Stephan Sapp, 55–59. San Francisco: American Society of Aging, 1999.

Tanakh: The Holy Scriptures: The new JPS translation according to the Traditional Hebrew Text (NJPS).

10

Transforming Suffering into Spiritual Energy

The Practice of "Dedicated Suffering"

—Jane Thibault, PhD

AGING AND SUFFERING—NEED FOR A NEW PARADIGM

> A human being would certainly not grow to be seventy or eighty years old if this longevity had no meaning for the species to which he belongs. The afternoon of human life must also have a significance of its own and cannot be merely a pitiful appendage to life's meaning.[1]

What is the purpose of our later years, the years that loom ahead after the tasks of child rearing and career development have been accomplished? Is the time after retirement a winding down of life's past pleasures or does it have a special purpose of its own? Might there be a spiritual call, an opportunity for growth, an invitation to take up new work, which can be heard most clearly and responded to most readily in later life?

Dismissing Carl Jung's assertion that old age has meaning and significance to society, Western culture does not look kindly on the aging process.

1. Jung, *Modern Man*, 108.

Try as we might to paint a brighter picture of later life, gerontologists have not yet been able to convince society that old age is something to anticipate with great joy! And there is considerable justification for this negative attitude toward aging, for despite the medical and social strides to keep people fit and functioning that have been made during the past half-century, some realities cannot be denied.

Among the starkest of these realities is the irrefutable fact that the longer we live, the nearer we are to death. Body parts and organ systems wear down at varying rates. We may have to endure life-threatening or chronic illnesses, which often cause a reduction of our vitality and sense of well-being due to pain or fatigue. Changes occur that reduce the pleasure we derive from our physical appearance (because only youthful beauty is valued by our culture). One of my young geriatrician colleagues is fond of saying, "After sixty it's 'patch, patch, patch.'" As a sixty-six year old I can attest to the fact that this has been true for me and for many of my sixty-something-plus friends. And I have to admit that the first of my need for "patches" came as a total surprise—eight months of chemotherapy for stage 4 non-Hodgkins lymphoma! Finally, friends, and relatives die or relocate, and sometimes we ourselves are forced to move to safer, more efficient housing where our living can be "assisted."

In short, we are confronted in our later years by many painful and unavoidable losses—of work, hobbies, friends, family, status, lifestyle, possessions, abilities of all kinds—those things we valued so greatly in our younger days, and which we so often use to define who we are as individuals.

Confrontation with this rather depressing prospect can cause great fear and dread for people facing or already experiencing their later years, and their responses to the threats of suffering in old age vary. Many are influenced by societal demands to be active and they believe that if they are not as frenetic as they were before retirement, they will be useless to society. Some become addicted to fitness behaviors while others fall into the depths of boredom, depression and suicidal despair. In past years the highest rates of suicide in the United States have been among male teenagers and among white males between the ages of seventy-five and eighty.[2] Now middle-aged people are joining these two groups. *New York Times* journalist Tara Parker-Pope reported:

> Suicide rates among middle-aged Americans have risen sharply
> in the past decade, prompting concern that a generation of baby
> boomers who have faced years of economic worry and easy ac-
> cess to prescription painkillers may be particularly vulnerable to

2. Osgood, *Suicide in the Elderly*, xi.

self-inflicted harm . . . The most pronounced increases were seen among men in their 50's, a group in which suicide rates jumped by nearly 50 percent, to about 30 per 300,000. For women, the largest increase was seen in those ages 60 to 64, among whom rates increased by nearly 60 percent, to 7.0 per 100,000 . . . the current numbers are, if anything, too low.[3]

As a member of a geriatric medical evaluation team for thirty years, one of my responsibilities was to assess family caregiver stress. One chilling statement I heard countless times from loving but exhausted caregivers was, "I've already told my kids—if this ever happens to me (illness, frailty, or dementia) take me behind the barn and shoot me!" When pressed, they'd admit that they wouldn't ask their child to kill them, but they wouldn't hesitate to commit suicide to relieve their family of the burden of care and themselves of meaningless suffering. Any response I could think of giving sounded hollow—I reasoned that the best I could do was offer a listening ear and provide resources and support groups.

And older adults themselves, those who do not consider suicide acceptable, struggle with their experience of suffering, trying to find palliation and meaning. How often have those of us who attend to the needs of older adults—professionally or personally—heard the following or similar words of anguish: "Why doesn't God take me? I'm of no use to anyone, including myself!" How do we respond? Are our responses comforting, encouraging, challenging, even believable? Do they enable the person to emerge from their despair to new meaning for their suffering? More often than not, the answer is "No!" When we don't know how to respond in a helpful way to the intense physical, emotional, spiritual or existential pain we encounter we often offer such statements as: "Why do *you* think God is keeping you here?" "You are here for a purpose, even though you may not know what it is!" "We still need your presence among us." "You can pray for us!" "God isn't finished with you yet!" "My life would be less if you weren't here." Even, "It's God's will." Sometimes these responses satisfy for the moment, but the comfort rarely lasts beyond our visit.

So the relationship between old age and the experience of a vast variety of pain and suffering is significant and has enormous societal as well as individual implications. Because the large population of baby boomers are looking at their parents and seeing their own future, pain and suffering are becoming a major source of medical, social, economic, and spiritual concern that will only increase over the coming half century. While suicide, euthanasia and physician-assisted death are highly debated solutions

3. Parker-Pope, "Suicide rates."

for the terminally ill at this time, society has not yet addressed the issues of pain and suffering in non-terminal older persons. The question arises: Are suicide and euthanasia the only emergent solutions available to older adults in persistent pain in the near future? What alternatives do we have for happy and meaningful late life (especially when I believe that the biological lifespan is 120)?

Finding an authentic and helpful answer to "Why doesn't God take me?" is an absolute necessity if we don't want to watch a whole generation die of hopelessness. But the person's ability to live a rich and meaningful life while suffering from persistent pain in any domain is an overwhelming physical, psychological, social, environmental, economic, and profoundly spiritual challenge. Pharmacological, psychological, and behavioral thera- pies may not alleviate all pain and do not deal with the "meaning" issues that accompany drawn out suffering. Few spiritual or religious responses or interventions are available to help the sufferer reconceptualize pain as meaningful to self and of potential benefit to others.

Because of the negative impact of unrelieved pain on the biosocial- spiritual well-being of the person, the management of persistent physical and emotional suffering is a major challenge to the helping professions as well as to the individual.[4] Palliative medication (often a source of con- troversy) and behavioral interventions (for which there is some evidence of effectiveness, especially in the treatment of musculoskeletal disorders[5]) are expensive and, therefore, largely unavailable to poor or poorly insured persons and those in medically underserved areas. In addition, chronic pain and suffering are a major expense to both patient and society in terms of personal productivity and financial cost of treatments, which are often only partially effective.

In his classic article, "The World of the Patient in Severe Pain of Long Duration," Lawrence LeShan writes:

> The meaning of pain has been approached by every great reli- gion and philosophy. In our own anti-metaphysical culture it is largely ignored. This lack of perceived meaning, of a culturally understood context, makes it much harder for the individual to deal with chronic pain. As the Nazis well understood and dem- onstrated, meaningless and purposeless torture is much harder for the person to accept and resist than is torture which the subject can place in a coherent frame of reference. A perceived senselessness in the universe weakens our belief that our efforts

4. Cassell, *Nature of Suffering*, 3–5, 51–58.
5. Van Tulder et al., "Low Back," 781.

have validity and point. They appear to be essentially futile. This makes it much harder to continue these efforts, including those of coping with pain and stress.[6,7]

ONE POSSIBILITY . . .

Might there be a transcendent, spiritual meaning or purpose that can be ascribed to pain and suffering, that offers sufferers a more positive way to conceptualize their pain? In Cassell's words, "Can the integrity of the person be restored in some other manner?" Can the person be enabled to find some way to cope with the suffering and not be destroyed by it? Since the publication of LeShan's article, a renewed interest in a spiritual approach to the healing or management of illness has occurred. Religion and spirituality play a significant part in the complementary, alternative, and integrative medicine movement and are gaining increased acceptance among mainstream clinicians.[8] Religions, spiritualities, and many philosophies are now valued because they attempt to give meaning to the suffering that exists in the world and offer ways to cope with it. Many of the spiritual coping techniques, such as meditation, mindfulness, and Tonglen breathing techniques call human beings to transcend their preoccupation with the "small" or "false" self in order to grow morally and spiritually and to help repair, heal, save, or enhance the world in whatever way they are able.

The ancient Catholic practice of "offering up" suffering, (which I have modernized and renamed "Dedicated Suffering") is another spiritual coping technique. Although largely ignored after Vatican II, the original devotional practice is still used occasionally and is believed by its practitioners to be a discipline leading to the spiritual transformation of both the sufferer and the one for whom the suffering is offered. In its traditional format, the person suffering (in any way, large or small) offers her actual pain to Christ, to be combined with his suffering for the continued redemption or healing of the world. In support of the renewal of the practice, Benedict XVI, Pope Emeritus, acknowledges its value in his 2007 encyclical, *Spe Salvi*:

> There used to be a form of devotion—perhaps less practiced today but quite widespread not long ago—that included the

6. LeShan, "World of the Patient," 274.

7. For another discussion on suffering see "Suffering in Caregiving and Receiving" in Richards chapter 6 "Care-Giving to Care-Sharing."

8. Ornstein and Swencionis, *The Healing Brain*; Benson, *Timeless Healing*; Koenig, *Is Religion Good*; and Jonas and Levin, *Essentials*.

idea of "offering up"; the minor daily hardships that continually strike at us like irritating "jabs," thereby giving them a meaning. Of course, there were some exaggerations and perhaps unhealthy applications of this devotion, but we need to ask ourselves whether there may not after all have been something essential and helpful contained within it. What does it mean to offer something up? Those who did so were convinced that they could insert these little annoyances into Christ's great "compassion" so that they somehow became part of the treasury of compassion so greatly needed by the human race. In his way, even the small inconveniences of daily life could acquire meaning and contribute to the economy of good and of human love. Maybe we should consider whether it might be judicious to revive this practice ourselves.[9]

REVIVING THE PRACTICE: FROM "OFFER IT UP" TO "DEDICATE YOUR SUFFERING"

Transforming Pain and Suffering into Positive, Loving Energy as a Gift for Others

In 1995, in near despair because I had no good response to "Why doesn't God take me?" and "If this happens to me, take me behind the barn and shoot me!" I decided to go out on a spiritual limb and resurrect the practice of "offering it up" by offering it as an intervention, along with the pain meds the physicians were offering. I decided on this particular intervention because I had had personal experience with it as a child. At the age of four I developed rheumatic fever, which was accompanied by great pain in all of my joints. The treatment at the time was penicillin and complete bed rest, and I was confined to painful immobilization for about six months. I was an only child of elderly parents, and my mother was particularly distressed by my complaining about the pain and my boredom. One day she brought a notepad and a pencil to me and told me to offer up my pain to God every time I wanted to complain about it. (In those days we Catholics offered up our pain to get souls out of Purgatory, so I took on the task of getting as many people out of Purgatory as I possibly could.) One day my pain-offerings resulted—I was convinced—in getting seventy-six poor souls out of Purgatory and into heaven. When I triumphantly told my mother that I couldn't wait to die to meet all these people, she realized she had gone a bit

---

9. Benedict XVI, *Spe Salve*, 84.

too far with this intervention and tried to come up with something else to divert my attention to my pain. Nothing else worked as well!

How It Works Today—Individual Counseling or Group Format

Recognizing that my mother had actually practiced good psychology by diverting and refocusing my attention, I wondered how I could update the practice for a new, scientifically inclined generation. The first thing to go was the label—"offer it up." Instead of talking about "offering it up" I changed the words to "dedicate your suffering." In presenting it to individuals I counseled and to people attending my workshops on suffering I guided them through the following thought process.

First I asked them to bring to mind some suffering they were currently experiencing or had experienced in the past. I then asked them to reflect on the following as they relate to their own lives.

Realities about Suffering in General:

1. Some form of suffering occurs in everyone's life. We are free to determine how we will respond to it.

2. Suffering feels bad—physically, emotionally, socially, and/or spiritually.

3. A powerful negative effect of personal suffering is that it pulls the sufferer into her/himself, away from the human community, focusing the person on self and creating a sense of isolation, alienation, and even depression.

4. Pain and suffering have very little meaning or value in today's society. Sufferers have little status, since they often cannot "contribute" to others through work or prayer. This lack of meaning can be a source of further suffering in itself.

5. Often, suffering people say they feel alienated from God and/or they find it difficult to pray in the way they are accustomed.

6. There are two kinds of suffering: our own and the pain we feel when we witness the suffering of others.

Traditional Jewish and Christian Teachings about the Value of Suffering

- Suffering can be educational and a source of growth. We may learn some lesson about our own life.

- Suffering can lead to empathy. By experiencing our own pain we may come to understand similar pain that others experience. This is the basis for the group-help movement, such as AA.

- Suffering can be a source of purification, remediation, rehabilitation, as in "no pain, no gain" when going through physical therapy.

- Suffering can be a way to atone, to make up for, transgressions, sins, and/or harmful behavior.

- Suffering can be redemptive, even beneficial in some way for others.

A New Way to Think about Pain and Suffering: As a Source of Loving Energy for Others (based on #5 above, that suffering can be beneficial in some way)

- We have a human obligation to attempt to alleviate suffering (both individually and via social justice activities) but in many cases there is some "left over" suffering that lingers, that cannot be alleviated, especially in later life. Grief and the pain of chronic illness are examples.

- Physical, emotional, social, and spiritual suffering (our own and the witness of others' pain) both create and expend enormous amounts of concentrated human energy, which is usually ignored, endured, subdued, or avoided—i.e., wasted. Why waste this energy? It can be "harvested" and "dedicated" (offered) as loving energy for the good of others. (This is actually a type of intercessory prayer, where the prayer is given by the body instead of the voice or mind.)

- We are physically as well as spiritually connected to one another:

  a. Quantum physics asserts the physical interconnectedness of all things at a sub-atomic level.

  b. Jesus acknowledges unity of all and states metaphorically that he is the vine and we are the branches.

  c. St. Paul, in Colossians chapter 1, verses 24–25 states, "I am rejoicing in my sufferings for your sake, and in my flesh I am completing what is lacking in Christ's afflictions for the sake of his body, the church."

d. Hopi Indians speak of the "web" of life.

e. The World Wide Web—the Internet—allows us to be intellectually and psychologically connected to one another via physical, electronic networks.

f. Energy medicine, a new branch on complementary medicine, focuses on the study and use of biological energy.

- The energy of suffering can be offered as positive energy directly to others or it can be given to God, G_d, the Creator, Higher Power, Jesus, Allah, in order to be transformed into loving energy for the well-being of others. This is a form of "redemptive suffering." It is also a type of intercessory prayer, using suffering energy, body energy, instead of word energy.

- When it is reconceptualized as a potential gift for someone, one's suffering energy can have meaning both for the self and for the larger community. It becomes a gift one has the power to give, reestablishing one's role in society, relieving the sense of isolation and alienation.

- The energy of suffering can be donated or dedicated as a gift on an individual basis or as a community, via a "Dedicated Suffering Group."

Dedicated Suffering Group Process

The following is the suggested process for a group, based on eighteen years of forming and leading DS groups:

1. Gather in small groups of three to ten people once each week. If the group does not meet in a retirement or nursing facility, it may help to "tack it on" to the beginning or end of another meeting, such as a Bible study.

2. Designate a leader who will also participate as a "sufferer." It does not have to the same person each week, not does it require special religious training or education.

3. Read or say an introductory prayer, according to the religion or philosophy of the participants, acknowledging that suffering is a form of energy that can be beneficial to others.

4. Go around the room clockwise, with each person stating simply in only one or two sentences, without comment by others, the predominant suffering she or he currently experiences. If there is no current suffering, persons may offer past suffering experiences.

5. After all have stated their pain, discuss to whom the gift of the collective energy of the group will be offered.

6. After the group has chosen a recipient, the leader says the following prayer of offering:

> Dear God, or Allah, Father, Creator, Jesus, Universe, we believe we have done all in our power to reduce our suffering, but it is not completely under our control. Please accept it and transform it into the energy of your loving compassion. Combine it with your infinite love and send your Spirit to deliver it as a gift to (name the person(s) or cause(s) *or to whomever you think needs it more.* Thank you for the privilege of participating with you in the work of loving all that is. Thank you for teaching us that our suffering, which we once thought was useless, has infinite value in the realm of God. Amen.

7. Take one minute to have everyone close their eyes and have them imagine the gift being given to the recipient.

8. Dismiss with mutual encouragement of practice this individually until the next group meeting.

Note: There are two guidelines for group practice: (1) this is gift or ministry for others, not therapy for participants. Do not offer the energy for anyone in the group. Participants should not be looking for personal positive changes in themselves. Although this may happen, it is not the purpose of the group. (2) Do not make the "cause" too large or the group of people to whom the energy is given too numerous.

In-depth Conceptual Foundations for the Practice of "Dedicated Suffering"

There is currently little evidence-based literature available to support the use of dedicated suffering. However, there exists both a spiritual and a research-based body of knowledge that lends credence indirectly to the physiological, psychological and spiritual rationale for the practice of "dedicated suffering." This includes the following:

Christianity

Traditional Roman Catholicism offers the theological concept of redemptive suffering (joining one's suffering with that of Christ for the completion of the kingdom of God). Scripturally, the theological basis is found in the writings of Paul, especially Colossians 1:24, where Paul states: "I rejoice in my sufferings for your sake, and in my flesh I am filling up what is lacking in the afflictions of Christ on behalf of his body, which is the church." According to general theological interpretation, Paul's claim does not mean that there is anything lacking in the redemptive act of Christ, but that the sufferings of anyone who unites them to Christ, help to heal the world, thereby shortening the time it takes for the kingdom to come to fullness and fruition. In the Gospel of John, 15:5, Jesus states "I am the vine, you are the branches" asserting the interconnectedness of all who are connected to him. Historically, "redemptive" suffering has been particularly well-practiced for hundreds of years by a number of religious orders, e.g., Cistercians (Trappists), Passionists, and Redemptorists, who base their mission and community life in large part of the theology of redemptive suffering.

In addition to the Orders, a lay society of chronically ill people, "The Catholic Union of the Sick (CUSA) was organized in 1947 to encourage sick and disabled persons of all ages to offer their pain for the benefit of others. As of 2006 it had more than 1200 members throughout the USA. CUSA's statement of purpose asserts that:

> CUSA is an active apostolate which unites its disabled or chronically ill members in the Cross of Christ, so that they "FIND PURPOSE IN SUFFERING." Physical disability or chronic illness is the sole requirement for membership. The CUSA attitude towards suffering is direct and positive. It is based on the union of all people in the Mystical Body of Christ. "So long as I must bear this cross," says the Cusan, "I will use it for other members of Christ's body." CUSAns believe that "there is much benefit to be gained for themselves, and for others, through their suffering."[10]

Dedicated suffering can be practiced by individuals or by groups of suffering people. The basis for the group practice of dedicated suffering lies in the following statement of Jesuit theologian and paleontologist, Pierre Teilhard de Chardin. It is his belief that the collective practice of dedicated suffering has the potential to spiritually transform the entire world. He asserts:

---

10. Jagdfeld, *The Cusan Magazine*, 1.

Human suffering, the sum total of suffering poured out at each moment over the whole earth is like a vast ocean. What makes up this immensity—is it blackness, emptiness, barren wastes? No, indeed. It is potential energy. Suffering holds hidden within it, in extreme intensity, the ascensional [ed. note: transformational] force of the world. The whole question is how to set this force free by making it conscious of its significance and potentialities. For if all the sick people in the world simultaneously were to turn their sufferings into a single shared longing for the speedy completion of the kingdom of God, what a vast leap toward God the world would thereby make![11]

According to Teilhard de Chardin, the group intent to offer suffering energy to others as loving energy has the potential to send a tremendous amount of positive, agenda-free love-energy into a world which needs it desperately.

Buddhism

In the Buddhist practice of Tonglen meditation, a practitioner does not have to be the sufferer, although he may be. In Tonglen, the meditator breathes in world suffering and breathes out relief to the world or to whoever needs relief from suffering. Tonglen is not identical to dedicated suffering, but shares its basis in the belief that spiritual energy (in the form of breath) can be offered as a gift of life to another.[12]

Judaism

The Jewish practice of Tikkun o'lam is the act of helping God repair, heal, transform, and perfect the world through one's work and actions. Here, no unseen energy is offered, as in Tonglen and dedicated suffering, but actual physical human energy is used. Tikkun o'lam shares the Buddhist and Christian belief that each person has the spiritual obligation and the mental and physical power to help heal the world's suffering.[13]

11. Teilhard de Chardin, *Hymn*, 93–94.
12. Chodron, *Start*, 6.
13. Dosick, *Living Judaism*, 37–38.

Quantum Theory of Physics

Inherent in quantum theory's concept of indeterminacy is the idea of non-locality—e.g., item A can simultaneously influence item B halfway around the world without an exchange of energy *as we currently know it*. This is closely associated with the functions of consciousness. In *The Conscious Universe*, Dean Radin makes the following basic suggestion about a quantum-based theory of consciousness: "as the mind moves, so moves matter." Radin theorizes that consciousness may have the following properties:

   a. "consciousness extends beyond the person and affects the probabilities of events;"

   b. "consciousness puts order into systems in proportion to the 'strength' of consciousness present;"

   c. "the strength of consciousness in a person changes from moment to moment, and is regulated by focus of attention;"

   d. "a group of individuals can be said to have 'group consciousness,' which strengthens when the group's attention is focused on a common object;'

   e. "when persons in a group are all attending to different things, the group consciousness and coherence is zero, producing what amounts to background noise;"

   f. "physical systems of all kinds respond to a consciousness field by becoming more ordered . . . when a group is actively focused on a common object, the 'group mind' momentarily has the power to organize."[14]

Radin quotes physicist Victor Mansfield, who theorizes that we inhabit "a radically interconnected and interdependent world, one so essentially connected at a deep level that the interconnections are more fundamental, more real than the independent existence of the parts."[15]

Energy Medicine

The basis of energy medicine is the use of the energies in and outside of the human body. Jonas and Crawford state: "There is evidence to suggest that mind and matter interact in a way that is consistent with the assumptions of distant healing. Mental intention has effects on non-living random

14. Radin, *Conscious Universe*, 160–61.

15. Mansfield, *Synchronicity*, 226.

systems (such as random number generators) and may have effects on living systems."[16]

Putting the above concepts of interconnectedness to practical application, the members of a "dedicated suffering group" simultaneously and intentionally focus their consciousness on their suffering. Then they choose to transform the energy generated by the collective suffering into positive energy for the well-being of one or more others. In effect, they create a field of consciousness that, according to quantum theory, has the power to effect the one(s) to whom they give their collective positive energy. The recipient is free to accept or reject the gift.

PRELIMINARY STUDIES

Parish-Based Practice of Dedicated Suffering

In 2007 I conducted a small, qualitative, non-randomized study of fifteen women who participated in a church-based "Dedicated Suffering Group" for twelve weeks. Results were:

- 100% of the participants reported experiencing a decrease in self-involvement and a reconnection with the human community which resulted in an overall feeling of renewed involvement in life.

- 90% reported a renewed sense of meaning and purpose to their lives. They had found an answer to the questions, "Why doesn't God take me?" and "Why am I here?"

- 84% reported a lessening of the sense of being a burden to others. They felt they had something to contribute to others.

- 10% reported a decrease in the experience of their pain or suffering, even though they realized this was not a purpose of the group.

Individual Use in a Hospital Setting

While there are many anecdotal accounts that the practice of redemptive suffering—"offering it up" is meaningful for many of the people who engage it, there is a scarcity of objective information or clinical evidence regarding it's therapeutic or spiritual usefulness, when performed either individually or in group. However, in 2007, under consultation with me, Chaplain Victoria Anne Lucas of Holy Cross Home Care and Hospice, Silver Spring,

16. Jonas and Levin, *Healing*, xvii.

Maryland, put the concept into individual practice with a variety of patients in a hospital setting as research for her Integrative Paper for the MA in Pastoral Ministry from Duquesne University. At the conclusion of the paper, entitled "The Spirituality of Suffering: The Individual Use of Dedicated Suffering as a Pastoral Care Technique at the Bedside," Chaplain Lucas writes:

> What I found in my exploration of Dedicated Suffering was one way to acknowledge the questions of theodicy, the terrible "why me," when no answers are possible. I discovered that when the patient or family member has accepted and made peace with their situation, the use of Dedicated Suffering may bring renewed meaning to their life, give them an action, a mission. Dedicated Suffering becomes a tool builder, the means with which a suffering patient or family member can become the "instrument of alleviation."[17]

"Dedicated Suffering" Group Experience in a Retirement Home

Dedicated suffering may be even more helpful when practiced in a group setting, especially by residents in retirement homes. I began my first dedicated suffering group when I was asked to help a group of nuns who were having a difficult time handling the many physical and psychological sufferings common to later life (but not common to the sufferer). Many were making frequent trips to physicians in a nearby city, a trip or more than fifty miles over narrow, winding roads; the mother superior was worried they were in danger of automobile accidents. Instead of providing individual or group counseling, I invited them to engage in a Dedicated Suffering Group. Thirteen nuns signed up and met weekly; I met monthly with them as a participant facilitator for a year. The mother superior kept track of the effects of the nuns' participation and the surprising results, which were:

a. The number of dangerous trips to out-of-town physicians decreased by 60%.

b. Verbal complaints (organ recitals) about aches and pains virtually ceased.

c. One withdrawn nun emerged from her self-imposed seclusion and began to visit the library each morning to read the paper, searching for needy people or world events that required her suffering energy.

17. Lucas, "The Spirituality of Suffering."

d. Finally, in a yearly survey of the mission assignments of the entire order, thirteen sisters claimed dedicated suffering as their mission.

Nursing Home Practice of "Dedicated Suffering"

In an article published in the *St. Anthony Messenger*, Virginia Froehle, RSM
reports on the experience or nursing home residents who participate in
weekly dedicated suffering groups in Cincinnati, Ohio and Louisville, Ken-
tucky. She writes about a new group's initial reactions:

> At first . . . some were afraid to focus on their suffering. But con-
> secrating it for the purpose of helping others offered a positive
> light. Many could then see the value of dedicating their suffer-
> ing as something holy . . . bonds have formed as residents join
> together in this kind of prayer. Although they do not discuss—
> only name—their suffering in the gathering, they are more
> aware of other's sufferings.[18]

Based on eighteen years of teaching dedicated suffering and leading groups,
the following are the general outcomes of participation:

1. The person or situation to whom loving energy is given may be helped.
    Note: The group is advised not to look for outcomes and for that rea-
    son, I have included in the offering prayer that God give it to the cho-
    sen person or anyone who needs the gift more.

2. The sufferer may experience a renewed sense of meaning and life
    purpose.

3. The sufferer may feel reconnected to the human community, with less
    self-preoccupation. Suffering may decrease, even though this is not to
    be expected nor is it the purpose of the practice.

IN SUMMARY

The use of the concept of dedicated suffering is not a panacea, nor is it appropriate for everyone in pain. However, it is one more tool in the arma-
mentarium of the pastor, chaplain, social worker—or any of us who care
for older adults who are suffering in any way. The only drawback to the use
of dedicated suffering is its potential to glorify suffering. However, in situations of residual, persistent physical and emotional pain, where all attempts

18. Froehle, "Dedicated Suffering," 42–46.

to alleviate the suffering have failed (situations which occur frequently in old age), the guided practice of dedicated suffering has the potential to engage the individual on a path of spiritual transformation through self-transcendence and the willingness to endure pain for the sake of another. This enables the person to recreate a life of meaning despite his or her suffering.

When clients are practicing Christians it can be noted that Jesus advised people to ask for what they needed, and told them that when two or three meet, he is there. Also recall the response to suffering by non-Christian theists (Buddhist, Judaism, etc.) earlier in this text. Connecting clients to their spiritual roots reinforces the spirituality/ministry of the practice. Remember, the actual benefits of practicing dedicated suffering as a group are the following:

1. Isolation that comes with the experience of pain is reduced.

2. Suffering is shared and thus "heard," again reducing the sense of isolation by increasing empathy.

3. Group practice enhances the impact of the action.

4. Individual practice is reinforced and encouraged by group practice.

REFERENCES

Benedict XVI. *Spe Salve*. San Francisco: Ignatius, 2007.

Benson, H. *Timeless Healing: The Power and Biology of Belief*. New York: Scribner's, 1996.

Cassell, E. J. *The Nature of Suffering*. New York: Oxford University Press, 1991.

Chodron, P. *Start Where You Are: A Guide to Compassionate Living*. Boston: Shambalah, 1994.

Dosick, W. *Living Judaism: The Complete Guide to Jewish Belief, Tradition, and Practice*. San Francisco: Harper, 1995.

Froehle, V. A. "Dedicated Suffering." *St. Anthony Messenger* (March 2010) 42–46.

Jagdfeld, L., ed. *The Cusan Magazine*. 50th jubilee issue (December 1993).

Jonas, W. B., and C. C. Crawford. *Healing, Intention, and Energy Medicine*. York, UK: Churchill Livingstone, 2003.

Jonas, W. B., and J. S. Levin, eds. *Essentials of Complementary and Alternative Medicine*. Philadelphia: Lippincott, Williams & Williams, 1999.

Jung, C. *Modern Man in Search of a Soul*. New York: Harcourt, Brace & World, 1993.

Koenig, H. *Is Religion Good for Your Health? The Effects of Religion on Physical and Mental Health*. New York: Haworth Pastoral, 1997.

LeShan, L. "The World of the Patient in Severe Pain of Long Duration." In *Stress and Survival: The Emotional Realities of Life-Threatening Illness*, edited by C. A. Garfield. St. Louis: DV Mosby, 1979.

Lucas, V. A. "The Spirituality of Suffering: The Use of Dedicated Suffering as a Pastoral Care Technique at the Bedside." Integrative Paper for the MA, Duquesne University, 2007.

Mansfield, Victor. *Synchronicity, Science and Soulmaking.* Chicago: Open Court, 1995.

Ornstein, R., and C. Swencionis, eds. *The Healing Brain: A Scientific Reader.* New York: Guildford, 1990.

Osgood, Nancy J. *Suicide in the Elderly: A Practitioner's Guide to Diagnosis and Mental Health Intervention.* Rockville, MD: Aspen Systems, 1985.

Parker-Pope, T. "Suicide Rates Rise Sharply in U.S." *New York Times,* May 2, 2013.

Radin, D. *The Conscious Universe.* San Francisco: Harper Edge, 1997.

Teilhard de Chardin, Pierre. *Hymn of The Universe.* New York: Harper & Row, 1965.

Van Tulder, M., and B. Koes. "Low Back Pain and Sciatica." *Clinical Evidence* 5 (2001).

Zohar, D. *The Quantum Self.* New York: Quill, William Morrow, 1990.

11

How Diminished Income Can Result in Whole Persons

—Donald Koepke, MDiv, BCC

Everything you undergo teaches you a lesson
The question is: Do you have the courage
and the strength to discover what lesson was taught?
Are you brave enough to make use of the wisdom you gained?[1]

PICTURE THE OFFICE OF Jane, an estate planner, or a social worker, or a therapist, or a clergy person, or a lawyer. In the office sits John and Mary, an elderly couple the other side of 85. "We don't know what we are going to do?" John explains. "My parents died at age 96 and were destitute and miserable. My wife is the last of her siblings. All of them, including her parents, died in their early 90s. We don't think that we have enough money to live that long." How does a provider of any discipline, like Jane above, effectively engage a person and their fear of not having enough money? The first step is to begin exploring cultural understandings of money.

---

1. Mueller, "11 Wise Lessons," n.p.

CULTURE AND MONEY

We are born into a culture defined by money. We all need it. We all seek it. We all want to keep it. We all are dependent on it for our future life and living. That is the American way, a culture based on capitalism that rewards success and productivity. In America we are confronted with the fact that: 11.7 % of Americans live in poverty, 70% of all wealth is controlled by 10% of the population, and the third most common reason for divorce is money and differing attitudes toward money.[2]

At the same time, as noted in the introduction, the experience of aging challenges all notions of success and productivity. Simple observation points to the notion that with length of years often comes a lessening of cognitive and often behavioral skills. If the person who is aging has a self-image that is dependent on cognition and being able to do, there is a conflict. So many older adults, particularly when they are physically challenged say, "Why am I here? If there is a God, why doesn't God just take me? I can't do anything anymore." Because of culture's emphasis upon money and the possession of it, these challenges to the aging self and self-image can be exacerbated to the max As Lynne Twist notes in her wonderful book, *The Soul of Money*,

> Whether we look at money in the context of our personal or family lives, the workplace, or in the health and welfare of nations, the same picture emerges: Money is the universally motivating, mischievous, miraculous, maligned and most misunderstood part of contemporary life. Rather than relating to money as a tool we created and control, we have come to relate to money as if it is a fact of nature, a force to be reckoned with. This stuff called money, mass produced tokens or paper bills with no more inherent power than a notepad or a Kleenex, has become the single most controlling force in our live. Money only has the power we assign to it, and we have assigned to it immense power. We have given it almost final authority. If we look only at behavior, it tells us that we have made money more important that we are, given it more meaning that human life. Humans have done and will do terrible things [to others and to themselves] in the name of money.[3]

Money, whether we have it or we don't, is not the problem. The problem is how we interpret that we have or do not have money. It was Paul who wrote a large portion of the Christian Scriptures who astutely observed:

2. Russo, *Money Keys*, 62–63.

3. Twist, *Soul of Money*, 7–8; words in brackets are mine.

"The love of money is the root of all kinds of evil."[4] It is not the money. It is the *love* of money. It is the irrational seeking of money that traps people, telling them that they are worthy or worthless, a person of power or weakness, one who is a success or a failure. This is one of the insidious messages that our money-driven culture imposes not only upon older adults but anyone of any age, an imposition that professionals like Jane have to consider as they engage the clients. Some words that clients might express in Jane's office express this feeling of being less than or incapable are: "The rich control all of the money and thus there is not enough to go around" or "I've made mistakes about money and it's tough to come back" or "I just don't know what to do in the area of money" or "I've cheated or failed with money and thus it's over for me."[5] The lack of money can be overwhelming and crushing. Jane needs to be ready to engage the client based on their perceptions and feelings, not on her understandings. Those understandings are probably are more educated and based on professional experience but that remains beside the point.

Money is a current, a carrier, a conduit for our intentions.
Money carries the imprimatur of our soul.[6]

The fear that one does not have enough money is also expressed in a profound sense of vulnerability. Most Americans will do just about anything not to feel vulnerable or at least not show others that they are vulnerable. Many cover that feeling through anger, resentment, and even a lashing out at others instead of looking at themselves. "It is my company's fault that I am in this mess" (implication: it is not my fault). "If the economy just had not tanked then we would be okay. People like me, the little people, cannot get ahead in this economy." Some of that anger might even be poured on the hapless service provider who is a safe, convenient target. But the vulnerability is there, the guilt is there, the sense of helplessness is there, whether or not the client wishes to own up to it. It is vital that Jane recognizes and engages vulnerability since it is deep, powerful, and very frightening to the client. As seen in both of my parents and the parents of my wife, it seems as though the fear of not having enough confronts many older adults in retirement.

---

4. 1 Tim 6:10 RSV.

5. For a deeper dialogue on the topic of scarcity, see Russo, *Soul of Money*, 43–66.

6. Quoted in Twist, *Soul of Money*, 97.

Many expressed beliefs and values are fueled by a denial or a fear of vulnerability. Thus to overtly take on a client's vulnerability is fraught with danger, something like playing with fire. Unless the client overtly indicates that he/she wants to explore this feeling, it is best for Jane to simply look at the client through "vulnerability glasses." Jane's response toward the client and the client's values and beliefs can informed and even sculpted by treating what is said with kindness and care knowing that they are treading on some deep, often unrecognized feelings that color everything that the client says and believes. Like recognizing the finitude of our bodies as we age, clients may also deny or rail against the limits that their financial resources place upon them.

THE THREE TOXIC MYTHS ABOUT MONEY

If a client believes, like Mary and John, that there is not enough money to last the rest of their lives, it might mean that they have accepted one or more of what Lynne Twist describes as the three toxic myths of money. It might be important to explore each of these myths with the client because any one of them on their own could be the lynch-pin of the client's anxiety and fear. The Three Toxic Myths are: 1) There is not enough; 2) More is better, and 3) That is just the way it is.[7]

Gigantic Lie #1: There Is not Enough.

Fear of not having enough money is based upon a belief that there is not enough money to go around and thus what one has must be protected and even hoarded. This myth about money suggests that financial viability is a matter of the survival of the fittest and the strongest. It fosters the belief that when it comes to money it is each one is on our own. Are not squirrels praised for gathering nuts for the coming winter when there are none to be found? Is it not prudent for every person to have a 401K as a hedge against being destitute in one's older years? Shouldn't older adults be prudent with their wealth since they are on a 'fixed income?" Money does not grow on trees, right? And yet, approaching financial issues from a belief in scarcity, from a belief that "there is not enough" can be debilitating and life-crushing. Lynne Twist describes this lie as playing musical chairs were participants compete for a chair knowing that there is one less than the number of players. Part of the fun of musical chairs is in the anxiety that is produced, which

7. Ibid., 48–55.

is fine for playing a game, but not so much fun for older adults who are concerned about money.[8] The fear of not having enough often drives people to spend more, desire more, seek more. It often causes them to perceive that their financial situation is worse than it really is.

I have met residents in retirement communities who continually fretted over not having enough money to live on but then, after they died, have left large sums to obscure family members. I remember one older adult who felt so insecure with her money that she did not allow herself the one luxury she craved: that of going to the hair dresser once a week. Sometimes the attitude of not having enough is caused by not understanding how money works in the real world. The clinical intervention might be as simple as developing a profit and loss statement noting the number of years it would take for investments and social security to run out. But for many older adults, some of whom have experienced real scarcity in life (i.e., the Depression) the fear of not having enough is emotional, not rational and thus cannot be lessened by cognitive means alone.

At the same time, the love of money, the desire for more, the belief that happiness requires a large enough bank account, masks something deeper: guilt, fear, and unfulfilled desire. When the need for more is expressed by John and Mary, perhaps it would be healthful for Jane to ask a simple question: "Why is having money so important to you? Of what are you afraid?" Often, usually, if the string of thought is followed the ultimate answer is our ego and the needs of our ego, not wanting to feel weak or incapable, or worse still, having people have pity on us.

Gigantic Lie #2: More is Better

Riches are not from abundance of worldly goods,
but from a contented mind.

—Mohammed PBUH[9]

A wealthy person is asked "In your view, at what point will you have enough money?" The person's simple reply was "Just a little more." This drive for more only fuels the fear of people like John and Mary, Jane's clients. They

8. Ibid., 49.
9. As quoted in Russo, *Money Keys*, 23.

fear that they do not have enough. But how much do they have already? How much has our culture of accumulation driven this fear? How much has our "throw away" society brought them to this place in their lives where they are confronted with the fact that they can no longer compete in the game of accumulating more. The game of "Keeping up with the Jones" leads us to define our lives, our worth, our "success" in terms of how much we have and how much we can hang on to.

In the Christian Scriptures, Jesus said: "A man's worth is not in the abundance of his possession."[10] Do people really need or even want everything that they have? One of the pains of entering a retirement community is that residents needs to downsize their living space and thus have to get rid of all sorts of stuff that they have accumulated over the years. But much of what some would call stuff is no longer simply stuff in the eyes of the resident. Instead each item is fraught with memories, even meaning and value. Some people see this downsizing process as a tragedy, crying over each item that must be left behind. Others, however, see this process as an unburdening, even a spiritual practice of weeding out the unneeded so that they might become aware of the freedom that this load-removing process creates. Because when the task is complete, when the resident has moved into the new, smaller home they are surrounded by the core of their lives having kept those things that are the most meaningful and fulfilling in their eyes. Gone might be the Van Gogh, but remaining are the photos of grandchildren and the wedding pictures that always bring a smile, or that special gift given by a spouse. They are surrounded by items that reflect the persons and events that have shaped and sculpted their lives.

The experience of divesting can also bring a sense of freedom, even peace. "It doesn't take as long to clean the house," exclaims one. "A few years ago," another said, "I was awakened by a small earthquake. Immediately I thought of my collection of music boxes. But then I remembered that I had given them to all of my family so I rolled over and went back to sleep." What did Porgy sing in Gershwin's *Porgy and Bess*: "I've got plenty of nothin' and nothin's plenty for me."[11] For many older adults those can be vital words by which to live.

10. Luke 12:15 RSV.

11. Gershwin's *Porgy and Bess*, quoted from www.oldielyrics.com/lyrics/brian_wilson/i_got_plenty_o_nuttin.html.

Gigantic Lie #3: That is Just the Way It Is

We have dreamed it: therefore it is. I have become convinced
that everything we think and feel is merely perception:
that our lives—individually and communally—are molded around
    such perception:
and that if we want to change, we must alter our perception.
When we give our energy to a different dream, the world is
    transformed.
To create a new world we must first create a new dream.

—John Perkins *The World As You Dream*[12]

Like Lie #2 above, Gigantic Lie #3 is also the result of a belief in scarcity. This lie says that everyone is stuck where they are and that there is nothing that can be done. Jane might hear from John and Mary: "I don't have enough money and that is just the way it is" or "If I can no longer play the game of accumulation, that is just the way it is" or "If I feel deflated and despairing over the loss of reputation and/or ego because of the lack of money, that is just the way it is. I am the victim of forces outside of myself. Without money I have no power to change my situation. These being my waning years I can't start over again like a younger person can do. I am just stuck with what I have, which is practically nothing."

That there is no way out of this difficult situation can be logical and even supported by what is seen and experienced by older persons. If I person can't hear, they can't hear and thus will feel left out of conversations. If a person is stricken with macular degeneration there is nothing that can be done but resign oneself to living a life that is by definition less-than. And it is this resignation, this inability to see beyond the present situation that makes a person feel hopeless, helpless, and cynical. So what can Jane do to engage John and Mary who are in such straits? The answer: reframe the situation by exploring what they continue to have, not what they don't have. Wealth, having enough, does not necessarily require more money than what we already have because we have rich resources that are more than money: meaning, love, giving, living positively, and the readiness to receive more such riches.

12. Quoted in Twist, *Soul of Money*, 174.

Two nurses (Highfield and Cason) provided a clinical model of spiritual needs that is helpful for all disciplines relating to older adults and very applicable to the discussion of "That's Just the Way it is." They suggest that there are four spiritual needs of the human person (note: not just the religious person). These spiritual needs are:

- Meaning and Purpose
- The Need to Give Love
- The Need to Receive Love
- The Need for an Open Future[13]

The first spiritual/human need, meaning and purpose provide a reason to live.[14] It was the philosopher Nietzsche who said: "He who has a why to live can bear with almost any how."[15] If I have a reason to get up in the morning I can deal with the lack of money in my life. If I have a reason to get up in the morning I can deal with any perception that I don't have enough money to complete my life. What is meaningful in life? The answer is in the eye of the beholder. Jane might choose to ask John and Mary where it is that they find meaning, purpose, and that sense of contented self. Anything can have meaning: having children, living in an intimate marital relationship, having valued friends with whom one can share what is on the heart, making lots of money, having lots of stuff. Meaning can come through gardening, playing golf, going to church, connecting with God though contemplative prayer. No action, no thing in life has intrinsic value. All meaning, all value, is attributed by the person themselves. Thus what is meaningful to one person might not be meaningful to another. The important question is however: from where and what do you gain your meaning?

The second spiritual/human need is "To Give Love" or to become aware that there is something or someone of importance that is beyond oneself and the needs of the moment. This must-in-life is often the least understood and the least explored of all four of the spiritual needs. Usually, when someone is in difficulty like John and Mary, the immediate response is to shower the person with care and concern. The person is hurting and there is a knee-jerk response to help. But what if the person really needs to be the giver and not the receiver? What if the issue in their life is not that they have too little money but that they have not given enough money and thus self away? "To Give Love" is to get outside the self and one's perceived need and

13. Highfield and Cason, "Spiritual Needs," 188.

14. See also James Ellor, chapter 2, "Finding Meaning in a Meaningless World."

15. Nietzsche, quoted at www.goodreads.com/quotes/137-he-who-has-a-why-to -live-for-can-bear.

consider the needs of another. Giving love might not mean giving money. It might be giving one's time, one's energy, one's attention, one's person. "To whom are you giving?" might be an important question for John and Mary to explore with Jane

The third spiritual/human need is "To Receive Love." Now this need might seem simple because everyone wants to be loved, right? Not really. For to allow a person to show love to you, you first have to be open to being loved. Being loved, and allowing oneself to be loved, can be frightening because it opens oneself to hurt and pain. If I allow you to love me, if I allow your love to become a part of me, you can then hurt me by leaving, by betraying, by ignoring, by loving another. In receiving love a person has to become vulnerable, open to sharing of oneself, open to allowing another person inside where one really lives. It can be downright frightening and paralyzing to receive love and much easier to deny one's vulnerability. Yet, it is a basic spiritual need of all human beings to be loved at least by one person. Without love a person can become despairing, hurtful, withdrawn, bitter, and even violent.

The final spiritual need is for "An Open Future." This is the need for a person to have hope even when the situation seems hopeless. This is the need to see a glimmer at the end of a dark tunnel that says that darkness is not the definition of life. For John and Mary, this is the need to transcend what is to embrace what is yet to come. What-is-to-come might be a financial windfall like winning the lottery. But more realistically it probably will come through the fulfillment of one or more of the other spiritual needs: acquiring meaning, loving another, being loved. These needs are the real needs of the human person. These needs are the doorway to quality of life meeting needs does not take money nor do they require money to fulfill. In fact, having lots of money might even be an impediment to fulfilling those needs as the heart of life becomes a focus on having and accumulating rather than on its creative use.

Jane would provide significant service if she explored these spiritual needs with her clients John and Mary. To be rich, as is having meaning in life, is in the eye of the beholder. Remember the last scene in that classic movie *It's a Wonderful Life*? Jimmy Stewart as George looks around at the many friends that are in his living room. Even with George's old house is still old, even though he still has money problems, his Medal-of-Honor brother makes a toast saying, "To my brother George: the richest man in town."[16] Such is the power of fulfilling the four spiritual needs of the human person. Remember the iconic speech made by Lou Gehrig of the New York Yankees

16. Quoted from http://www.imdb.com/title/tt0038650/quotes.

on his last day in baseball? He was stricken with ALS (which now bears his name) and struggling with the effects of the disease. Gehrig said, "I might have been given a bad break, but I've got an awful lot to live for."[17] A person can be poor in our understanding but rich in his understanding. They can envision light at the end of the tunnel even if we can see no light. "That's the Way it is" does not have to be defining for today or tomorrow.

Karen Russo, writes of twin girls, Positive-Little-Karen and Not-So-Positive-Little-Karen who wake up on their tenth birthday. They are told that there is a present for them in the barn. Expecting it to be a pony they rush out to find only a pile of manure. The Not-So-Positive-Little-Karen complains about never getting anything good for her birthdays. But the Positive Twin claps her hands and exclaims: "There must be a pony here somewhere!"[18] There is an old cliché that reminds us that "Sh_t Happens." When life turns brown, dirty and smelly we can choose what the event means. We can choose only to see the pile of sh_t, or we can begin to look for the pony. The future is as open if we wish it to be.

THE ROLE OF THE SERVICE PROVIDER

What is the role of the lawyer, social worker, therapist, nurse, clergyperson as they engage older adults regarding the role of money in their lives? How can they facilitate a discussion without imposing their perspective, or any other perspective for that matter, on the client(s)?

Hint #1: Don't Try to Fix the Problem

The first and most important hint is to stifle the knee-jerk response that is inherent within any service profession dealing with older adults: the need to fix the problem. The truth is that no provider can fix any problem in another person. That person, no matter what their age or condition, is the only person who has the power and the knowledge to solve the problem. The client comes to a professional not for answers but insight, perspective, and a way of becoming aware of what is already present within them. They have the power to choose their reactions, interpretations, attitudes, and responses to life and create meaning out of our experiences. This perspective is especially important to remember when dealing with late-life dwindling

17. Said at Lou Gehrig Appreciation day at Yankee Stadium, on July 4, 1939 after having been diagnosed with ALS. See http://www.baseball-almanac.com/quotes/quogehr.shtml.

18. Russo, *Money Keys*, 64.

resources. How we respond grows out of our conscious and unconscious core beliefs.[19] Clients have the power to create meaning in their lives that is "meaning-management," which is as important as "money-management."[20]

Hint #2: Limitations and Vulnerabilities are Doorways to Wholeness

Sometimes our beliefs about money
are based upon a period of life
that that is no longer true.

—Cameron, *The Prosperous Heart*

People don't like limits on their freedom. Nor do people of any age like to feel vulnerable. And yet, it is these things that we so diligently avoid or deny that lead us to a new plan of living, a new sense of connection, a greater belief in self, a more solid experience of connection with others. To put it simply: Limitations and vulnerabilities are doorways to wholeness. Remember the famous paradigm voiced by the philosopher Hegel: Thesis, Antithesis, and Synthesis.[21] Thesis is the starting point: what the client has believed to be true, lasting, and reliable like, "If I am careful about spending I will have enough money for the rest of my life." But then a new experience or new information arises: a stock market crash, a house loses value, or there are unexpected health care expenses and the old thesis no longer seems valid. The client enters a state of antithesis that challenges the once reliable thesis. Internal conflict arises and personal confidence plummets, sending them to the provider's office where, hopefully, insight will come that leads to a synthesis of the old belief and the new experience. Thus answers to money problems are not found by denying or avoiding the pain that the problems cause. Instead wholeness, truth, and self are found by entering the pain, allowing the pain to reveal inner resources and by evaluating long held beliefs that at one time worked but no longer in this time and this situation. In the 1970s and 1980s there was a fad called values clarification whereby

19. For a more detailed discussion, see Paul Dobies, chapter 3, "Spirituality and the Brain: We See Only in Part."

20. Russo, *Money Keys*, 54.

21. Hegel, *Phenomenology of the Spirit*.

participants would enter into an existential process whereby they are able to get in touch with what they value in life. The process in the provider's office is like a giant personal process of value-clarification in which the person end up confirming the old beliefs or adopting new ones. The important realization is that the beliefs and values that come out of the crucible of not having enough money are the client's personal "property" for this time and this place. The challenges of aging, no matter what they might be, are "one of the ways the soul nudges itself into attention to the spirit. Aging and its challenges forces us to decide what is important in life."[22]

Hint #3: Watch Your Language

How something is said is often more important than what is said. A valuable insight can be lost due to a word or phrase that triggers a reaction that is different than the one that is expected. A couple of examples come from Stueve.[23]

- Clients are people with complex problems, not problem people. Use language that validates their efforts, passion and desires. Before they entered an office they have already tried to solve the issue but their efforts and ideas haven't worked.

- Good personal connecting begins with humility, a willingness to learn from the experience and insights that can be found in older adults, even those with money problems. Good personal connecting requires an openness to listen without judgment or arrogance.

- Ask "What happened?" rather than "What is wrong with you?" or just "What's wrong?" Don't see them as diminished because they have money problems. We all do, even service providers.

- Be conversational, a person of calm in a sea of crisis and chaos. Some people call it being a "non-anxious presence" that not only allows the client to vent emotions but models a calm exploration of the situation.

- Use the language of the client rather than language and professional terminology that was learned in school. For example, match the client's tone and idiom. If the client uses slang the provider might want to use it as well. The point is that if the client's language is used, the client will understand, which is the point, right?

22. Moore, *Care of the Soul*, 216.
23. Stueve, "Companioning People."

- Recognize and affirm the client's assets, strengths and resources. They have been and probably will be the client's best way of addressing the situation. It is easier to say "That's very perceptive" or "I like your creativity" or even "I knew that you would come up with something that will help you survive."

- Contrary to much "professional advice" consider stripping away some of your personal insulation. Professionals are taught to be just that: professional, stingy about sharing feelings and experiences about the role of money in their own lives. This advice is based on enabling the professional to be more objective than emotional. However, see the client's situation as an opportunity for you to learn, for you to go deeper into yourself, for you to evaluate long held beliefs of which you might or might not be aware. Don't be afraid to disclose something of yourself as long as you are comfortable doing so and it is helpful for the client and not your own cathartic musings.

- Companion the client. Enter into his/her humanity from the place of your own humanity. "You are not alone in this experience, I am here for you" can go a long way towards building confidence and trust.

- Get in touch with their core values and beliefs. Help them think about choices and options. Strategies for such engagement are in the next section but words like the following might bear fruit: "If you made this decision, what would it be like?" or "If you could wave a magic wand, what would life be like?"

- Many people going through financial crisis feel little control over their situation. They feel that any authority that is supposed to help are distant and out of touch with little understanding of their situation. Often they will express deep negative feelings about self and/or others. So remember:

  1. The present is most important. Guide conversation towards staying in the present. Some episodes of crisis demand immediate action but some do not. Be discerning.

  2. Assist the client to see the forest instead of the trees.

  3. Again, don't try to fix. Only the client can fix.

- Be careful not to get too far ahead of the client in thought or outcome. Again, the provider is a guide who leads the client to self-discovery. While providing information may be part of the focus, it is not the objective of interactions.

ENGAGING THE CLIENT ABOUT MONEY

How can a provider like Jane engage client(s) about money since money is one of the personal and guarded parts of the human person? Engaging the client about money takes time. To do an adequate job it might take as many as three one-hour sessions. Those sessions can be divided into three: 1) gathering personal information and family-of-origin questions, 2) Judith Peck's values-clarification exercise, and 3) Judith Peck's process-clarification exercise.

Session One: Gathering Personal Information and Family-of-Origin Questions

Money is like an iron ring
we put through our nose.
It is now leading us around wherever it wants.
We just forgot that we are the ones who designed it.

—Mark Kinney[24]

To begin with, gathering some personal information is quite standard in an intake process: name, address, email, phone, names and ages of persons living in the client's home, names and ages of family members living outside the client's home, names of parents and other who were part of the client's family-of-origin.

Second, listen to the client as the client expresses why they have sought assistance and how they feel about it. Remembering that you can't fix the problem, that limitations and vulnerabilities are doorways to wholeness, and that the language you use sets a tone. Share with the client some of your core principles regarding money. You might use Lynne Twist's three lies about money: 1) there is not enough, 2) more is better, and 3) that is just the way it is. Ask the client about their willingness to engage in a three session exploration of the role of money in their lives. If they are in agreement, begin by completing and then discussion the following questions:

---

24. Quoted in Twist, *Soul of Money*, 3.

Family-of-Origin Attitudes Regarding Money

1. When you were very young what do you remember about the place of money in your family?

2. As you got older, were you ever surprised to discover that your family did/did not have enough money?

3. As a child who made the money decisions in your family?

4. What role did other members in the family have regarding the use of money in your family of origin?

5. As a child, what did you have to do to receive family money for your own use?

6. How old were you when you received an allowance?

7. As a child, I perceived that my family was poor/middle class/upper class/rich.

8. What was the highest grade/degree achieved by your father? Mother?

9. Complete this sentence: One of the events of the past that has affected my view of money in my life was . . .

10. How did your family-of-origin feel about debt?

Session Two: Clarifying Values Regarding Money

Judith Peck, in *Money and Meaning: New Ways to Have Conversations about Money with Your Clients*, suggests that instead of offering solutions to the client's money problems, whether real or perceived, a change in the way of thinking about money should be presented. She advocates for a values-based approach that can be constantly revisited and revised. In the introduction to this book, spirituality was defined as core beliefs and values. It is these core beliefs that need to be explored. Only then can the client decide if his/her money woes are as life-threatening as they appear.

Again clients usually enter Jane's office steeped in cultural values and beliefs about money. At this point, those cultural values and beliefs are not working. So Peck suggests that instead of addressing the issue of money directly in cognitive ways through budget training, and education in economic values, that Jane help the client(s) become aware of their core values and beliefs. Then ask the client(s) if present behavior and feelings about match up to the goals in life inherent in the client's core beliefs and values, in other words, their spirituality. Peck suggests that there are three stages of talking about money.[25]

1. Make the person's value system explicit by raising those values into consciousness and clarifying them.

2. Apply the explicit values to financial decisions and address any inherent contradictions in the client's life.

3. If desired by the client and possible in this particular situation, transform the client's values around money.

4. The process of bringing a person's value system to awareness and consciousness is done through two card sort activities used over two one-hour sessions.[26] One set of cards explores values that drive our behavior and attitudes about money. The second set is designed to discover how financial decisions are made rather than why we make such decisions. Using the cards provides a neutral safe place to share values and attitudes about money because the clients feel that they are talking about what is on the cards not themselves directly. The values cards include areas of importance: education, work, philanthropy, relationships, material possessions, spirituality, financial responsibility, physical needs, personal values, public services, recreations, economics, and ethical values. Process card are: reflective thinking, inclusive values, exclusive values, dialogue, transparency, empowerment, and equality.

The process of using the cards is very simple.

- The client(s) are given time to look at the cards in order to become familiar with the content.

- The clients then sort the cards into two piles: Important Values and Unimportant Values.

- The clients are then instructed to that the "Important Values" pile and narrow it down to the top four values. This task can be difficult since the clients need to distinguish between core values and situational values. Core values inform behavior no matter what the situation (home, work, doing taxes, balancing the checkbook, deciding on a large purchase, i.e., new car, etc.). Situational values are more fluid. They exist for a specific period of time or a specific situation. For example, when

25. Peck, *Money and Meaning*, 13–20.

26. Providers can download both the values cards and the process cards at www.wiley.come/go/moneyandmeaning.

a problem arises the person can often confuse situational values with core values. Such a dichotomy usually ends up in behaviors that are not always expressive of core values. Remember there are no "right" answers only the client's answer. If the client has a spouse or a life-partner that person must participate in the exercise as well.

- A discussion is encouraged about the final four values that are chosen. Are there any surprises? What about the values that did not make the final cut to become one of the final four? If the client is a couple, what is different between the partners? What is similar?

Now for step two. The goal is to explore what values effected a recent financial decision.

1. Reshuffle all of the cards

2. Picture one of the most recent financial decisions.

3. With that picture in mind, again divide the values cards into two piles: important and unimportant.

4. Take the important pile and continue to sort until the final four values that effected the recent financial decision are revealed.

5. Is there alignment or discrepancy between the values that were chosen in part one and part two? Talking about any alignment and/or discrepancy reveals the link between money and core beliefs. The client(s) is asked to interpret the final four with the feelings/experience surrounding his/her struggle with money. Which of the final four have anything to do with money? How could those core values be fulfilled without money? What does the client's core values as revealed above say about the feeling of scarcity that often drives financial insecurity and fear? If not, what is more important than money? What does this exercise reveal about the place of money in life?

Session Three: Clarifying Values of Financial Decision-Making

In session three, the same process is followed as in the second session. The only difference is the use of the process cards instead of the values cards. Again, the goal is to reveal core ways in which decisions are made both in a general way and by picturing a recent financial decision, how financial decisions are made. Providers like Jane might not feel as though they have the time for Peck's process. It probably does require three sessions, one to secure personal information and receive the client's initial perspective(s) regarding their money issues. The second two sessions, however, are also helpful and instructive to older adults. Perhaps a staff person can be trained to conference with the clients in session two and three giving Jane a summary of what was accomplished. Part of the training might be reading a couple of books from the bibliography as personal preparation. Of the entire list I would choose Twist, *The Soul of Money* and Russo, *The Money Keys*. No matter how it is done, exploring attitudes about money is both vital and time consuming. That's just the way it is.

One of the blessings of later life is coming to the realization that all of the trinkets in our life have been fun to possess but they do not define us. There is more to our life than "stuff" even if that stuff is money. Personhood is found in our core beliefs, our core values, our spirituality. Our intrinsic value comes not from our checkbook but from within us as we live by what we believe and value. For some people these beliefs and values are expressed in religion and religious practice. For others that core is articulated through music, or art, or building big buildings, or being an important cog in our country's economic machine by driving a truck or planting and harvesting food. Yes, money and the making of money is an important part of life. But is it the essential part of life, particularly for Jane's client(s)? Only the client(s) can answer that question, but any provider of older adult services can provide significant support in the client(s) discovery of what is fundamental for them.

In closing I have two offerings, one a story, the other a prayer. I hope that both are received as they are offered: as an expression and a summary of much that has been shared in this chapter.

A STORY ABOUT LIFE AND POSSESSIONS

Recently a family put up a hummingbird feeder with four feeding stations. Almost immediately, it became popular with the hummingbirds that lived in the area. Two, three, or even four birds would feed at one time. The feeder would be refilled at least once a day.

Suddenly the usage decreased to almost nothing. The feeder needed filling only about once a week. The reason for the decreased usage soon became apparent. A male bird had taken over the feeder as his property. He was now the only hummingbird who used it. He would feed and then sit in a nearby tree, rising to attack any bird that approached his feeder. Guard duty occupied his every waking hour. He was an effective guard. The only time another bird got to use the feeder was when the self-appointed owner was momentarily gone to chase away an intruder.[27]

That hummingbird was teaching a valuable lesson. By choosing to assume ownership of the feeder, he forfeited his freedom. He was no longer free to come and go as he wished. He was tied to the work of guarding his feeder, his *stuff*. He was possessed by his possessions.

The following prayer by the Christian mystic and noted author on spirituality and prayer, Henri Nouwen, expresses much of what has been said throughout this chapter and, I believe, an appropriate stance for all to take, older adults as well as their service providers.

> Dear God/Spirit of the Universe/Creator/Allah/G_d
> I am so afraid to open my clinched fists!
> Who will I be when I have nothing left to hold on to?
> Who will I be when I stand before you with empty hands?
> Please help me to gradually open my hands
> and to discover that I am not what I own,
> but what you want to give me.[28]

REFERENCES

Cameron, Julia. *The Prosperous Heart: Creating a Life of "Enough."* New York: Penguin, 2010.

Hegel, Georg Fredrick. *The Phenomenology of the Spirit.* Translated by J. B. Baillie. N.p.: Digigreads, 2010.

Highfield, M. E., and C. Cason. "Spiritual Needs of Patients: Are They Recognized?" *Cancer Nursing* 6/3 (June 1983) 187–92.

Peck, Judith Stern. *Money and Meaning: New Ways to Have Conversations About Money with Your Clients.* Hoboken, NJ: Wiley, 2008.

Moody, Harry, and David Carroll. *The Five Stages of the Soul.* New York: Anchor, 1997.

Moore, Thomas. *The Care of the Soul.* New York: HarperCollins, 1992.

Mueller, Steve. "11 Wise Lessons—Essential Wisdom for Life." August 15, 2012. http://www.planetofsuccess.com/blog/2012/11-wise-lessons/.

Nouwen, Henri. *The Only Necessary Thing: A Prayerful Life.* New York: Crossroads, 1999.

Russo, Karen. *The Money Keys: Unlocking Peace, Freedom and Real Financial Power.* Scottsdale, AZ: Life Success, 2007.

Shinn, Florence Scoval. *The Complete Works of Florence Scoval Shinn.* Mineola, NY: Dover, 2010.

Stueve, Barry. "Companioning People in the Culture of Poverty." Web seminar sponsored by the Association of Professional Chaplains, July 25, 2013.

27. Unpublished sermon, Rev. Lyn Crow, Emmanuel Episcopal Church, Fullerton, CA. October 13, 2013.

28. Nouwen, *Only Necessary Thing.*

Twist, Lynne. *Soul of Money: Transforming Your Relationship with Money and Life.* New York: Norton, 2003.

12

Death and Dying
The Final Act of Living

—G. Jay Westbrook, MSG

PURPOSE

The purpose of this chapter is to use stories, case studies, vignettes, and narratives in the style of Native American storytellers to:

1. comfort the disturbed, and disturb the comfortable

2. present a number of common and not-so-common end-of-life situations

3. offer an array of "take home and use today" spiritual tools, stories, approaches, and perspectives for your consideration—arrows in your quiver, if you will—for which you might reach when encountering similar end-of-life situations

4. inspire you, whomever you might be, whatever discipline or role(s) you might occupy, to incorporate the spiritual—always—into your work

5. encourage you to pause, if only for a moment, to see on which side of the door the hinges are located (more on this later), for in the momentary pause we find the always and forever of now, the alpha and omega of now, the living and dying of now.

INTRODUCTION

I'm not sure why, but I'm feeling moved to begin and end this chapter with stories of dying prisoners, and the spirituality with which they die, and/or the spiritual experience they afford others.

And please don't worry that this chapter will focus solely on the currently or formerly incarcerated. Sandwiched between their stories will be many stories of the never-incarcerated, and the spiritual tools they and I have employed, at various points, as we co-journeyed towards their death.

A MURDERER SEEKS REDEMPTION: WHO'S SUFFERING SPIRITUALLY? WHO HAS THE SPIRITUAL DILEMMA?

Our patient had committed murder as a young man, served thirty-five years behind bars, been a free man for thirteen years, and was now in our hospital—dying with an agonizing metastatic cancer.

As clinical director of the hospital's Palliative Care Service, I'd been called in to specifically address his extensive pain-management issues. The moment I stepped off the elevator, I heard muffled screams, screams that became louder and louder as I neared our patient's room. A blanket taped over the patient's door, and moistened towels under his door, did little to contain the sounds of his suffering from the physical pain of his cancer.

Once I looked at the chart, the problem was obvious; there were absolutely no pain medications being given to this man. I entered his room, to assess his pain and have a conversation, prior to commencing his pain management.

In conversation, our patient revealed that he had refused all pain medication, and that he intended to continue to do so. He was lucid, understood the consequences of his decision, and possessed decision-making capacity. Of course, the question was why he would make such a choice.

He explained that his God was a judgmental, unforgiving, and punishing God, and he knew that after his death God would have him suffer horribly, for an eternity, because of the murder he committed. His thinking was that if he could suffer enough here, while still alive, it might reduce the post-death suffering for which he knew he was destined.

Once this information was available to the team, each discipline—physicians, nurses, chaplains, and social workers—offered support, but tried to convince him that he was wrong: his choice was wrong, his concept of God was wrong, his way of trying to right the scales was wrong, his suffering was wrong, etc. People spoke of how much he was suffering, not just physically, but spiritually and existentially, and spoke of his spiritual dilemma. Finally, some people shook their heads and commented on how sad it was that this man had failed to discover the loving and forgiving nature of God.

There's so much going on in this story. It seems to me that great spiritual arrogance was being practiced, of the "my concept of God is right, and yours is wrong" variety, and it was being practiced by both "sides." Rigid beliefs, closed minds, and hardened hearts are seldom compatible with new vision or new experience. My favorite Herbert Spencer quote is: "There is a principle which is a bar against all information, which is proof against all arguments, and which cannot fail to keep a man in everlasting ignorance—that principle is contempt prior to investigation."[1]

I do not believe that our patient had a spiritual dilemma, nor do I believe he was suffering spiritually. He had a spiritual situation—how to reduce his post-death suffering. He had a spiritual solution—balance the scales by enduring some physical suffering here. His situation and solution were compatible with his belief system and his value system, and he was convinced that his solution would work. Therefore, he embraced his physical suffering, and was pleased to be able to use that physical suffering to accomplish his spiritual goals.

I believe it was the clinical team members who were suffering spiritually and who had the spiritual dilemma. Their dilemma was "how do we convince someone, who is resistant to our intervention, to allow us to end their needless suffering?" when in fact, the patient saw his suffering as "needed," not "needless." We do not get to determine for another what is needed or what is needless. The team's spiritual suffering came out of our difficulty accessing the great humility, compassion, and restraint required to bear witness to another's suffering, and do no more unless invited to do so. This situation demanded that we lay down our tool kits, and simply sit with a compassionate presence, for ourselves, for our patient, and for all who suffer.

Finally, our patient died the death as he wanted: in exquisite pain and physical suffering. He died teaching us about compassionate presence and bearing witness. I can only pray his suffering accomplished the "righting of the scales" he was so convinced would occur.

1. Most commonly attributed to Herbert Spencer in the book, *Alcoholics Anonymous*. It was used exactly as written about in the personal stories section of the first edition in 1939 and in "Appendix II: Spiritual Experience" in all subsequent editions.

MY STORY
THE BROKEN ROAD BECOMES A SPIRITUAL JOURNEY

I was raised in a devoutly atheist home. I had drilled into my head that there is no God, that God is nothing more than a technique invented to control the masses, and that belief in any God would just make me weak.

My mother abandoned the family when I was five months old. My father remarried just as I turned three, and he and my stepmom wanted to focus on careers. So they placed me in the home of "friends of the family." For the next three years I was tortured, raped, beaten, and isolated on a daily basis in that home. I lived, slept, ate, and toileted in a pitch-black closet and was taken out once daily to be washed, beaten, and raped by three adult perpetrators.

When I finally was pulled out of that situation, I was pretty broken, and continued to be a target for perpetrators. As I grew up, I turned to alcohol and drugs to medicate my feelings. They helped, but made me stupid and led to bad decision-making, and those decisions put me in front of a power greater than myself. He wore a flowing black robe, slammed his gavel down, and sentenced me to state prison. Although I thought of myself as a tough guy, it took only five hours before I was gang-raped for the first time, and it continued throughout my incarceration.

Upon my release, I was broken on every level on which a man can be broken—physically, emotionally, and spiritually. I was filled with self-pity, self-righteousness, judgment, blame, shame, and cowardice. I was not a vision for you. I blamed a God, in whom I did not believe, for everything bad that had happened to me—as a child, and as a young man.

After prison, I acquired an education, and earned lots of letters after my name, as well as professional success and respect. I simultaneously lived with a deep-seated spiritual malady of "no God." That malady produced a larger and larger God-sized hole in my gut that I tried to fill with substances and behaviors that weren't God, and that left me increasingly more miserable. Finally, on the day of a well-planned suicide, I picked up the phone, called a twelve-step hotline, and within ninety minutes I was in a twelve-step meeting for the first time. And in that meeting, I felt the breath of a God, in whom I did not believe, blowing on me with a gentleness that I had not earned and did not deserve. I called that breath of God "Grace." That was December 2, 1988, and I have been clean and sober since that first meeting.

While the God consciousness did not stick, I did become a struggling seeker. I realized the immaturity of my spiritual past: praying to a God in whom I did not believe ("Please God, get me out of this one," or "Please God, don't let the liquor store close before I get there.") and blaming a God in whom I did not believe for everything bad that had ever happened to me, while crediting him for none of the good.

My first sober God—or more correctly, my first God in sobriety—was just the "Group Of Drunks" in my twelve-step meeting. Then God became the mercy, compassion, and love in my heart. I remember speaking at a meeting on skid row, and telling of my childhood incest, prison trauma, and my current struggle to find a personal God. After the meeting, an old, dirty, stinky, toothless, homeless woman approached me and queried whether she could ask me a question, to which I replied, "of course." She then said, "What must it be like for such a nice young man like you to have to wear diapers?" "Lady, I don't wear diapers," I replied with some irritation, to which she said, "Well, I heard what you said happened when you weren't nothin' but a little boy, and what those men did to you in the jail house, and that must have torn you up down there [gesturing]—how could you not wear diapers, unless [pause] there is a God?" She then cackled like a witch, turned, and walked away. I was speechless. Upon consideration, I decided I did not want her God, one that would allow me to be raped as a child, but would spare me the humiliation of having to wear diapers. However, what she did give me was the pause, the gift of uncertainty about my simple concept of God, and the certainty that there was a God and that it was not me.

At the same time, I moved into bedside end-of-life work, and it quickly and undeniably became clear that the place where life and death meet is filled with God. I acquired many Buddhist tools to use in my work, but continued to seek a personal God that "worked" for me, given my childhood, prison, and other experiences. I finally found a God, one who is omnipresent and all loving, but who does not intervene, a God who designed us perfectly, but gave us free will, a God who co-journeys with me and who co-suffers with me, a God who looked at me being raped at three, four, and five years old and wept at my suffering, but who looked at my rapists and wept just as hard at their suffering, at each of them having moved so far from his grace. This God resonated with me, made sense in light of my experiences, and allowed a deeply personal relationship. I know today that God created me with everything I needed for resiliency, and created my rapists with everything they needed for redemption; I pray they reached for it. I know I did.

My favorite country western group is Rascal Flatts, my favorite song "Bless the Broken Road."[2] While I would never wish my background on anyone, you could not get me to give it up. It is the "Broken Road," my "Broken

2. Boyd, Robert E., Marcus Hummon, and Jeff Hanna. "Bless the Broken Road." Originally sung by the Nitty Gritty Band, more recently by Rascal Flatts. For lyrics and a Rascal Flatts performance, see http://www.azlyrics.com/lyrics/rascalflatts/blessthebrokenroad.html.

Road," that led me straight to God. Also, the telling of my story, usually in the third person, has been invaluable in working with dying and grieving patients who are attached to a "why me?" or "it's not fair" posture.

Two final things come to mind: I was at a twelve-step meeting in Branson, Missouri listening to messages of recovery being delivered in an accent my ears were not used to hearing, and at a pace far slower than my ears were used to listening. However, I clearly heard one of the attendees when he shared, "God doesn't call the equipped; rather, he equips the called." I have shared this wisdom with many of my patients, and their families, and they have found comfort in that thought.

Finally, I love the link between these first two stories. In mine (the second), I speak of finding a God who is a co-journeying, non-intervening co-sufferer. My personal experience with that God, both equipped and allowed me—as described in the first story—to "access the great humility, compassion, and restraint required to bear witness to another's suffering, and [to] do no more . . . [to] simply sit with a compassionate presence, for ourselves, for our patient, and for all who suffer." "God bless the broken road that led me straight to you."

COME BEFORE WINTER—A METAPHOR FOR NOW

Historically, "come before winter" were the words written by the disciple Paul in the Christian Scriptures, while in prison in Rome. He asked another disciple, Timothy, to bring him blankets and something to write with and something to write on. He also asked simply for Timothy's presence and companionship.

In my [end-of-life] work, "come before winter" has come to mean "say it now" or "do it now," whatever "it" might be. In other words, say or do it now, because you may never again have the chance. And, if things progress more slowly than anticipated, you can say or do them again. But, if things progress more quickly, the opportunity to say or do them may disappear.

It's not a bad way to lead our lives, to stay thoroughly current and "complete" with others, especially loved ones, leaving nothing important unsaid or put off until later. We have this moment, and this moment alone; all the rest is uncertain. Seize the moment. Come before winter.

Reframing—A Life so Sweet, A Life too Short

Reframing is one of the most important tools I have with which to address suffering—mine or that of others. Reframing is simply finding another way to tell the story, another way to look at the situation. And, whenever possible, a way in which—at the least—I am not a victim, and—at the most—where I am a hero (although not all stories lend themselves to this "victim to hero" transformation—case in point).

At five months into their first pregnancy, a young (nineteen and twenty), married, (very) Catholic couple came to the hospital for a prenatal checkup. They were close to their God, comforted, strengthened, and sustained by that God. They maintained a deep personal relationship with him. After the checkup, they were told that their baby would be born with a heart defect that would take his life in hours to days, and that it was untreatable. They were then given the option of terminating the pregnancy. They declined that option saying they wanted their baby to be born so that he could have an identity.

The Palliative Care Service should have been notified at that point, so that we would have had four months to work with this young family on their anticipatory grief. Four months later, on a Tuesday afternoon, we were told that a woman was delivering a full-term baby who would die very soon, and were asked to provide bereavement support. The baby was baptized in the delivery room, placed on DNR (Do Not Resuscitate) status and, while appearing healthy, was moving quickly towards death.

We spent Tuesday evening and most of Wednesday and Thursday with this young family. We were able to send them home early Friday morning with pediatric hospice, and the baby died late Friday night—never having known anything but love, sweetness, being held, and being sung to his entire, sweet—but far too short—life.

On Thursday, while still at the hospital, mom handed the baby off to dad and asked me if we could speak in the hallway. She led the way out of the room and part way down the hall. She then whirled, and half screaming, half sobbing, wailed "Why? Why would God take my baby, my only baby? He must hate me, and I hate him." At that point, she was crying too hard to move any more words out. I waited a moment, led with a defense-lowering statement, and then provided this reframing: "I could be wrong, but is it possible that it's the heart defect taking your baby's life, and God will be there to receive him?" I wanted to say so much more, but I needed to be silent so she could process what I had offered. It took almost fifteen seconds, and she then embraced the reframing I had offered. At a time when she most needed her God, instead of being in an adversarial relationship with that God, she was back in a loving and supported relationship with him.

I am not a scholar of Catholicism, and to this day do not know if what I offered was accurate: does God take, or does the disease take and God receives? What I do know is that I said, "I could be wrong" and "is it possible?"

and those allowed me comfort in what I offered, and gratitude that my re-framing allowed her to be back in a loving relationship with her God.

A Parable of Faith, Still Making the Rounds

Over the years, I have heard this fable many times, with various settings and details, but the message is always simple and clear:

A sick man turned to his doctor, as the doctor was preparing to leave the exam room and said, "Doctor, I'm afraid to die. Tell me what lies on the other side."

Very quietly, the doctor said, "I do not know."

"You don't know? You're a Christian man and a physician, and you don't know what's on the other side?"

The doctor was holding the handle of the door, from the other side of which came a sound of scratching and whining. As the doctor opened the door, a dog sprang into the room and leaped on him with an eager show of glee and affection.

Turning to the patient, the doctor said, "Did you observe my dog's behavior? He's never been in this room before; he didn't know what was inside. He knew nothing except that his master was here, and when the door opened, he sprang in without fear, without hesitation.

So, I know little of what is on the other side of death, but I do know one thing—I know my Master is there, and that is enough."

This is a powerful and quick story to use with a person who is trying to "figure it out," who wants to know the facts, who believes that they have to understand it all and be certain, and to control what's happening. It reminds me of the Buddhist saying, "relax, nothing is under control."

A Mom's Rugged Dying—Changed by her Children and Tibetan Buddhist Ah Breath

The overhead speakers requested—no, demanded—"Palliative Care to 2-Northeast; Palliative Care to 2-Northeast." My Palliative Care coordina-tor, Carmen, and I arrived a few minutes later. The charge nurse said, "the new patient, a young woman, in room 5 is dying; her family's in there, and we don't know what to do. Can you help?"

A quick look at the chart revealed a stage 4 cancer that had spread to the lungs, a prognosis of imminent death, and both oxygen and as-needed pain medication orders in place. A quick look at the patient revealed a young woman (twenty-nine years old), in pain, wearing an oxygen mask, terrified, wide-eyed, suffering, actively dying and panting rapidly—both because of her high degree of anxiety and the tumor burden in her lungs. She was staring across the room, at her family—husband, six-year-old son and eight-year-old daughter—who were standing against the far wall, looking equally terrified and wide-eyed, and suffering in their separation from the person they loved, as well as their inability to help.

Carmen escorted the family into the hallway where we could speak with them, and I assured the patient that we would quickly make her comfortable, and then bring her family back to her. Two minutes later, orders were in place for more morphine, both for pain and to ease her breathing, and to replace her oxygen mask—which was separating her from her family—with little nasal canullas, as no amount of oxygen would make a difference in her imminent outcome.

We asked the family if they knew what was going on, and both kids answered, "yes, mommy has cancer." We then asked if they knew what was happening, and the daughter responded, "my mom is going to die." When we asked if they knew when she was going to die, again both children whispered "soon." With the asking and answering of those three questions, we knew the family's knowledge level, and knew we could speak to them very directly.

We told the family they were correct, and that while we couldn't change the fact that their mommy/wife was dying, we could teach them some things they could do that would help their mom/wife die much more gently, and they indicated a strong desire to be taught those tools.

First, we explained the importance of saying those things that were deep and important, but which may have gone previously unsaid—things like "I love you, I'm sorry for . . . I forgive you for . . . I don't know if I ever said how proud I was when you . . . or I don't know if I ever said how much I appreciated the way you always . . ." We also told them that while those messages were best delivered one-on-one, we would be pleased to accompany the kids if they wanted us to.

Immediately, the eight-year-old daughter said, "I want to go first, and I want to go alone." She walked bravely into her mom's room and came back out, several minutes later, with tears running down her cheeks. The husband went next, also alone, and also returned several minutes later with tears running down his cheeks. The six-year-old son went last, and asked me to accompany him. He tentatively entered the room, told his mom how much he loved her, and that he was sorry for stealing change from her purse.

We regrouped in the hallway, and decided to teach this family the "Ah Breath" practice—a Tibetan Buddhist breathing practice to enhance bonding and connectedness. It also has a "side effect" of slowing and making more even the listener's breathing. While changing her breathing pattern was important, the primary purpose of the exercise was the bonding and connectedness, especially with someone who felt distant and unreachable in the moment.

As this family was Korean and Methodist, we chose to omit "Tibetan" and "Buddhist" from our description of the practice, and just described it as "a breathing exercise that will help you help mommy." I said, "When we go back into the room, I want you to get up on the bed, and just watch mommy's breathing. When you see the pattern of her breathing, try to match yours to hers—when she breathes in, you breathe in; when she breathes out, you breathe out. And, if she's breathing too fast for you to keep up, then it's okay for you to breathe once in the same time that she takes two or three little breaths. Then, when you've matched your breathing to hers, I want you to make the 'Ah' sound on your out breath—not a little whispered 'Ah,' but a big 'Ah' that rides out on your breath so that mommy can hear it. Do you think you can do that?" All three shook their heads "yes."

We entered the room, and the kids climbed up on the bed and took their mom's hands—the daughter holding mom's left hand, the son her right. The husband stood behind the kids, his left hand on his wife's right shoulder, and his right hand on his children. They commenced the exercise—first observing mom's breathing, then matching it—and then, tentatively at first, then more confidently and with greater volume, making the "Ah" sound on their out breaths. As Carmen and I backed out of the room, we heard three voices, chanting over and over, progressively more and more slowly, "Ah"—"Ah"—"Ah"—"Ah"—"Ah." The slowing of their "Ahs" told us that mom's breathing was slowing and becoming more even, exactly as we had told them it would in response to the Ah Breath practice. Then, the sounds stopped, and we knew this young wife and mother had died. Her husband and children walked out of the room in tears, never acknowledged us, and simply walked off the unit and out of the hospital. The nurses entered the room, and in a kind and dignified manner, do what nurses do at such a time.

Fast-forward three weeks: Carmen and I were sitting in the Palliative Care office, and heard a knock. It was the husband/father of the above story. We greeted one another, and then the room fell silent as he looked deeply into our eyes. His chin commenced to quiver, tears spilled from his eyes, and he fought to maintain composure sufficient to allow him to get his words from his heart to his mouth to our ears. He said, "Three weeks ago, you did what the doctors and the nurses had been unable to do. You changed the way my wife died. And perhaps even more importantly, you changed—forever—my children's lives. When you found us, we were all suffering, across the room from one another, frightened, and separated. In just a few moments, you taught my children how to change the way their mother died; she died tenderly and gently, and that is because of what you taught them to do. Their lives will never be the same, will always be richer, and we are forever in your debt. How can we repay you?" Through my tears, I responded, "you just have."

A Mother's "Hate and Abandonment"— Transformed Through the Gift of Uncertainty

There was a man who got sober in Alcoholics Anonymous when he was in his early thirties. While he stayed sober, he was very slow to work the steps, and even slower to work his ninth step—the step in which alcoholics make direct amends to those they've harmed.

Over the years, he seemed very attached and eager to share his story. It was a story of how his mother abandoned him, failed to protect him, hated him, and loved his older brother more than she loved him. The story was told with such regularity, that many listeners felt they could recite the story themselves.

When the man was about nine years sober, he discovered his mother was dying of cancer, and was motivated to go see her and make his ninth-step amends. He said to her, "I used the things you did when I was a child—favoring my brother, abandoning me to boarding school, failing to protect me from school yard bullies, and hating me—as an excuse to justify my bad behavior. I was withholding, punishing, judgmental, bitter, unforgiving, and gossiped about your bad behavior to anyone who would listen. It was wrong for me to do those things, and I apologize. It is my intent to not repeat these behaviors. Are there any other ways I've harmed you, and what can I do to set right these wrongs?"

With tears in her eyes, but not traveling down her face, his mother replied. She said, "Oh sweetheart, you have it so wrong. After your father died, I remarried, and the man I married was a monster. He beat me mercilessly and sexually ravaged your older brother. As you grew older, I knew you were next, and that I couldn't stop him. So, I sent you to boarding school, not to abandon you, but to protect you. I did so because I loved you, not because I hated you. And I always loved you and your brother equally. Finally, as for what you can do to set right these wrongs, here's what you can do: in the couple months of life I have left, squeeze in everything you withheld from me over the decades with your arrogant certainty that I was a monster and you were a victim. When you figure out how to do that, call me."

He returned home and to his AA meetings. He spoke of feeling sad, defeated, humiliated, and worthless. To make it worse, his mother died two weeks later, far more quickly than expected. I did some grief work with him, and he fell in love with some words I had written: "As sobriety became a way of life, humility and curiosity conspired to steal my certainty and to provide the gift of uncertainty, from which softness, openness, humor, and opportunity flowed." He commenced to become attached to his new story, that his amends had done more harm than good, and had actually led to his mother's accelerated death. I was able to help him see that "certainty" was his problem, that he was just applying it to a different story line, and that his solution was to embrace the gift an uncertainty. He has finally been able to recognize the corrosive nature of certainty, and slowly moved closer to valuing that which uncertainty allows and fosters.

A Near-Drowning—Language of the Heart and Locating the Hinges

Southern California Septembers can be brutally hot, and Labor Day weekend 2006 was no exception. The problem with triple-digit heat is that the swimming pools call to the children, and sadly, they respond—sometimes with tragic results. Our story revolves around a family of a mom, a dad, and five daughters.

The Friday before Labor Day, the second eldest daughter left to commence her first year at university the following Tuesday. On Saturday, mom, dad, and the eldest daughter went off to work, leaving their eleven-year-old, four-year-old, and nineteen-month-old (Leanna) at home. In spite of the eleven-year-old's maturity, they asked two teenage girls from next door to babysit.

They were in and out of the pool through the morning, but as the day—and the heat—progressed, the two teenage girls said, "we're going inside to watch videos with the baby." Assuming they meant Leanna, the eleven-year-old stopped being vigilant. Fifteen minutes later, she walked in the house, saw the two babysitters watching videos with the four-year-old, and commenced a panicked search for her youngest sister, whom she found at the bottom of the hot tub.

The eleven-year-old screamed for 911, pulled her sister from the hot tub, and started CPR, to no avail. Paramedics arrived and were also unable to resuscitate Leanna. They transported her to the hospital, where she was placed on a ventilator and admitted to the pediatric ICU.

Over the next three days of observation and testing, it became clear that the near-drowning had permanently destroyed all but the slightest bit of brain stem activity, meaning Leanna was never coming back. Our Palliative Care Service was asked to lead the very difficult conversation with Leanna's family on Tuesday evening. After acknowledging the tragedy of the situation, we opened the meeting by saying, "It's important for you to understand that there are no right or wrong decisions here, no good or bad decisions, just decisions that more or less closely mirror your values as a family. We are going to describe each of the options you have, tell you about the benefits and burdens of each option, answer any and all of your questions, and at that point, you will be in a position to make an informed decision. And we promise you, whatever that decision is, we will honor and respect it." We then went on to describe their options in a manner that normalized each of the possible choices. We gave them both time and privacy, and accepted their unanimous decision to remove Leanna from the ventilator.

A light morphine drip was started, and Leanna was taken off the vent Tuesday night. We were with the family late into the night, all day and evening Wednesday, and returned very early Thursday morning. We were told Leanna had died about three hours earlier, and were again asked for our help. The ICU team said. "It's been three hours, and we can't get the parents to give up Leanna's body, in spite of having held her for too long." We said we'd see what we could do. Elizabeth (the Palliative Care therapist) and I walked to the door, looked to the left and to the right to see on which side of the door the hinges were located, and then entered the room. About three minutes later, mom and dad placed Leanna's body in my arms; Elizabeth put her arms around them, and walked them out of that room and out of the hospital. I continued to hold Leanna, thinking that if these grieving parents got to the elevator and turned around and came back, they would not find their daughter anywhere but where they had left her—in my arms.

About fifteen minutes later, Elizabeth returned. We placed Leanna in her bed and the nurses came in to again, kindly and with dignity, do what they had to do. As we exited the room, we were barraged with thanks and questions about how we were able to so quickly change the parents' minds. We asked for about twenty or thirty minutes to debrief, asked them to think of their questions and problems with this case, and told them we'd return in half an hour to debrief this difficult case and answer their questions.

When we returned, there were essentially three questions, asked in various ways, only two of which we were able to answer meaningfully. The one we felt we could not answer was, "when you're in a room, and a mother is sobbing uncontrollably over the impending death of her baby, how do you stay in the room?" The question was so foreign, that we were at a loss about how to answer it. All we could say was, "Somebody needs to bear witness to her suffering. Whether you watch quietly, with a compassionate presence, from across the room, or go to the mom and place your hand on her shoulder, or you whisper in her ear—and I trust you will intuitively know which of these is right for you and for her—you need to stay." It seems to me this was a pretty unsatisfactory answer, but the only one I had. As I gave it, my internal voice kept screaming that it was the question that was wrong, not the answer—instead of asking "how you stay in the room when . . ." I wanted to whisper, "how do you *not* stay in the room when a mom is sobbing uncontrollably over the impending death of her baby." I regret not moving those words from my internal to my external voice.

The second question was, "when you walk into the room of a dying child, and each of the family members is in a different place—physically and emotionally—who do you approach first, and what do you say?" Great question! More detail was provided, about the bedside mother sobbing, the father shaking with anger in the corner, the grandmother in a second corner looking as though she might pass out, the uncle channel surfing on the (thank God) muted television, and the aunt standing alone muttering to herself. I responded that I walked to the door, looked to the left and the right to see on which side of the doors the hinges were located, and then entered the room and said just one word, a single word that created a uni-fied group completely focused on me. That word was "Leanna." As I walked toward her, I said, "Leanna, you are such a beautiful angel, and you must be so comforted having your whole family here loving you and supporting one another." They were not, and I could not have told them what to do without offending them and, most likely, meeting resistance. However, I could speak to them through Leanna, set an expectation to which I believed they would rise, and subtly remind them of what was important in this situation. I call this technique "communication by proxy"—communicating to the family through words spoken to the patient. It is a highly effective and very gentle technique.

Their last question was, "when a parent has held the dead body of their baby too long, how do you get them to give up that body?" This time I had no problem telling them that it was the question that was the problem: that parents don't give up their babies and that as soon as you ask them to, you have set yourself up for failure. I also reminded them that these parents had held nineteen-month-old Leanna far too short, not too long. Their response was, "Yeah, but you walked into that room and three minutes later you got them to do what we were unable to convince them to do. What did you say?"

I responded, "Elizabeth and I walked to the room, paused in the door-way, and looked to the right and the left to see on which side of the door the hinges were located. Then, we —" At that point, they interrupted asking, "What's with the hinges?" I explained it was a tool shared with me by Zen Hospice Project of San Francisco, a centering tool to empower me to walk into a room fully present. I explained that it did not matter on which of the door the hinges were located. Rather, it was a vehicle to pause and make certain not only that I was fully present, but that I was walking into the room with the eight elements of presence: 1) *vulnerability* (to make me accessible to them), 2) *privilege* (a sense of privilege to get to serve them), 3) *invitation* (for them to join me), 4) *attentiveness* (God gave me two eyes and one mouth, two ears and one mouth—perhaps for a reason), 5) *mercy*, 6) *compassion*, 7) *respect*, and 8) *silence* (initially), and that these eight elements would allow me to *respond in* the situation, rather than *react to* the situation. It is an extremely powerful centering tool, one which I use before entering almost any room—not just the rooms of patients, but in my personal life as well—using it each day before entering my own home, after a day of driving from one dying patient's home to another.

Anyway, let's get back to the story. So Elizabeth and I centered and entered the room, initially in silence. We met the gaze of mom and dad, and they asked everyone else to leave the room. So it was mom, dad, Leanna, Elizabeth, and me. I opened my conversation with a defense-lowering statement, saying, "You get to do whatever you want. I have a concern, which I will share with you in a moment. You know, Leanna is such a beautiful angel, and I know you've taken many photographs of her with your hearts. Well, she's been dead about two or three hours now, and her body is starting to change. My concern is that those perfect photographs in your hearts are going to be replaced with images that really aren't Leanna. So, are you willing to put her little body in my arms and allow Elizabeth to walk you out of this room and out of this hospital?" I was finished, and needed to stand in silence as they processed what I had said. They never answered me—with words. Instead they looked back at Leanna, sang another chorus of the lullaby they'd been whispering to her, stood up, walked across the room, placed her body in my arms, kissed her, and allowed Elizabeth to escort them out of the room.

Speaking the Language of the Heart creates the comfort and security to perform amazingly courageous and difficult acts. I hope I have role-modeled well, for you, Language of the Heart.

Dying Behind Bars in the Deep South
—"God has no grandkids . . ."

In the last couple of decades, we have seen a real growth in the number of prisons, across the country, that have created in-house hospice programs, for inmates who will die behind bars. In some of those prisons, the percentage of inmates who will die behind bars can be as high as 89% of the inmate population. And while many of those hospice programs have been created for cost-containment reasons, almost all have resulted in a reduction of prison violence by changing the social milieu of the institution. I have been able to spend a little of my time as an educator and consultant for the creation or improvement of hospice programs in the corrections community.

One of the prisons I visit is a maximum-security prison in the Deep South. It is in a state with a death penalty, and is a prison in which there is an active death chamber. I have stood in that death chamber, and the energy is palpable. I will also tell you that I have stood in that death chamber knowing that had I been caught, tried, convicted, and sentenced there, for crimes I committed in California (see "My Story" above), I could have found myself in that death chamber under very different circumstances, and y'all would have had a different author for this chapter. I am humbled, and so grateful for my life.

I remember standing in that death chamber with the warden, and asking him what crimes the last three men executed in that room had committed. Bad question—because he told me, and the haunting images of the personal brutality he described have never left my head. After describing those crimes, he then turned to me and said, "But you know, Jay, while I'm not unwilling to carry out the court-mandated consequences of the prisoner's behavior, with every man who is executed in this room, I hold his hand, tell him he's loved and that he is not alone." My thought was that this warden really lives the words, that if you have ever heard me speak, you have heard me say, and they are, "God has no grandkids, only kids, and God doesn't make junk. And while many have gone out into the world trying to validate—through their behavior—their belief that when God made them he made junk, they are wrong—because the truth is that God has no grandkids, only kids, and God doesn't make junk."

SUMMARY

I hope this non-traditional chapter has accomplished what I promised:

1. comforted the disturbed, and disturbed the comfortable

2. presented a number of common and not-so-common end-of-life situations

3. offered an array of "take home and use today" spiritual tools, approaches, and perspectives for your consideration—arrows in your quiver, if you will—for which you might reach when encountering similar end-of-life situations:

   a. access the great humility, compassion, and restraint required to bear witness to another's suffering

      i. do no more unless invited to do so

      ii. sit with a compassionate presence for ourselves, our patients, and all who suffer

   b. Grace

   c. co-journeying and co-suffering

   d. Come Before Winter

   e. reframing

   f. move to the Master, without fear or hesitation

   g. deliver previously undelivered significant emotional statements

   h. the Gift of Uncertainty

   i. Ah Breath

   j. Language of the Heart

   k. communication by proxy

   l. know on which side of the door the hinges are located

   m. God has no grandkids—only kids, and God doesn't make junk

4. inspired you, whomever you might be, whatever discipline or role(s) you might occupy, to incorporate the spiritual—always—into your work

5. encouraged you to pause, if only for a moment, to see on which side of the door the hinges are located, for in the momentary pause we find the always and forever of now, the alpha and omega of now, the living and dying of now.

God bless the broken road that led me straight to you.

REFERENCES

Anonymous. *Alcoholics Anonymous*. New York: AA World Services, 1939.

Epilogue

Looking in a Mirror
What Do I Want to Be When I Grow Up

—Nancy Gordon, MSLS, MDiv, and Donald Koepke, MDiv, BCC

To care one must offer one's own vulnerable self to others as a source of healing. To care for aging, therefore, means first of all to enter into close contact with your own aging self, to sense your own time, and to experience the movements of your own life cycle. And how can we be fully present to the elderly when we are hiding from our own aging? How can we listen to their pains when their stories open wounds in us that we are trying to cover up? How can we offer companionship when we want to keep our own aging self out of the room, and how can we gently touch the vulnerable spots in old people's lives when we have armored our own vulnerable self with fear and blindness? Only as we enter into solidarity with the aging and speak out of common experience, can we help others to discover the freedom of old age.[1]

—Henri Nouwen and Walter Gaffney

1. Nouwen and Gaffney, *Aging*, 97–99.

NANCY'S STORY

When I first read these words, I was fifty-one and had only recently started working full-time with older adults. As I read the rest of the passage that contained these words and continued to reiterate them, I became convinced the Nouwen and Gaffney had stated a challenging, profound truth. I heard a call in these words, a call to let the barriers down and to become friends with my own aging self—a call to be aware of my own time in life and the movements of my life cycle.

I've carried this challenge in my heart and mind these last sixteen years, as I served in a large retirement community and as director of the CLH Center for Spirituality and Aging. What does it mean, to "enter into close contact with your own aging self"? What does it mean to "make ourselves available to the experience of becoming old"? Nouwen invites us to welcome this aging self—this stranger, an intruder—to make this stranger "first a part of our inner self and a welcome friend who feels at home in our own house."

As a leading-edge baby boomer, I must confess that in my youth and young adulthood, I couldn't imagine getting old. My whole growing up was about being a part of the biggest, younger generation to hit our land. Even though I majored in history in college, I had no vision for the place of older adults in society and apart from grandparents, and great-aunts and great-uncles, in my own life. Even when I went to seminary in midlife and some of my seminary friends were doing their field education in a retirement community, I couldn't imagine that being my ministry.

But then it was. I found myself experiencing a profound sense of dislocation, a sense of having lost the map for my life. I heard Nouwen's challenge and I listened to the older adults I saw and worked with every day. And a new question began to arise: What kind of older adult did I want to be? And how was I going to get there? What was the new map for the rest of my life?

I began by deciding that my age was nothing to hide. I had never colored my hair and as the dark brown began to gray, I let it and didn't try to cover it up. I decided that one of the ways to honor the elders I served and to befriend my own aging self, was not to deny the effect of passing years on my hair and my body. As I told my daughters, "I earned every one of these gray hairs."

Coming from a family that placed great value on intellectual ability, the prospect of Alzheimer's disease was one of my deepest fears. But as I began to bring worship experiences to the places where folks with Alzheimer's and other dementias lived, I quickly realized that my words and intellect were not nearly as helpful as the ability to connect in other ways. I explored a way of doing worship that required far fewer words and provided a visual and tactile element. And I realized that it was only as I set my fears aside and really attempted to relate to those right in front of me, could I be at all effective. And that work in turn made me less afraid of whom I might be even if I lost my memory and my ability reason things out. I am beginning to befriend the possible future self who can't remember and can't think.

Aside from Nouwen, another one of my earliest guides in aging and serving the aging has been Kathleen Fischer, whose book *Winter Grace* is widely cited and praised. In the book she speaks of needing a spirituality of aging that holds together both the gains and losses of the aging processes. Without holding the two together, even if in tension, we fall into the happy face successful aging crowd, or we're part of the general cultural bias that casts everything about aging in terms of debilitation and loss. As I worked with older adults, I watched for the ones who seemed to be holding together both the losses and gains of aging.

Carl, in particular, impressed me. I ran into him in our main atrium one day and he was holding a picture of his mother and father and another couple, dressed to the nines, embarking on a boat ride in the pond at Garfield Park in the city of Chicago in 1902. While Carl held this picture and told me about it, he said repeatedly, "I am so blessed." Now I knew that Carl had some great difficulties and losses in his life. He'd lost a finger in a work accident. His only daughter died as a freshman in college from polio. His wife of many years had died several years earlier. He sometimes suffered from episodes of debilitating depression. Yet here he was, telling me how blessed he was, how enjoyable he was finding it to look at his family pictures, to remember the lives that had preceded his and been linked to his.

Carl was one of those who was able to hold together losses and gains of aging and able to say, "It's been a blessed life." Part of that came from his Lutheran faith which he'd practiced his whole life. But part of it too came from the choices he'd made and continued to make. He chose to be open to new experiences. For example after a pumpkin decorating contest one year he said, "I'm 92 years old and I'd never decorated a pumpkin before. I'm already thinking about how to decorate it next year." The next year he and his friend Lewis decorated bride and groom pumpkins and won the prize. He participated in lots of activities—some with great meaning and purpose, and other that were just fun. The night before he died he was dancing to the music being played in the atrium.

When I think of my own aging self, I hope that I like Carl, can continue to embrace new experiences and have fun, and count my life as blessed even as I navigate the losses that have already occurred and those that will no doubt occur in the future. And I hope that I can continue the journey with good humor and grace.

> To receive the elderly into our inner self, however, is far from easy. Old age is hidden not just from our eyes, but more from our feelings. In our deepest self we keep living with the illusion that we will always be the same. We not only tend to deny the real existence of old men and women living in their closed rooms and nursing homes, but also the old man or woman who is slowly awakening in our own center. *They are strangers, and strangers are fearful. They are intruders threatening to rob us of what we consider our own.*[2]

LOOKING IN THE MIRROR: YOUR STORY? (DON)

Are you afraid of your own aging? It seems as though most people in our culture deny, avoid, and even run from aging as if it were an outbreak of Ebola. At a November 1999 presentation for the CLH Center for Spirituality and Aging, Jane Thibault posited this question: "There is an old Jewish birthday blessing: 'May you live to be 120.' How many of us would feel blessed and how many of us would feel cursed?"[3] To the extent that you feel cursed you have succumbed to the anti-aging paradigm of America. Jane then asked, how do you feel with you tell someone your age and they reply, "You don't look _____." Every time you feel pleased and complimented by that comment you are caving into our anti-age culture.

The reality is that we, as professionals engaging older adults, do know why we are so afraid to age: we encounter the challenges of aging every day at our work. We cannot escape the realities that we would rather ignore: finiteness, vulnerability, and a culture fascinated with youth, even as our demographics grow ever older. The challenges of older age were described throughout this book. Cordula Dick-Muehlke shared the struggles behind dementia, specifically Alzheimer's. When you enter a "Memory Assist" unit, does a knot grow in your stomach as your unconscious mind shouts, "Could that be me someday? Is that the way my life is going to end?"

And when Marty Richards and Giovanna Piazza write about the challenges of caregiving, the burden, the feeling of being minimized or the frustration of being used, the threat to the primary relationship—don't our hearts cry for caregiver and care-receiver alike?

2. Ibid., 101; author's italics.
3. Thibault, "Toward a Sprituality."

Nancy Gordon powerfully advocated for older adult programming that is based upon meaning-making rather than merely entertainment. Don't we all want more in our lives when we're old than Bingo and watching TV?

Rabbi Address lifted up rituals as a means of meaning-making and life fulfillment. What are the rituals that make sense to you, empower you, fill you, energize you?

Jane Thibault spoke of suffering (life is suffering say the Buddhists) while Don Koepke confronted the place of money in our lives and the question of having enough for our "golden years." You have heard that fear from many, but is it a worry for you as well?

Last, but not least, Jay Westbrook closed with the most frightening issue of aging: death and dying, something that is constantly in the back of each of our minds. How are you going to make friends with your own death?

So we, as professionals in the field, understand aging at least cognitively if not existentially. But one question remains: how are you and I going to handle these challenges of aging? Admitting that I am aging is vital, but so is coming to grips with this personal existential reality. The truth is that we are going to try to made sense out of our aging using the glasses of our personal spirituality whatever that spirituality might be: theist/non-theist, Christian, Muslim, Jewish, Buddhist, Hindu, metaphysical. It is my strong perspective that while a person may not be a part of what culture would say is religion, they do have spirituality. Be it money, fame, power, desire—something deep within, some core belief, influences every thought, feeling and behavior that we call "me."

Thus, in the introduction, I defined spirituality as an individual's core beliefs that are the interplay of all of our life experiences, aging included. McGee and Pargament suggest that spirituality is what we hold sacred, our "sacred cows" if you will, that belief, action, feeling that is most important in our lives. Ellor speaks in terms of those perspectives that bring meaning to our lives while Paul Dobies puts forth the notion that spirituality is like driving the car in contrast to merely owning the car. The point is, every author, in every chapter, believes that one's spirituality is what enables a coping and even a growing as one ages. A chaplain once quipped: "I like talking with older adults because they ask better questions."

So what is your view of your own aging, and how does your spirituality help you to make sense of your aging and cope with the challenges of aging? I am sure that you have observed people who are aging with grace, embracing what is, even if they don't like it, and those who fight their aging and rail at its limits and even the destruction their lives-as-they-were. Some seem to have simply given up in resignation. What have they taught you? What have you learned from them? Remember Erik Erikson and his eight stages of human development? Erikson suggested that in the final stage of human development the person struggles with evaluating their life by asking "Have I lived my life with integrity?" If the answer is "No," their journey is truncated and ends in despair.[4] Is this the answer of many of the older adults that we have encountered? Is this what you want to be when you grow up?

Other older adults whom we have engaged seem to be fully engaged with living their life as-it-is-now, rather than pining away at the life that is no longer present. These people seem to find new ways to have meaning, new perspectives to embrace, new people to know. These are the people who begin to water color at seventy-five or to learn Spanish at eighty. These are the people who enjoy computers and connect with family and friends around the world. These are the people who are motivated to attend physical fitness classes, if necessary in their wheelchairs. Some are the people haven't decided between integrity and despair as of yet and thus gravitate to those who have decided. We all know them. We all have admired them. Why are they thriving in the same setting where others are declining? Why do they believe that the best day in their life is today or tomorrow rather than some day in the distant past? What floats their boat, making it into a cabin cruiser rather than a life-jacket?

AGING AND SPIRITUALITY IN PRACTICE (NANCY)

> Thus care for the elderly means, first of all, to make ourselves available to the experience of becoming old. Only he who has recognized the relativity of his own life can bring a smile to the face a man who feels the closeness of death . . . No old man or woman will ever feel free to reveal his or her hidden anxieties or deepest desires when they only trigger off uneasy feelings in those who are trying to listen. It is no secret that many of our suggestions, advice, admonitions, and good words are often offered in order to keep distance rather than to allow closeness. When we are primarily concerned with giving old people something to do, offering them entertainment and distractions, we might avoid the painful realization that most people do not want to distracted but heard, not entertained but sustained.[5]

4. Erikson, *Childhood*, 242.
5. Nouwen and Gaffney, *Aging*, 102–3.

As I (Nancy) think of Carl, and others whose boat is a cabin cruiser and not a life jacket (to use Don's metaphor), it has occurred to me that these older adults have incorporated spiritual practices (intentionally or unintentionally) into their lives that have sustained them in their aging journey. And as I reflected on Carl and other older adults who I admired for their spunk, creativity, and caring, I began to take an inventory of my life.

I realized that left to my own devices, I could very easily become a very crabby, solitary old woman. And I began to think about the spiritual practices that would help me navigate the aging journey with grace and humor. Practices that would help me be an aging person that I would want to live with and that others would want to have as part of their life. Practices that would make me like the person I saw in the mirror.

When I was asked to write a piece a couple of years ago on spirituality and aging, I interpreted the request to be: "Please provide us with the spiritual answer that is going to make aging not be aging, that will make aging look not like getting old." I knew this was not possible. But as I thought about it, I realized that while there was no spiritual answer that would make everything about aging okay, there were spiritual practices that could provide sustenance for the journey. So I came up with a list of suggested practices. But the practices I came up with I was really writing for myself—they were the practices that I realized I needed to enable me to continue to make friends with my aging self—so that self didn't have to be banished to some dark corner of my life, but could be embraced and welcomed.

I referenced these practices in my chapter on programming, but I want to say just a few words about them here. I started with "Breathe." Breathing is a practice that reminds me that I live in a body, and as someone who lives in my head a lot, I need reminders of the importance of this body, the address for my soul. If I were to write these practices today, I would include physical activity as another practice to help me embrace and care for my physical being.

"Practicing gratitude" and "practicing kindness" are two of the best ways that I, in Frankl's words, can "choose my attitude" (and thus create meaning) towards the circumstances that I can't change and have no power over.[6] I can almost always find something to be thankful for; I can almost always find a way to be kind. "Practicing wonder" opens me up to see beauty and experience the awe of a world and universe far bigger than myself. "Practicing creativity" and "practicing making music" puts me in touch with sources of energy and joy that are available to me all the time, but that frequently get lost and ignored. "Practicing releasing" allows me to let go

6. Frankl, *Man's Search*, 116.

of things, grudges, attitudes that are weighing me down and impeding my aging journey. "Practicing connecting" reminds me that relationships are precious and that even though many are lost due to death, relocations, and other life changes, there are still so many fascinating people who are also looking to connect and share this journey with me. And "practicing resting" reminds me that the world can get along without me for a few hours, while I stop and restore my soul. The practice of rest is a way of living into being, not doing, and it prepares me for the day that may come, when all I can do is rest. Together these practices connect my spirituality with my aging life. They are the practices that give me hope and courage for my own aging journey. And they give me the ability to truly be present with others share this aging journey.

IN CONCLUSION (DON)

In the book, *Religious and Spiritual Aspects of Human Service Practice*, the authors, James Ellor, F. Ellen Netting, and Jane Thibault share a Personal Inventory for Human Service Providers.[7] Nancy and I have adapted the inventory in the hopes that it will help you get in touch with your own spirituality in aging. Read the entire inventory at least once and then gently return to each question with an open, questioning, searching heart of one who wishes to be known, especially by you.

Becoming Sware of My Spirituality

1. Do I experience a personal need for the spiritual? Have I recognized an urge or desire for self-transcendence, ultimate meaning, or a relationship with a higher power? Is there something, someone, or some idea/perspective that gives my life meaning and acts as a guide for my decisions/behaviors and a filter for my emotions?

2. How intense is my urge toward the spiritual or transcendent dimension of my life?

3. How have I expressed this spiritual urge? How I repressed it? Do I have an outlet to express this urge?

4. To what degree do I express my spirituality through formal religious activity? What non-religious ways do I allow my spiritual perspective

---

7. Ellor et al., *Understanding Religious*, 121–25.

to be nurtured and grown? Why have I chosen this particular community or tradition?

5. How do I use my spirituality to interpret/cope with my journey of aging? To what extent do I feel that my way of expressing my spirituality is the 'best" or "better" or the "preferred" way? How do I avoid imposing my spiritual perspectives, my opinions on life and living, on my clients?

6. How do I feel about serving a client whose spiritual and/or religious views are diametrically opposed to my own?

7. To what extent am I willing to learn about the basic spiritual/religious views of my client if they are different than my own?

8. To what extent am I willing to include other professionals with expertise in religion and spirituality as my supervisors or consultants?

9. To what extent do I feel a need to share my spiritual or religious insights with clients?

10. If I do not believe in self-transcendence, am I willing to help a client find their own transcendent meaning in life?

We leave you now with a poem that I found a site on the internet that quoted an unknown author.[8] It is a picture of truly making friends with our aging self. We think that it is a fitting conclusion to *The Essential Spirit: Providing Wholistic Service to and with Older Adults.*

On Being Called Old

As I've aged, I've become kinder to myself,
    and less critical of myself.
    I've become my own friend.

I have seen too many dear friends leave this world, too soon;
    before they understood the great freedom that comes with aging?

Whose business is it, if I choose to read, or play on the computer
    until 4 AM, or sleep until noon?
      I will dance with myself to those wonderful tunes of the 50, 60 &70's,
        and if I, at the same time, wish to weep over a lost love, I will.
      I will walk the beach, in a swim suit that is stretched over a bulging body,

8. Author Unknown, as quoted in "On Aging —and Being Called Old." http://www.smilegodlovesyou.org/jokes.seniors.html.

and will dive into the waves with abandon, if I choose to,
despite the pitying glances from the jet set.
They, too, will get old.

I know I am sometimes forgetful.
But then again, some of life is just as well forgotten.
And, I eventually remember the important things.
Sure, over the years, my heart has been broken.
How can your heart not break, when you lose a loved one,
or when a child suffers,
or even when somebody's beloved pet gets hit by a car?
But, broken hearts are what give us strength, and understanding,
and compassion.
A heart never broken, is pristine, and sterile,
and will never know the joy of being imperfect.

I am so blessed to have lived long enough to have my hair turning gray,
and to have my youthful laughs be forever etched
into deep grooves on my face.
So many have never laughed, and so many have died
before their hair could turn silver.

As you get older, it is easier to be positive.
You care less about what other people think.
I don't question myself anymore.
I've even earned the right to be wrong.

So, to answer your question, I like being old.
It has set me free. I like the person I have become.
I am not going to live forever, but while I am still here,
I will not waste time lamenting what could have been,
or worrying about what will be.
And I shall eat dessert every single day (if I feel like it).

Author Unknown.
As quoted in "On Aging—and Being Called Old"
www.smilegodlovesyou.org/jokes.seniors.html

REFERENCES

Ellor, James W., F. Ellen Netting, and Jane M. Thibault. *Understanding Religious and Spiritual Aspects of Human Service Practice*. Columbia: University of South Carolina Press, 1999.

Erikson, Erik. *Childhood and Society*. London: Vintage, 1995.

Frankl, Viktor. *Man's Search for Meaning*. New York: Simon & Schuster, 1959.

Nouwen, Henri J. M., and Walter J. Gaffney. *Aging: The Fulfillment of Life*. New York: Image, 1974.

Thibault, Jane. "Towards a Spirituality of Aging." Plenary presentation at the first symposium sponsored by the CLH Center for Spirituality in Aging, November, 1999.

Yalom, Irvin. *Existential Psychotherapy*. New York: Basic, 1980.

Contributors

Rabbi Richard Address, DMin, PhD (honorary from HUC-JIR 1999)—Has served congregations in California and New Jersey as well as serving as Director for Family Concerns for Union for Reform Judaism. He serves as Founder and Director of Jewish Sacred Aging and www.jewishsacredaging.com and is the author of *Seekers of Meaning: Baby Boomers, Judaism and the Pursuit of Healthy Aging.*

Cordula Dick-Muehlke, PhD—Professional Consultant Dementia and Aging, Former University of California, Irvine, Director of Education Mind Research Unit, former executive director of Alzheimer's Family Services Center.

Paul Dobies, OD—Assistant professor, College of Optometry, Western University of Health Science.

James Ellor, PhD, DMin, LCSW, ACSW, BCD, DCSW, CSW-G—Professor of Social Work, Baylor University, a leading authority on the work of Viktor Frankl, author of several books including, *Methods in Religion, Spirituality and Aging.* London: Routledge, 2009, and "Spiritual and Religious Growth," In *Perspectives on Productive Aging: Social Work with the New Aged*, edited by L. W. Kaye. Washington, DC: NASW, 2005.

Nancy Gordon, MSLS, MDiv—Director of the CLH Center for Spirituality in Aging, Member of Governing Council, the Forum on Religion, Spirituality and Aging of the American Society on Aging, former director of Growth Opportunities at Friendship Village of Schaumburg, IL.

Donald Koepke, MDiv, BCC—Founding Director of the CLH Center for Spirituality in Aging (retired), former secretary of the National Interfaith Coalition on Aging, present editor of published materials for the Forum on Religion, Spirituality and Aging, author of several journal articles and book chapters, and editor of *Ministering to Older Adults: The Building Blocks.*

Giovanna Piazza, MDiv, BCC—Ordained in the Ecumenical Catholic Church, Spiritual Director.

Kenneth Pargament, PhD—Professor of Psychology, Bowling Green State University, teacher, researcher in spirituality in aging, author (among others) of *Spiritually Integrated Psychotherapy.*

Peggy Price, DMin—Minister Emeritus, Center for Spiritual Living, Seal Beach, California. Ambassador, Advisory Board, Parliament of the World's Religions; founding member and Past President Greater Huntington Beach Interfaith Council; Member Advisory Council Association for Global New Thought; Member Interfaith and Intercultural Committee Centers for Spiritual Living.

Jocelyn McGee, PhD—Associate Professor, University of Alaska. Development of non-pharmacological clinical interventions for persons with dementia and/or other complex chronic medical conditions and their family caregivers; spirituality and health outcomes.

Marty Richards, LICSW—Lifelong gerontologist, past chair of the Forum on Religion, Spirituality and Aging of the American Society on Aging. Author of *Caresharing: A Reciprocal Approach to Care Giving and Care Receiving.*

Aaron Silverbook, BS—A graduate student in the Master of Science in Clinical Psychology at the University of Alaska Anchorage. BS in Psychology from the University of Alaska Anchorage.

Jane Thibault, PhD—Clinical Professor and Clinical Gerontologist, University of Louisville School of Family Medicine and Geriatrics. Author of many books on aging including: *A Deepening Love Affair—The Gift of God in Later Life* and *No Act of Love is Ever Wasted: The Spirituality of Caring for Persons with Dementia,* plus an upcoming book on dedicated suffering.

G. Jay Westbrook, MSG—A multiple award-winning clinician and speaker, visiting faculty scholar at Harvard Medical School, and a specialist in end-of-life care and education. He holds an MS in Gerontology, is a Grief Recovery Specialist, an R.N., and a Certified Hospice and Palliative Nurse. He is nationally recognized as an expert on the constellation of issues surrounding end-of-life, and is both a national speaker and a bedside clinician.